INSIDE CHARTER SCHOOLS

Edited by Bruce Fuller

Inside Charter Schools

The Paradox of Radical
Decentralization

HARVARD UNIVERSITY PRESS

Cambridge, Massachusetts, and London, England   2000

A version of Chapter 4 appeared as "Starting from Scratch" in the *Boston Globe Magazine*, June 15, 1997. Reprinted courtesy of *The Boston Globe*.

Library of Congress Cataloging-in-Publication Data

Inside charter schools : the paradox of radical decentralization / edited by Bruce Fuller.
    p. cm.
  Includes bibliographical references and index.
  ISBN 0-674-00325-X (alk. paper)
  1. Charter schools—United States. 2. Schools—Decentralization—United States.
  3. Education and state—United States. I. Fuller, Bruce.
  LB2806.36 .I57 2000
  371.01—dc21   00-056713

The public good is a dangerous concept. Asking people to act in the public good and not in their self-interest asks them to leave a terrain in which their everyday experience gives them relatively reliable messages on what is good for them . . . The unsettled, contested nature of the concept is part of the unsettled, contested nature of politics itself.

Jane Mansbridge, 1998

Contents

Acknowledgments

In this book we invite you to peek inside and explore the vibrant lives of charter schools. Not yet a decade old, this burgeoning number of alternative schools—supported by public funds but less encumbered by the education bureaucracy—has gained a bizarre band of political supporters. From corporate leaders to black liberationists, from progressive teachers to the religious right, everyone seems to be hopeful about the promise of charter schools.

When it comes to the topic of charter schools, and the broader issue of school choice, emotional polemics and faith-filled claims are already in abundant supply. Yet the debate is impoverished by a lack of dispassionate evidence. Three years ago my research group at Berkeley came together with fellow researchers, motivated by the desire to gather sound evidence on what life is really like inside these human-scale, often fragile organizations.

What forms of social participation are being invented? What joys and disappointments are felt by the parents and teachers who have created charters schools? Are new and effective forms of teaching and learning really spawned inside these little education greenhouses? And the big question: What happens when government radically decenters public authority, forms of public accountability, and the allocation of public funds?

Few analysts have been putting such tough questions to this robust movement. In fact, the more I talk with earnest advocates the more I am reminded of Pope John Paul II, who has reformed the Vatican's centuries-old rules for how to canonize new saints, abolishing the ancient role of "devil's advocate," the counselor who mounted the strongest argument against new candidates for sainthood.[1]

Charter school enthusiasts, along with their pro–school-choice comrades, have forgotten the need for a devil's advocate, a loyal opposition. This book strives to get beyond theory and ideology, bringing to life the daily problems, dilemmas, and successes of this colorful panoply of alternative schools. It's up to you to decide whether the proponents' claims for charters are accurate or not.

The contributors to this volume do not take a uniform perspective on charter schools. This book is largely the result of a conversation with tandem groups of scholars. The first group was based at the University of California, Berkeley. Eric Rofes and Patty Yancey recently completed work for their Ph.D., having focused their thesis research on charter schools. Patty went on to join the national charter school evaluation team headed by Paul Berman, and then took a teaching post at the University of San Francisco. Eric presently teaches at California State University, Humboldt. My Berkeley colleagues also include two doctoral students, Luis Huerta and Edward Wexler. We conducted intensive studies of a handful of charter schools in northern California between 1996 and 1999.

The second research group was led by Amy Stuart Wells at the University of California, Los Angeles. Amy was completing her extensive study of charter schools in California as this book was taking shape. Jennifer Jellison Holme and Ash Vasudeva were members of the UCLA-based project.

When I lived outside of Cambridge, Massachusetts, I always enjoyed reading Kate Zernike's careful analysis of education and wider cultural issues in the *Boston Globe*. She, too, caught the charter school bug, then applied her journalist's eye to capturing the details and texture of daily life inside one school in Chelmsford, Massachusetts.

These contributors collectively have spent years inside charter schools around the United States. We have all arrived at somewhat differing conclusions about the promise and perils of these schools. I see charters as an attempt to radically decentralize public education, with all the excitement and risk this entails. I believe that in part we are replaying an old historical tune, seeking a return to a more human-scale way of raising out children. But the colorful array of charter advocates, the legal structure ensuring ongoing public support, the pluralistic rise of multiethnic power centers in cities, and the steady demise of large public bureaucracies all represent new and unprecedented forces for decentralization. Other contributors are more optimistic than I, seeing charters as a mechanism for finally challenging hopelessly hog-tied school systems and for empowering largely disenfranchised communities. Still others believe that I'm too soft on charters—too trusting of their intentions, too neglectful of their shortcomings.

This book would never have come together if not for the selfless work and always supportive criticism of two people. David Ruenzel served as our Berkeley editor and adviser, pushing all of us to organize our arguments and fresh data with greater clarity and punch. David, a contributing editor for *Education Week,* brought to the project a level of expertise, gentle candor, and discipline that I will long remember. Elizabeth Knoll at Harvard University Press is always a positive and engaging force to reckon with. She encouraged us to articulate the broader political and institutional questions within which debates around charter schools are situated. As a careful reader and inventive thinker, Elizabeth kept us focused on the essential arguments and our own evidence contained within the school case studies. She also found two extraordinarily thoughtful reviewers to whom we are indebted as well.

Martin Carnoy, Dan Perlstein, David Tyack, and Carol Weiss generously read chunks of the manuscript, setting us straight on facts and prodding us to think about the issues from new vantage points. A special thanks to our steadfast and accurate transcriber, Jessica Quindel, who labored over hundreds of hours of audio tapes and converted them into volumes of text, which were used to amplify the rich voices of the actors within the schools. Julie Ericksen Hagen superbly edited the final manuscript.

Let me sketch a few autobiographical notes to help you understand my own perspective. Much of my current thinking on democracy and decentralization stems from my graduate student days at Stanford University. David Tyack convinced me that "the one best system" had pluses and minuses, but that if democratic participation was a policy priority, alternative forms of governance had to be found. This blended with my interest in the Carter administration's efforts to decentralize drop-out prevention and youth employment programs via small-scale community organizations that to this day remain variably rooted in their ethnic neighborhoods. And John W. Meyer taught me that the vertical movement of "power" downward and the exercise of participatory symbols do not mean that teachers or classrooms will change all that much.

In those wonderfully random moves that often follow graduate school, I first went to the World Bank and then to the Graduate School of Education at Harvard. In both settings I pursued the issue of decentralization, looking especially at how different types of families respond to schools and family-support programs when these organizations become more detached from the central state. With partner Susan Holloway and remarkable colleagues Dick Elmore, Gary Orfield, and Judy Singer, I studied the effects of market-oriented policies in the public schools and in the early-education and child-care sector. I also explored, with Magdalena Rivarola, the politics and implementation conflicts that arose within Nicaragua's post-Sandinista push to decentralize its schools.

A few discrete lessons have emerged from this tortured trek across a variety of community-level organizations and institutional worlds. First, the spread and quality of alternative organizations—from charter schools to child-care centers—is shaped only in part by policy. The economic dynamics of communities, as well as their cultural norms, exert far more telling forces. Second, moving power and responsibility down the governance chain often has little substantive effect on what frontline workers really do with students or clients. The scripts and institutionalized forms of action that guide what teachers do, for example, live on independently, in spite of where the "governors" reside in the organization. Third, the distribution of policy power is not a zero-sum game. We can strengthen central elements of government *and* nurture richer participation in civil society or within neighborhood schools. The central state can become more effective, perhaps leaner and smarter, at the same time that parents and village-level educators gain more discretion and professionalism.

A heartfelt thank you goes to those who have supported this research program financially. Fieldwork and literature reviews by my Berkeley team were funded by two foundations. Special thanks go to the Hewlett Foundation's Ray Bacchetti, who has long supported my research home, the institute dubbed Policy Analysis for California Education (PACE). Ray has trusted us to pursue issues that are on the horizon and hold long-term significance. The Stuart Foundation also has supported our work on school choice. Ted Lobman is a wonderfully cantankerous colleague and financial supporter. Elizabeth Burr and Susan Puryear contributed enormously to an earlier report that helped pull together much of the empirical work reviewed herein; it was thoughtfully reviewed by Howard Fuller, Jane Henderson, Ellen Hershey, Allan Odden, and Terry Moe.[2] This diversity of perspectives—exercised by the book's reviewers and contributors as well—has greatly enriched our exploration of the political questions raised by the charter-school movement and the daily dynamics found inside the schools themselves.

Note that three of our case study schools preferred anonymity. Endnotes indicate those chapters in which pseudonyms were used.

Finally, I dedicate this book to my late father, Robert D. Fuller. He taught me, through his example, the importance of asking tough questions of individuals and organizations without ever losing respect for them. My dad was quite a democrat. Thank you all.

BRUCE FULLER

INSIDE CHARTER SCHOOLS

Introduction: Growing Charter Schools, Decentering the State

BRUCE FULLER

Margarita Ortíz was a hero long before she started a charter school. Whenever she entered a classroom or assembly, Ortíz signaled a warm sense of caring, quickly engaging the issue at hand. She was consumed by a commitment to her teachers and students, children who flocked to her school from the rising number of Latino households packed on top of each other in apartments and tiny postwar houses not more than a mile from downtown Oakland, California. Ortíz, a longtime elementary school principal, was trusted by these immigrant parents, who struggled to raise their children right, a difficult task in this concrete-gray patchwork of city blocks chopped into disparate pieces by freeway on-ramps and overpasses, surrounded by neglected and drooping chain-link fences.

Affection for Ortíz grew even deeper as she boldly led the emancipation struggle—arm in arm with the parish priest, the city's corporate leaders, and outspoken parents—to create one of California's first charter schools in 1993. This slight woman with fading auburn hair had become a Che Guevara of sorts, leading a civil war over school reform and neighborhood control.

The war against the Oakland school board had grown ugly in the late 1980s and early 1990s; the board was seen by Ortíz and her allies as imperial, uncaring, and unresponsive. The middle school into which children were sucked was viewed by parents as mediocre in quality and simply dangerous for Latino and black youths, who inevitably became affiliated with quarreling gangs.

Then the door to freedom opened a bit. In 1992, the California legislature approved the nation's second charter school bill, essentially allowing local

activists and educators to break from their school district and reject the volu-
minous education code and union agreements and still reap full public funding for a home-grown alternative school. These new schools are literally
chartered by education authorities to operate in a largely autonomous manner. Unlike private schools, charter schools receive the same per-pupil funding from the government as any garden-variety public school.

But the Oakland school board refused to grant a charter for a new middle
school; it said no to Ortíz and her comrades. The board was caught up in its
own bureaucratic aloofness and penned in by the teacher union that feared
the emerging threat posed by the new charters.

Ortíz then figured out that Sacramento's charter law provided more than
one way to secede from the education establishment. So she went to the
priest, the city's fledgling Latino leadership, and well-heeled conservatives
who backed school choice. Together they moved the county education office
to approve their license for liberation. In 1993 the Amigos Charter Academy
opened in the backyard of the neighborhood's Catholic church. The escape
to freedom had been won.[1]

Talking to the Enemy

By time I began visiting Amigos Charter in the fall of 1996, along with graduate students Luis Huerta and Eddie Wexler, the heady days of liberation
were somewhat forgotten—although the war stories remained. But it was
the prospect of needing to return *from* freedom that Ortíz found most troubling.

Organizational victories had been won. Control of Amigos was indeed
radically decentralized. The parent-and-staff governing board hired the
teachers, constructed the budget, and was in the process of restructuring the
curriculum. Ortíz had truly blasted free from the sluggish downtown bureaucracy.

But Margarita Ortíz was troubled by a recent epiphany: Amigos could not
survive economically unless she talked to the enemy—the administration of
the Oakland public schools. She was both angry and befuddled when we
first met, crammed into her tiny office in a corner of a tin trailer, situated on
a barren patchwork of land adjacent to the Port of Oakland. Her school
could not afford an estimated $12,000 for liability insurance. If the school
district superintendent would approve it, Amigos would have to pay just

$350 into the districtwide insurance pool. The downtown office was also withholding various resources, from bilingual education funding to use of a special education teacher.

During our first year at Amigos, Ortíz won most of these battles. She rebuilt bridges to the school district. She pressed the flesh with foundation staff. She kept working her contacts with the corporate world, securing land, equipment, and political support. But by the following year, 1997, Ortíz was gone, suffering from burn out and her own family struggles. By the time we completed our fieldwork in 1999, we had met three principals in three years. The school had moved twice. We counted seventeen different teachers who had cycled through Amigos' six or seven teaching posts.

The succession of principals, including one English-speaking *gringa,* each sought help from other collective authorities. The Coalition for Essential Schools provided organizational consultants, seeking to cut down on staff turnover and retrieve the fleeting spirit of camaraderie. State and federal grants were sought to gain funding outside the local school financing formula. Amigos also asked the University of California for help in developing evidence of its effectiveness as it approached the five-year mark, at which time it was due for rechartering. But we found that the downtown schools office had literally purged its records of five years of Amigos students, seeing Amigos as a private school, not a public one. The Amigos leadership had neither assessed its children's learning in a consistent manner nor kept comparable records of test scores or dropout rates.

The Tandem Ironies of Radical Decentralization

This story kept running through my mind as I began to sketch this book and distill lessons from our fieldwork. It captures two issues faced by charter school enthusiasts, the most recent in a long line of Americans who have wanted to further decentralize the state.

First, the escape to freedom is always exhilarating, in this case not only for the grassroots founders of charter schools but also for the wider circle of public school critics and advocates for school choice who believe that the only way to fix government is to radically decenter it, disassembling the stultifying elements of bureaucracy. The rub is, as Eric Fromm argued a half-century ago, that the liberating escape from strong institutions, and the psychological desire for more personal autonomy, are often followed by alienation from the common values and virtues that those institutions help to sustain. Charter school founders—leading their human-scale institutions and, in the aggregate, the charge to decentralize government—may paradoxically erode the strength of public authority and the very agencies on which their local livelihood depends. For if charter schools are essentially to serve the "tribal" agendas of well-off white parents, faithful home schoolers, La Raza devotees, black nationalists, even Mormons and Muslims, then why would society continue to support the public purposes that hold together public education? If we are to elect the proud pursuit of private interests in a revamped education marketplace, and to hell with the other guy, then why would a no-longer-civil society tax itself to support *public* schools? And once we all win our own private places, like private clubs surrounded by high walls, who will be left behind to rely on public spaces?

The second issue stems from the fact that building a warm, nurturing community within these human-scale schools, which average fewer than 200 students, is quite rewarding. This book's case studies invite you into a colorful garden of charter schools, where you will see inventive pedagogy, strong ways of raising kids, and educators who are unsurpassed in their commitment to learning and a variety of moral values.

Yet we also discover a classic tension between *democratizing* civil society and building *effective* public institutions. Despite Margarita Ortíz's idealism and artful capacity to build a warm little greenhouse, she had designed no viable way of knowing whether her students were learning. Yes, kids could speak Spanish freely. Yes, dumbed-down bilingual curricula had been abolished. Yes, grandmothers were watering the garden and singing praise for this island of safety in a treacherous inner-city environment. But were children actually learning more? To this day, even after Amigos was rechartered for another five years, we don't know.

Thus a second paradox speaks to whether the very advocates of local empowerment and the radical deconstruction of the modern state will unknowingly advance greater inequality. The broader school choice movement, upon which charter schools are founded, has gained many adherents on the political right and left. About one-fourth of all children no longer attend their assigned neighborhood school, a remarkable departure from the basic tenets of the common-school movement. But is this push to replace state-led school reform with the market model really leading to more effective forms of schooling? Or do school choice advocates simply offer the illusion of choice—now providing McDonald's, Burger King, *and* Wendy's—

without really improving teaching and learning, without addressing the underlying causes of unequal schooling in America?

The Promise and Perils of Decentering the State

The Oakland charter story is revealing in yet another way. It demonstrates the difficulty of arriving at crisp answers to these broad political and educational quandaries. Will charter schools aid and abet those who simply wish to disassemble the modern state, who yearn for a return to tribal forms of society characterized by insularity and distrust? Or will charter schools and a widening array of school choices raise kids' achievement and, more broadly, our faith that government can lend a steady hand? Will charter schools truly empower local activists and inventive educators, while delivering on their promise of quality schools for blue-collar and impoverished families? Or do we see charter schools resegregating students along economic and racial lines, widening the chasm that already divides the rich from the poor in America?

This volume puts forward emerging evidence and detailed case studies, contributing pieces to help solve this intriguing puzzle. But charter schools are so diverse—our cases include a teacher cooperative in rural Minnesota, an urban back-to-basics school in Michigan, and a devout group of home schoolers in California—that it's difficult to advance generalized claims about this far-flung movement. My approach, then, is to place charter schools, and their energetic leaders, within the broader political debate over how best to improve public education, be it to privatize and "voucherize" the system or to entrust moderate governors who are now leading the charge with state efforts at accountability and reform. In short, should government move toward a headless state, simply trusting market-oriented policy remedies? Or can government become mindful, leaner, and smarter as it cajoles and supports local schools in their efforts to improve?

For the past two decades, beginning with Ronald Reagan's ascendance to the presidency, we have witnessed an intense push to radically decentralize and disassemble central forms of government. This can be seen, for example, in Washington's moves to decentralize family welfare programs, giving authority to states and then to counties. We now have a Supreme Court that appears to be reconstructing a nineteenth-century conception of states' rights, diminishing Washington's political authority. We have seen the rise and fall of those who argued that privatization of health care would lead to

reform and higher quality services. Now we see a more intriguing movement, pushed by activists on the political right and left, to deconstruct the
cumbersome institution of public education via charter schools, open enrollment schemes, and vouchers.

Detailing the ideological context in which the charter schools are sprout-
ing is crucial, yet still insufficient, to fully inform your own assessment of
the movement. I aim to be more Socratic than didactic. That is, I hope to
describe the charter movement's roots, scope, and its emerging consequences—for kids, parents, and, yes, politicians. I want to put the movement on a clearly drawn political map so that we can better understand its
significance and underlying codes. With the rise of education as the domestic policy issue, every major policy device attracts symbols and rhetoric like a
magnet—symbols and rhetoric that must be scrutinized and deciphered.

Yet the parallel story pertains to what goes on inside charter schools. The
daily life of teachers and kids in these alternative schools, as well as the
structure of pedagogy and socialization, is every bit as important as the
broader policy wars. The hope and hype around charter schools has been so
colorful and pervasive, yet most people have had slight opportunity to actually step inside a school, look around, and see what this educational promised land is all about.

A Robust Movement, One Decade Old

What are the core features of a charter school? Let's define the beast. These
schools are often described as publicly funded independent schools. Charter
school founders, after winning approval of their bid before a school board,
can operate semi-autonomously from their state's education code and regulatory strings for three to twenty years. The basic level of per-pupil spending
allocated to regular public schools is also allocated to the new charter school,
although contention persists over funding for the "categorical aid" programs, which range from special education to gifted and talented programs.
In most states, charter schools can avoid teachers' unions. The charter
school's local board—or corporate office, if run by a firm—hires and fires the
principal as well as the teaching staff.

A local school district or state education board, depending on state legislation, can grant a charter to a small band of local teachers to break away from
the district (these are called *conversion charters*); it can also grant a charter to
parents, community activists, or clusters of educators and corporate entre-

preneurs to craft an entirely new school *(start-up charters).* The theory of action underlying charter schools is that they will be more innovative, effective, and accountable than bureaucratically managed neighborhood schools. Charters are to be reviewed periodically, and evidence of effectiveness is allegedly put forward. Since charter schools are directly accountable to their students and parents—be they working-class Latinos, evangelical Christians, or affluent whites in gated communities—the assumption is that their directors and teachers will be responsive and inventive in advancing preferred ways of raising and teaching children.

Rooted in the alternative school movement of the 1960s, and profiting from the subsequent enthusiasm over school-level control as manifested in Chicago and the small schools of New York City, the charter mechanism was first shaped by the Minnesota legislature in 1991. By decade's end, more than 1,600 charter schools were operating in thirty-four states and the District of Columbia, serving almost 400,000 students. Enrollments in charter schools will likely top a half-million children in the 2000–2001 school year.

What's striking about many charter school founders is that they are dedicated to much more than simply raising children's test scores. This may not even be an immediate concern. Instead, they talk about how kids should be raised, the cultural content of the curriculum, the democratic or authoritative ways in which teachers relate to parents. At the charter movement's heart is a brightly colored pastiche—or, better put, a variegated set of small murals—advancing particular ways of embedding schooling within ethnic, religious, and class-based forms of child rearing. I discovered in recent years that policy wonks talk about how charters enact the best facets of *market choice.* But in fact grassroots advocates and school directors speak of inventing *new communities* for learning and socialization.

Despite these ambitious aims and the hopeful rhetoric, we still know very little about what unfolds inside charter schools. Are worthwhile ideals effectively brought to life through innovative pedagogies and classroom practices? How are the promised forms of democratic participation among teachers and parents enacted, and with what effects on teachers and their teaching? Are charter schools advancing faith in public education or simply eroding the ideals of America's common-school movement that have persisted for a century and a half? And, yes, one bottom line: Do charter schools really raise children's learning curves? What exactly are students learning in these schools, which may focus on anything from phonics to La Raza political themes, from black identity to Christian fundamentalism?

What Rendition of Democracy for America?

A vastly wider sea—upon which charter schools are tossed about—might represent the broader question: What kind of democracy do we Americans really want to build? I don't mean this in an abstract sense. I mean it school by school, block by block. The feisty charter movement manifests a recurring impulse among Americans to advance democracy with a small *d*. In a wonderfully odd and unpredictable manner, former President George Bush's old hope for "a thousand points of light" has come true in the education arena: the Clinton administration aimed to fund 3,000 new charter schools. One Republican leader, George W. Bush, wants to loan charter schools another $2 billion to grow even more, not satisfied with only a thousand points of flickering light.

Indeed, the institution of public schooling has long played a leading role on the political stage where we struggle to improve our two-century-old democracy. The one-room schoolhouse of nineteenth-century rural America fit well with what I call "village republicanism," displaying idealized scenes of local control, quaint ways of raising kids, and a social fabric with few colors and mostly smooth edges. But this didn't work when the show began to run in urban America: Catholics and Protestants fought over how to socialize youngsters. Corporate elites wrung their hands over the seeming inefficiencies of small schools and the problem of educating immigrant children. Districts were consolidated; downtown school administrations grew and grew.

By the 1960s, as urban "systems" and regulatory lines grew, they seemed to disempower school principals and parents, alienating teachers and students alike. The tandem policy aims of maximizing local participation and engineering school reforms from on high, in the name of boosting schools' technical effectiveness, seemed like a pipe dream, even contradictory. The public school system, once viewed as the institution that would advance village democracy, has come to be viewed in many communities as insular, antidemocratic, and ineffective.

One reason the school's role is so perplexing is that "democracy" is in the eye of the beholder. For many, democracy speaks mainly to the sacred freedom of the individual, including the advancing of both civil rights and one's unimpaired ability to conquer unfettered markets. For others, the key elements of democracy are linked to communal aspirations: small-town participation in civic issues, or a cosmopolitan tolerance of pluralistic groups that unite around various public interests and public projects.

John Dewey argued that social participation and engagement, the necessary counters to the centrifugal forces of individualism and economic freedom, do not come naturally. Legitimated forms of public authority and agency—including a progressive array of public schools—were necessary to build a democracy that would provide supportive, tolerant communities. Applying this idea to a structure of governance, James Madison insisted that multiple layers of government and checks and balances would ensure that local tribes would not eclipse a society's broader public interests. This distribution of public power would also ensure that local authorities would be held accountable by higher levels of government, a principle now resonating within school reform circles and the burgeoning standards movement. To borrow from sociologist Anthony Giddens' conception of social architecture, no abstracted structure of democracy exists apart from the day-to-day social participation of individuals within their neighborhoods and nations. Yes, democracy includes individual rights. But individual rights must be balanced with the communal spirit of participation and social engagement.[2]

The movers and shakers advancing the charter movement are energized by alternative conceptions of democracy. They are caught between the pursuit of very local communal interests—such as, How do we best raise our children, and within what kind of social organization?—and the attention to shared public interests that invariably impinge on individualistic impulses. At Amigos Charter Academy, students could speak Spanish everywhere, inside and outside the classroom. This signaled a new identity. But some parents worried that this would not help their youngsters get ahead once they left this warm cocoon and entered the regular high school. The dogged push by conservatives for a common curriculum that emphasizes the Western heritage, or for enforced English-only instruction, illustrates how the dominant culture can press for a particular "common good" that may no longer be commonly held in nonmajority communities. How do more participatory schools define what is truly democratic in settling these disputes between public and private?

In the Wild West of the charter school world—especially in Arizona and California where the number of charters is growing exponentially—we now have taxpayer-supported education companies that enroll home-schooled kids over the Web (and collect $6,500 per child from the state). We have back-to-basics charter schools in African American communities, dedicated to strict discipline and didactics. The question is not whether particular communities should have the civil right to create such schools. The pressing issue is whether your tax dollars and mine should subsidize such tribal forms of community.

Will Charter Schools and Choice Advocates Address Inequality?

Any honest proponent of local democracy must raise the question of equity and justice. Any policy leader who argues that simply reforming what goes on inside schools will make America a more fair society—without addressing child poverty and deeper inequalities—is trying to fool you. To expect that the learning curves of kids from working-class and starkly poor backgrounds will rise substantially simply through better schooling, without attacking root causes, namely the economic insecurity and constrained opportunities facing low-income parents, is policy hogwash. It ignores a half-century of empirical research.

The gap between the haves and have-nots is widening in America. The richest 2.7 million Americans, the top 1 percent, together had as many after-tax dollars to spend in 1999 as did the bottom 100 million citizens. This ratio has doubled since 1977.[3] A recent *Los Angeles Times* survey revealed that one quarter of all residents of Orange County live in gated communities.[4] Will a weaker state and greater faith in markets reverse these escalating levels of inequality and the troubling drift toward two Americas that never see each other?

Yes, schools can play an important role in making our society more fair. But let's not forget that a student's social-class background—gauged by his or her mother's education level, family income, and ethnicity—are the strongest predictors of his or her test scores. The average African American second grader in this country reads at a proficiency level that is already one year behind the typical Anglo child.[5]

I agree with school choice advocates that poor and blue-collar parents should be given the same options that affluent parents can pursue by moving to leafy suburban communities that have good schools. But the charter movement largely sidesteps structural forms of inequality. Its rhetoric is more like Booker T. Washington's: grit your teeth and pull yourself up by your bootstraps. They wrongly see the problem as only local. If we simply gain control of our schools, or modestly boost parents' purchasing power with a voucher, deeper forms of inequality—in wage structures, job opportunities, and pro-education family practices—can be ignored.

This book is structured to place charter schools within the broader issue of how government is to be recrafted in the new century and the constituent role played by the push for school choice. My contributors and I invite you inside six wonderfully diverse schools that capture the breadth of the movement, replete with all its beauty marks and warts.

We do not offer easy answers. Instead, we aim to be informative and provocative, placing the charter movement in historical and political context. I ask whether state-led school reform is a viable alternative to school choice and charter schools. And the book's contributors illuminate the promise and perils of life inside these intriguing alternative schools. Together, we press the advocates to demonstrate how charter schools will deliver on their twin promise: more democratic participation at the grassroots, and as better schools that teach and help raise children more effectively. If charters cannot demonstrate that they have achieved these things, then this experiment in radically decentralizing public authority will have failed.

CHAPTER 1

The Public Square, Big or Small?
Charter Schools in Political Context

BRUCE FULLER

Summers in Berkeley are rather mellow. A thousand flowers, all metaphors aside, literally blossom, adding color and texture to the warm hillsides and petite meadows on which the university sits, cooled by wisps of fog that sweep across San Francisco Bay. But in the summer of 1997, during a conference of charter school activists, union lobbyists, and policy wonks from around the country, the climate quickly turned chilly.

Eric Rofes and his grad student colleagues had convinced me to host this week-long summit meeting of sorts. Our aim was to pull true believers together with leading educators skeptical of school choice—two camps with divergent perspectives on how to improve public education. We wanted to have a frank discussion of the pluses and minuses of the charter school movement. My opening role was to review early research on the effects of previous choice experiments, then to encourage reflection on how we could minimize such negative effects as the sorting of children along social-class lines and the tendency of charter advocates to overlook achievement results or, more precisely, the lack of evidence on this topic.

I could barely finish my remarks before the director of a right-wing San Francisco think tank sharply objected to my questions about whether charters were really publicly accountable, and whether fringe groups, like the Church of Scientology, should win taxpayer funds to advance their ideologies. She asked, "Isn't it time that we really question the wisdom of separating church from state?" I was speechless: I couldn't remember any time in my 25-year career that someone had explicitly argued to repeal the establishment clause.

Then I was hit from the left by a young African American man, clad in jeans, dreadlocks down to his shoulders. This parent organizer of a new Los Angeles charter school talked with precision and emotion about the mediocrity of urban schools. I had spoken of Milwaukee's Afrocentric private schools, financed by vouchers, and the ironic image of Republicans Lamar Alexander and William Bennett in navy blue suits and black ties celebrating the liberating effect of school vouchers while standing in front of posters bearing the images of Malcolm X and Eldridge Cleaver. But this fellow didn't appreciate my sense of humor. Because I asked tough questions of charter schools, I apparently stood for the status quo.

As the week's debates unfolded, it struck me that the activists who were creating and running charter schools did not necessarily see themselves as members of a politically unified movement, a common "institution" that should be judged by universal benchmarks. Rather, they expressed human-scale visions around which parents or fellow educators rallied: a charter based in a San Diego shopping mall, a school in Los Angeles set up by black activists frustrated with the moribund public schools, even a "virtual charter" on the Web, where students never even see their teachers.

Should they be held accountable for the aggregate effects of charter schools writ large? The people gazing back at me with a doubtful look in their eyes shared one heartfelt position: they were against the notion of the "one best system" of schooling, as historian David Tyack famously put it. Perhaps they were yearning for a return to the one-room schoolhouse, literally and figuratively, a particular rendition of what *their* bounded community should look like, capturing how their tribe wants to raise its children.

This group of seventy-odd activists certainly represented a feisty pastiche of social communities marked by religious, ethnic, regional, and class diversity. If they had ever read the likes of Michael Cohen or Jennifer O'Day on "systemic reform"—with all their talk of methodically rearranging the disparate pieces of the school institution—these radical decentralists had certainly concluded that it was incremental nonsense. These neighborhood leaders cared most about how to craft their own schools, inside their own communities.

Whether or not these local activists conceive of themselves as members of a broader movement, that is indeed what they are. Policymakers and interest groups—including state charter associations, who now hire lobbyists—clearly conceive of charter schools as a new, inventive sector of education. As with earlier forms of school choice, certain reformers, political actors, and foundation and corporate donors have come together to form networks, aiming to mobilize resources to aid the movement. This is how a unified identity and the organization of political strategy coalesces.

Proponents preach that charter schools—as a distinct institutional form—

are one remedy to enliven public education. Inevitably the charter movement will be judged not only by its internal diversity but also by its overall ability to attract families and push children's learning curves upward. For these reasons, we can see the movement as a fledgling institution, then set it in the context of broader efforts to decentralize key functions of the state.

I should be clear that my normative aim is to help the movement get a fair shot at true reform, organizational change that advances both democratic participation *and* children's learning. Yet high hopes must be tempered with sound evaluation and unrelenting attention to evidence. The skeletal remains of earlier generations of "reform" already litter the dusty plains of public education. I am firm in my insistence that evidence be used to separate high hopes from real results.

Charter Schools in Tandem Contexts

This chapter focuses on the twin contexts in which the decade-old charter school movement is embedded, including both the historical soil and the contemporary nutrients that have fed the robust growth of these very local alternative schools.

Charters are first embedded in the broader school choice movement, stemming from an odd marriage between American conservatives' affection for the individualistic pursuit of private interests via markets, and liberals' growing impatience with ineffective urban school systems. This chapter details the multiple political and educational forces that have led many to abandon the modern tenets of the common school and instead advance pro-school-choice policies, from vouchers to charter schools, that have sprouted over the past four decades.

Second, I argue that both the charter and parental choice movements are embedded in a wider debate over how civil society can construct warmer and more supportive forms of community. One major discovery from our work inside charter schools—detailed in the case studies that comprise this book's midsection—is that charter founders and families talk mostly about creating or preserving their *community*, eager to draw boundaries around their new schools within which like-minded parents and teachers can reside. The market-oriented imagery of parents shopping around at different schools in pursuit of private interests just doesn't match the communal forms of discourse that characterize what many parents and teachers say about charter schools.

The charter movement, despite much of the rhetoric from proponents and opponents, is not about detonating centers of public authority. That is, the contest does not concern whether collective groups should be chartered by society to receive public funding, teach our children, and set norms for how youngsters are socialized in their neighborhood. The political question, rather, is about *where* these nodes of public authority should be located, ranging from Washington to state capitals to local school boards to the radically decentralized alternative: the village's charter school. It's also about *who* should control the cultural and curricular content and social rules that are learned by our children.

These issues are central to how we raise children and the power parents retain over this fundamental human process. They have been debated since the advent of the modern state two centuries ago, which, in America, dispersed power and public resources down to local school offices. What often goes unsaid is that these debates are over basic issues of *social organization,* not the creation of idealized free markets that are void of public authority. I argue that charter schools, like other forms of school choice, spring from particular communities and interest groups motivated by the desire to allocate public resources and regulate social behavior in *particular* ways. They do operate from a greater faith in market mechanisms, but the origins and effects of charter schools are embedded in political-economic contexts and local cultures, not in the individualistic nirvana envisioned by Adam Smith. This is because raising children remains a very social activity, reaching across America's social-class and ethnic archipelagos.

I begin the analysis with the question: What are the political and institutional origins of the charter school movement? Why have thousands of parents and neighborhood activists—from suburban housewives to inner-city descendants of Chicago's Saul Alinsky—joined with teachers to create these alternative schools? And why have centrist politicians joined the movement—ironically using the soapbox and public purse made available by the government—to support radical decentralization? Is this creation of small, even tribal, public squares bounded by ethnicity, social class, or religion a viable way to enrich communities? Or is it part of a political agenda bent on eroding the larger public square, the foundations of a common good to which the modern state has been committed for more than two centuries?

The basic facts about charter schools are then put on the table, one decade into this robust movement. I detail the growth of charter schools and their enrollments, then review initial empirical assessments of whether these small institutions boost parents' enthusiasm and hard-core involvement and raise student achievement. I also ask whether parents are equally concerned with finding a safe and culturally convergent way of raising their children, independent of whether their youngsters' test scores rise.

The origins and force of charter schools cannot be fully described without seeing their place in the broader issue of school choice, viewing charters as a crucial part of the debate over how government can effectively reform public education. This leads to another emerging element of the policy context: the rise of state-led accountability programs, pushed by governors and legislators of varying political stripes. As active-state reforms take hold in California, Connecticut, North Carolina, and Texas—and show bottomline results in terms of boosting achievement—the relative viability of charters and stronger forms of privatization, like vouchers, comes into question. The newfound faith in centralized reform strategies further places in context the push to radically decenter the state.

Finally, I summarize distinct lessons learned that contemporary decentralists might consider. These lessons stem from the nation's almost half-century of experience with school choice and the longer running quandary over how government and schools are pushed to either reinforce pluralistic but separate local villages or promote a more integrated, perhaps more homogenous, modern society. These lessons should be kept in mind as we invite you inside the six diverse charter schools.

Individual Empowerment or the Common Good?
The Conflicting Origins of Charter Schools

To explain why charter schools have inspired such fervor and faith, it's useful to begin the story with the 1960s' idea of "empowerment." Under the Great Society's organizational assumptions, central government could target aid and open new political space for ethnic and social-class groups historically excluded from the American dream. The Tennessee Valley Authority had aimed to provide development assistance for poor whites of Appalachia. Project Head Start went further south to open preschools and fund community action agencies for poor blacks. The Office of Economic Opportunity, guided by Sargent Shriver and Christopher Jencks, offered school vouchers to poor families in the Alum Rock schools just south of San Jose, California.

In each case, empowerment meant an end run around white local governments that had shown little political will, or simply held scarce resources, to lend a steady hand to impoverished families. These communities were not simply the objectified "targets" of government assistance, they were awarded resources to organize their own neighborhoods and engage in local action. These "community action agencies," as the federal legislation termed them, represented an alternative to the traditional arrangement of local political power and public services.

This was a sharp departure from how the modern state had historically and tacitly viewed empowerment. From the French and American revolutions forward, centralized or federalist political structures built social institutions—schools and universities—to advance a common language and cultural tenets, knowledge of civic responsibilities, and the skills required to participate in free labor markets. The assumption was that Balkanized tribes and disenfranchised classes could be pulled toward the society's center, or into the mainstream, through participation in these institutions. Leaders of the institutions, acting alongside government leaders, would build a large "public square"—a Durkheimian conception of the "common good"—be it focused on capitalist expansion, fairness and due process, or broadening economic opportunity and racial integration.

Critical thinkers, such as Antonio Gramsci, have emphasized the limitations of the big-public-square conception of civil society, in terms of both who gets to define its workings and cultural content and whether this expansive public park can truly welcome all groups. This involves a historical institutional contest about which the school choice debate is but one contemporary manifestation.[1] Modern institution building moves from the assumption that local public squares are backward, a drag on an integrated economy, and corrosive of the Rousseau-like social contract under which individuals are granted rights and entitlements by pledging allegiance to the nation-state. Under the terms of this deal, from the early nineteenth century forward, civil and international disputes were to be settled through more civilized, less coercive means, via democratic debate and political compromise.[2] Class and tribal conflicts would be mediated within large public institutions, including an expanded common school system and uniform (middle-class) ways of socializing children.

But at what level of government or public authority should the common good be defined? America's distinctly federalist structure, for instance, granting states authority over public education, has led to many disputes over who may shape the content of schooling and rule this very local institution on a day-to-day basis.

Nineteenth-century advocates of a uniform system of common schools were major players in this distinctly American contest between central and local institution building. Rural and urban republicans (with a small *r*) fought to retain their one-room schoolhouses, run by village councils. But these scattered little schools in the midnineteenth century were unfairly financed, drew poorly educated teachers, and failed to advance a uniform set of Protestant values and dictates for "good citizenship." The steady systemization of public education brought remarkable gains in equity and quality. It also brought uniformity and a loose bureaucratic form of accountability, whereby teachers and school principals were pushed to follow central regulations and mechanical ways of organizing classrooms.[3]

Empowerment as Liberation from Public Institutions

During the 1960s and 1970s government agencies were determined to experiment with human-scale institutions that were rooted in ethnic neighborhoods, not in the big public square. Then a new and even more dramatic conception of empowerment emerged in the 1980s: true empowerment of parents would come only when they were allowed to exit the dominant institution, their assigned neighborhood school.

In a telling twist of the tale, the political right took control of the empowerment story line. Ronald Reagan and Margaret Thatcher rose to power largely by arguing that the postwar central state was exercising undue economic power and that "social engineering" had resulted in two fatal maladies. First, the rights and freedom of individuals were being curtailed by national and state governments that were pushing to regulate ever-expanding slices of economic and social life. Second, two generations of deficit spending were eroding the national economy, signaling the decline of both the fiscal and the moral fiber of American society. In effect, fiscal conservatism was fused to the perennial cause of individual rights to advance conservative political and cultural change.

This classically liberal framing of right and wrong—individual freedom and laissez-faire economics versus state planning and social programs—would structure much of the school reform debate. The new policy discourse dropped the earlier progressive elements of community empowerment and democratic participation, aimed at transforming society, in favor of a story about "devolving" the state's authority and delivering Adam Smith's dream of ever-widening market choices. Conservatives argued that a lack of accountability and competition were the culprits, not family poverty, unequal school financing, or uneven teacher quality.

Importantly, the newfound meaning of empowerment, voiced by the Reagan conservatives, held no clear role for the state in improving local schools, other than pushing forward on tax credits for affluent parents who sent their children to private schools and liberating parents from neighborhood schools through school choice. Eighteenth-century liberalism and liberationist rhetoric were the proper elixir, according to the Republican agenda in the 1980s. As the market metaphor fused with a cultural battle against the "educrats" and "secular humanists," a more focused school reform agenda emerged from the right. Market-oriented reforms—vouchers, charter schools, open enrollment schemes—were designed to pressure bureaucratic school managers to compete and be held *directly accountable* to parents.

A capstone for this period was the 1990 book *Politics, Markets, and America's Schools* by John Chubb and Terry Moe, two political scientists who clearly articulated this fresh diagnosis of the political constraints strangling public education.[4] Opening Pandora's box, they argued that democratic pressures from interest groups—ranging from teachers' unions to parents of disabled kids—had resulted in a panoply of highly regulated programs that served to undercut the power of typical parents to effect change. School principals inside their neighborhood schools were hog-tied by a hopeless array of government rules and union contracts that prevented them from exacting sharper accountability from their teachers. With no ability to exit, parents were seen as trapped in bureaucratized school systems that had come to serve their employees first, students and parents a distant second.

You may disagree with their market-oriented remedies, like vouchers, but Chubb and Moe's analysis is indisputably penetrating. As education interest groups organize at national, state, and local levels, various programs and regulations rain down on school principals and teachers. This serves to disempower grassroots educators, since they must work within the boxes and rules set by actors who work in the downtown office or the state capital. When special interests lead to an array of categorical programs—from bilingual to special education—governed far from the neighborhood school, teachers and principals lose much of their discretion. In turn, the school becomes isolated from its community, unable to respond to the values of neighborhood parents.

The only way to beat bureaucracy and its habit of rule making from afar, Chubb and Moe argued, is to sever schools from it, radically decentralizing management. The ultimate form of decentered public authority is represented by vouchers. This is the way to liberate individual parents to pursue their private agenda for their child. The state sanctions the pursuit not of the broad common good but of private interests.

Charter schools also represent a major step forward in the eyes of these critics. Parents are able to exit their neighborhood school, and local activists have wide latitude in crafting a school organization that can better nestle into local preferences and social values. The movement is imbued with the crisp imagery of the empowerment metaphor, ringing out with classic tones of liberation. Listen to the words of William Weld, former Massachusetts governor, now a board member of Edison Schools Inc.: "Changes in education are coming as surely as the Berlin Wall went down."[5]

No doubt the state's "liberation" of parents from the old compulsion to send one's child to the assigned neighborhood schools has unleashed rising demand for charter and magnet schools, cross-district choice schemes, and vouchers. (Later I will discuss the finding that fully one quarter of the nation's 52 million school children no longer attended their assigned school.) But that's where the market dynamic begins and ends. The deeper social process involved is how parents, teachers, and children create new associations and construct formal organizations called charter schools. I hesitate to use the words *reinventing community*. But indeed the story revealed inside our case-study schools, and among the neighborhood activists powering them, centers on the search for safer and more invigorating social collectives.

The story told by policy elites and national activists is one replete with market symbols: a virtuous campaign to liberate disaffected parents from the monopoly of public schooling, thereby unlocking the chains and shackles that keep parents and kids in their mediocre neighborhood schools. Elements of this plot do occasionally appear in the local stories told in our later chapters. Yet these local actors also strive to enact the ideals of local democracy—whether it's through a conserving or a transformational conception of learning and child rearing. In the discourse of these local activists, the individualistic values emphasized by an Adam Smith or a Milton Friedman are rarely to be found. It is a central irony that newfound market rules in education may feed the return of premodern tribes, not the idealized pursuit of free-thinking utilitarians.

Building Community: From the Center or the Ground Up?

Charter school advocates, as they advance small public squares, are joining a debate that has rocked America's schools for more than a century and a half.

By the 1840s the village republicans were energized mainly by Protestant reformers who worried that the fledgling education sector was fracturing between private schools for the haves and impoverished village schools for the have-nots. The westward movement of pioneers and farmers threatened to fray the cultural and political fabric of the young nation even further, not to mention the threat from the southern states, who sought to preserve a fundamentally different order.

This led New England reformers, such as Horace Mann, to advance the idea of the common school, which was to be embodied in state- or locally financed schoolhouses that would share the same textbooks, form of moral socialization, and conventional pedagogical techniques. Other civic leaders in rural America and budding cities opposed giving state government more authority over their sacred schools. These are the ancestors of contemporary decentralists, including charter school advocates.

The common schools would advance a unifying commitment to Protestant values, shared political rights and responsibilities, and a cultural frame that recognized religion yet organized the commonweal around the virtues of democracy and giving young people utilitarian skills for the commercializing economy. In the words of social historian Carl Kaestle, "Initial acceptance of the state common-school systems was encouraged by Americans' commitment to republican government, by the dominance of Protestant culture, and by the development of capitalism . . . [I]n translating [these] values into public policy, leaders were guided by a particular ideology. The reform version of this ideology called for state-regulated common schools to integrate and assimilate a diverse population into the nation's political, economic, and cultural institutions."[6]

Kaestle illuminates the ideals and political forces that fueled the common school movement from the 1840s forward, forces that now shape the sometimes contradictory reform stance taken by contemporary moderates and center-right Republicans. In 1998, for instance, then-governor Pete Wilson in California pushed centralized curricular standards and uniform pedagogical practices such as forbidding any language in the classroom other than English. Yet at the same time, Mr. Wilson pushed to radically decentralize school control and budgeting to parent-dominated councils.

Similarly, George W. Bush has advocated a stronger role for Washington in organizing tests and standards, and he also promotes vouchers for parents when these stiff accountability measures don't lift low-performing schools. Such a two-pronged strategy would be a return to a centrally enforced curriculum and shared set of social values, while at the same time permitting parents to pursue their own preferences via vouchers.

On the one hand, we see policy elites eagerly trying to set certain learning outcomes and sanction official forms of knowledge. On the other hand, a populist tack is taken to empower parents and demolish the authority of professional educators and local policymakers. Governor Wilson, for instance, proudly talked of how he had imported his model from Britain after meeting with Margaret Thatcher and the *Economist* magazine's editorial board.[7] Wilson's state board of education also purged historical figures like Mahatma Gandhi from the social studies textbooks, replacing them with contemporary notables like astronaut Sally Ride and actor John Wayne.

Horace Mann would certainly have sung praise for John Engler, John Rowland, and Tommy Thompson, other Republican governors who have recently advanced the power of their state's government to dictate what is to be taught in millions of classrooms, and how. Listen to one Republican legislator who authored California's new mandate on teachers to instruct early language skills exclusively through phonics: "K–12 classrooms are not free-speech zones where anyone can teach what they please. We have a set of standards that people have to follow."[8] So much for a tempered, Jeffersonian conception of democracy.

This policy strategy descends directly from a genealogy, originating in America with the common school, that assumes a strong state bent on legitimizing a conception of the common good. State governments under the Constitution now push to legislate a universal curriculum and achievement standards. These core elements of the classroom contain "official" forms of knowledge that now, in the case of history, include some multicultural and ideological themes, yet cannot veer far from the Anglo-European cultural frame. The state then enforces universal ways of judging the performance of children through standardized tests. Emile Durkheim, one nineteenth-century architect of the modern state, would applaud contemporary moderates who are earnestly trying to encircle and rope in the disparate cultural elements of American society, advancing the idea of one big public square.

But charter school advocates oppose this recurring lunge toward uniformity, central standards, regulated accountability. Their logic of action resembles the Chubb and Moe thesis. Empower parents to choose, win state financing of alternative schools, and shake free of centralized rules. In turn, a thousand flowers will blossom.

Organizing for Individual Empowerment

The broader school choice movement is powered by widespread and diffuse constituencies. But centers of power and capital have emerged within the movement, similar to the nodes of influence found within public education. Any analysis of the charter school uprising must recognize the heavy-duty political and corporate forces that have grown stronger over the past decade. And charter activists are rooted in this wider school choice movement, which focuses not only on opening school options for families but also on business options for private firms that increasingly create and manage charter schools.

Choice advocates ironically talk of individual freedom unencumbered by organizations, but they themselves are often funded by corporate leaders and conservative foundations. I must smile whenever conservatives like William Bennett or George Will bemoan the alleged rise of "group rights," as if American society was ever a Norman Rockwell painting of innocent individuals moving about in neighborhoods and markets, unbothered by institutions, social inequities, or interest groups. The school choice battle is being fought among firms, corporate moguls, teachers' unions, and institutions, not among the innocent village republicans of yesteryear who pieced together their one-room schoolhouses brick by brick.

A truly bizarre set of political bedfellows now pushes to expand charter schools and widen school options in general. Beyond such corporate reformers as Hollywood agent Michael Ovitz and Wal-Mart's John Walton, there are moderates, like Los Angeles mayor Richard Riordan. Even black progressives, such as Atlanta mayor Andrew Young, now support privately financed voucher programs: "What happened to IBM when Apple started making computers?"[9] At a recent ceremony in Los Angeles, more than 3,700 kids from low-income and working-class families were awarded their vouchers by Ovitz and his buddy, Magic Johnson. Even Oprah sent words of support.

Or take activist Catholic priests bent on challenging mediocre public schools. At his wit's end over the unequal funding and sluggish management of Chicago's inner-city schools, South Side priest Michael Pfleger has talked of converting Catholic schools into taxpayer-supported charter schools. Black minister and former member of Congress Floyd Flake, a strident backer of vouchers for poor kids, is pushing the same idea under New

York's new charter school law.[10] At a 1999 conference of Catholic school leaders titled "Catholic Schools and School Choice: Partners for Justice," Bishop Robert J. Banks of Green Bay, Wisconsin, declared that "justice demands that this nation do something to make choice more possible for all of our people."[11] Ohio's Republican senator George V. Voinovich was given an award by the Catholic association for his vigorous support of Cleveland's voucher program.

By equating "justice" with charter schools and vouchers, Catholic educators are solidifying an alliance with political conservatives who have now shifted their focus from tuition tax credits (pushed by the Reagan-Bush White House, they would have benefited affluent families) to vouchers and school choice specifically for poor families. By building bridges between inner-city Catholics with corporate elites, choice advocates are attempting to define a broader public interest. Instead of promoting market remedies to aid affluent suburbanites, they appear to be helping low-income families escape from mediocre to downright dangerous urban schools. Perhaps the Catholic leadership is also getting the last laugh, after having been smashed politically a century and half ago by the New England bluebloods who pushed for Protestant-led common schools.

The diverse constituencies now backing the use of public dollars for communal purposes must be recognized and respected. This rainbow coalition of advocates contends that school choice will advance equity and opportunity for urban children and families. We will return to whether the evidence to date substantiates this claim of more equal outcomes for kids.

It is the political paradox that remains most salient. As charter advocates push to allocate more public funds for radically decentralized schools, the central state is distracted from attacking the more fundamental causes of low student performance: persistent inequalities in school financing and stubbornly high rates of child poverty, even during economic booms. And these are problems that the corporate community has shown little interest in addressing seriously.

I hasten to add that we have seen both conservatives and centrists like Bill Clinton and California governor Gray Davis push to consolidate school curricula and mandate new standards, as well as to end the social promotion of students from one grade level to the next. These reformers, not unlike the Republican moderates, want to reform every classroom by firing a silver bullet, be it reducing the average number of students in classrooms, "ending" social promotion, or requiring phonics as the sacred form of instruction.

Then, alluding to market magic, we hear Bill Clinton, speaking in San Carlos at California's first charter school, claiming, "Charter schools are living proof of what parents and teachers can do to reinvigorate public education. They keep their charters only so long as their customers are satisfied they're doing a good job."[12] It is this jumping between centralized remedies and faith in market solutions that is bewildering. The schizophrenic symbolism pleases many political camps. What works, policywise, for children and teachers remains unknown.

Political scientist Lawrence Mead makes the important point that the more political leaders use the state's organizational levers to enforce a certain moral message—whether it is "tough love" and welfare reform, pushing one "official language," or pushing kids to prove their worth via higher test scores—the more credibility government enjoys as the legitimate civic stage on which social issues are debated and settled. Thus in some policy sectors we see the state becoming more authoritative and less classically liberal or tolerant.[13]

In the education arena, the school choice battle is being waged as an attack against big government, at the same time that central public agencies push popular school reforms that even conservatives now want to champion. As with past generations of school reform, countervailing forces are bringing centralizing and decentralizing reforms simultaneously. In short, a new form of the "common good" is being coconstructed: proponents of state-led reform argue for more centralized accountability and a narrower curricular agenda for the schools, enforced by state capitals. At the same time, moderates increasingly support educational policies that devolve authority away from the state, down to local groups.

Will Charter Schools Subvert the Common Good?

Charter schools—as the latest political impulse for radically decentering government—manifest two intriguing paradoxes. The first speaks to how choice advocates attempt to mobilize organs of the state that may in the long run destroy its central heart. That is, the charter movement—now sanctified as the centrists' rendition of school choice—may contribute to the dismantling of the modern state's political foundations.

The post-Enlightenment social contract that emerged in western Europe by the late eighteenth century recast the central state's role in civil society. The individual was eager to win civil rights and protections, along with wider avenues for getting ahead. Governments that were struggling to become more democratic, less feudal, or less dominated by the church, aimed to more effectively democratize economic participation and widen their popular legitimacy. Political thinkers such as Rousseau and, later, Durkheim, realized that the central state organization had to be effective to ensure participatory rights for the individual, to rein in recalcitrant provinces, and to advance economic development.[14] But in the decentralized political culture of early America, a crucial political question was never really resolved: within what level(s) of government do we lodge the moral authority and economic resources to deliver on the promises contained in the modern social contract?

It's useful to see these new alternative schools—chartered by state governments or school districts—in terms of how the British throne once chartered new commercial establishments. The prior institutional condition that lent the charter real meaning was that the British state held ample political authority and economic resources. The small firm or public organization receiving the charter is then sustained by the legitimacy of the central authority granting it.

The contemporary dilemma is linked to the fact that the center may no longer be holding. As the politicization of cultural groups intensifies across America—and I include ethnic, linguistic, religious, and gendered forms of culture and particular beliefs about child rearing—we see growing disaffection with public schools that often remain governed by faceless and impersonal bureaucracies. In a sense this is a hopeful sign of local democratic action by a variety of groups that have not historically had the ability to challenge impenetrable institutions. At the same time, these institutions—schools, universities, government—hold public resources, regulate how taxpayer dollars are used (however unevenly), and occasionally express an interest in greater equity of opportunity. And if the center doesn't hold, then the state's stimulation of human-scale and innovative organizations—like charter schools—will lose credibility and meaning. Think about how the public sees the quality of trade schools or some child-care centers: when the state's quality standards are weak or monitoring is lax, the credibility of the state *and* the local organizations sinks like a rock.

Proponents of school choice tend to see the distribution of power and resources as a zero-sum game: Washington and state capitals must give up authority if local agencies and individual charter schools are to gain clout. Choice advocates have become almost monotheistic in this regard, believing that salvation comes only through faith in the most decentralized form of association possible: parent-dominated school-level councils (the first iteration of school reform in Chicago), or through isolated parents acting in markets. Even locally elected school boards are viewed as suspect, either seen as harboring imperial bureaucracies or being in the pocket of the vilified teachers' unions.[15]

The second paradox of the charter school movement is a corollary of the first. In their progressive push to empower families who have access only to mediocre neighborhood schools, moderates who advocate choice may undermine the state's capacity to address underlying inequalities. The right's zero-sum framing of the issue, whereby parental choice is opposed to "government monopoly" and the public sector in general, is unfortunate. It distracts us from the crucial question of what the central state can do to address the structural causes of the learning gap between children from rich families and those from poor families.

The politics of choice are intriguing, as support grows among urban and blue-collar parents who have typically backed strong states, not radical decentralization. These constituencies, including prolabor and minority voters, have usually concurred with the equalizing power of a social-democratic state, advancing stronger health insurance, progressive tax structures, and low-cost public universities. Yet recent polls show growing support for vouchers among Latino and African American parents, urban constituencies surrounded by troubled schools. Yet conservatives may be narrowing their appeal by setting school choice against the central state's authority, certainly an opposition that many parents and independent voters, simply interested in better schools for children, may not endorse.

The charter school movement—as it plays out inside neighborhoods—is better seen not as a dispute pitting individual (market) freedoms against the central authority of government or even professional educators. Instead it resembles what University of Chicago philosopher Martin E. Marty calls the consequential political war between "tribalism" and "totalism"; that is, a dispute over the *level of social organization* within which we lodge moral authority and public funding. This is not an entirely new kind of battle. Even fellow republicans Thomas Jefferson and James Madison fudged in their general suspicion of a strong central government. Under some conditions they agreed with the Federalists, who aimed to pull America's states and communities together into one indivisible nation, *e pluribus unum*.[16]

The historical form of decentralization—when examined in America's urban school systems—has not proved to work well. The management of urban schools is a mess in many cases. The school boards in Los Angeles, Kansas City, and New York, for example, are really regional political bodies, offering a stage on which diverse groups attempt to nudge their public schools in one direction or another. But exacting real accountability and more demanding levels of performance from teachers is almost impossible when these elected boards find themselves restricted by state education codes, union contracts, and highly regulated categorical aid programs.[17] Sadly, this governance arrangement typically yields thin analysis and thinly veiled lip service paid to school accountability. Nor is it easy to find more than a few parents who participate in this highly bureaucratized form of school decision making. We have procedural democracy on high, often pushed around by regional or statewide interest groups, then below we see very little spirited involvement by community members inside of schools, with the possible exception of affluent parents. Various polls and community studies detail the frustration and fears expressed by urban parents who see their neighborhood schools as unsafe and ineffective places for their children to learn.[18]

It is understandable—as anyone who has struggled to raise children knows—that parents are eager to bring up their kids within a familiar community. A return to the one-room schoolhouse is an attractive ideal, for it keeps our communal customs, moral beliefs, language, and forms of literacy within the four walls of that little schoolhouse just down the street. But all tribes are *not* created equal: some elders hold more wealth than others; the parents in some tribes hold better jobs and are better educated than those in other tribes. The retreat into our own schoolhouses—an isolationist rendition of village republicanism—may be good for local community building. But it denies the fact that only in a larger public square can the structural (cross-community) causes of inequality be addressed: family poverty, the hollowing out of inner cities, and resulting inequities in how schools are financed.

The Origins and Contours of Charter Schools

Like most educational "innovations," the basics of charter schools are not altogether new. Historian David Tyack, after reviewing an earlier draft of this chapter, postulated that charter advocates are reinventing the one-room schoolhouse. This may be only part of the story.

I do agree that skepticism over government and its often unresponsive institutions is renewing a commitment to village republicanism and the search for small-town community. But never before have we seen such a rainbow of particular local groups—expressing ethnic identities, religious convictions, pedagogical or child rearing philosophies—creating their own schools and pushing hard on the state to extract more public resources for their diverse organizations. Indeed, this is not a localism held together by the retrieval of a common nineteenth-century cultural frame, given form and unity through the common school. The new village republicanism renews faith in the virtues of human-scale schooling, but its contemporary rendition relaxes the assumption that a shared cultural frame and unifying public scheme are necessary to improve the local conditions under which we raise our children.

In my search to better understand charter activists' faith in radical decentralization, I keep returning to Madison's dispute with Jefferson, a bone of contention that intensified between the two in the early 1800s. Jefferson claimed, in historian Joseph Ellis's words, "that the individual is the sovereign unit of society; his natural state is freedom from and equality with other individuals."[19] Always defferential to his mentor, Madison was an early Republican, steadily needling the Federalists, like Alexander Hamilton and George Washington, who believed that states rights were fine so long as they did not undercut the essential authority of the nationwide common good.

Yet Madison sought a distribution of public authority—both vertically across levels and horizontally among branches—that would ensure strong leadership with accountability. He was heavily influenced by David Hume's thinking and repeatedly cited Hume's essay on political philosophy, *Idea of a Perfect Commonwealth*. After the collapse of the original states-rights compact, the Articles of Confederation, Madison headed for the constitutional convention aiming "to inculcate and enlighten [the delegates'] sense of national interest," as historian Jack Rakove puts it.[20] In the following three decades, even while serving in Jefferson's cabinet, Madison would push to strengthen the notion of judicial review, and he even challenged his old mentor to recognize that the central government must deliver on its sovereignty, enacting a uniform system of national laws governing transport and trade.

The charter movement represents a contemporary thrust not simply toward states' rights; it is a grassroots and corporate fusion moving to decenter public authority even below the level of local school boards. Frenchman Alexis de Tocqueville would be even more astonished if he were to visit America in the early twenty-first century. Not even Jefferson could have imagined how present-day reformers are challenging the commonweal, pushing to radically disassemble public institutions and the shared interests for which they used to stand.

How Are Charter Schools Different?

Perhaps what most distinguishes charter schools is that they are not subject to the mountains of statutory rules, program regulations, and union contracts that often confound school boards and principals who dare to consider serious reforms. Nor are charter school directors typically required to follow personnel practices that have accrued, like layers of crustaceans on a seaside boulder, inside school administrations.[21]

Charter schools have discretion over which children they accept. Legislation often requires that a lottery be used if applicants outnumber available classroom slots, but the much more consequential dynamic is that charters usually invite just certain types of families to participate, whether they be classified by race, religious affiliation, or philosophical commitment to strict discipline or innovative pedagogy. Charter schools, almost by their special-mission definition, are rarely inclusive institutions. One postmodern reality, or maybe premodern, is that building a tight community requires limited inclusiveness.

It is important to grasp the political innovation inherent in the charter mechanism. I want to spotlight two facets of the new school politics. First, charter schools are largely supported by public funds, yet only minimally accountable to public authority. This is symptomatic of how eager state policymakers and citizens have grown when it comes to sparking organizational innovation and new options for families who are fed up with their neighborhood school. We will describe how accountability is supposed to work, relying on a review every three or five years by the chartering agency of each school. But our case studies also detail rechartering efforts at two schools where very little hard evidence was put forward to document their effectiveness in raising children's achievement. Testimonials were abundant. Parental satisfaction often registered off the charts. Mayoral candidates dropped by to weigh in. But these half-baked attempts to sustain a school's charter often resembled the soft-headed means by which mediocre public schools survive politically.

Second, control over each charter school moves beneath, and unfolds independently from, the local school board or state education department. Village-level school boards, such as those that run charter schools, are certainly not unprecedented in American education. The one-room schoolhouse found in the nineteenth-century Midwest was typically governed by a village council, not by an administrative apparatus encompassing hundreds of schools, now so typical in contemporary urban districts. But even common-school boards were elected at large by the entire community, which ensured at least some political pluralism in civic debates.

Charter schools, in contrast, are controlled by loyalists to a particular school, usually founders, active parents, and teachers. Few argue that a Catholic parish, hospital, or a McDonald's franchise should operate with autonomy from the larger organization that pays the bills or enforces quality control. But this is precisely the license that charter school proponents have won from the state. Indeed, charters are designed to mimic private schools in their relative autonomy from local public authorities. In the case studies, you will discover how organizational autonomy is a double-edged sword.

The Royal Charter Is Reborn

A government charter is an "authorization from a central or parent organization to establish a new branch . . . [or] to give a special favor or privilege to."[22] The trading companies that settled Connecticut and Virginia, for instance, were granted royal charters by the British Crown. Banks, shoemakers, and factory owners were originally awarded charters by the state to operate in civil society. Colonial charters were granted to pursue private interests, yet government retained the ability to control actions that could impinge on the collective good as defined by the state.

This pivotal idea of a charter—whereby the imperial nation-state licenses an agent to pursue defined economic or political interests with limited autonomy—has been born anew. In 1975 a little-known educator, Ray Budde, spoke at an obscure academic conference. It was at the Society for General Systems Research—a banal setting for what became such a revolutionary political mechanism—that Budde put forward his simple idea. Originally his notion was essentially to charter teachers, giving them freedom from district regulations and rigid school norms to create innovative pedagogical programs. One of Budde's examples was for a teacher to take the earth-shaking step of increasing a high school class period from 50 to 120 minutes in length—what has since become known as "block scheduling."[23]

Ironically it was the late Al Shanker, long-time president of the American Federation of Teachers (AFT), who let the charter genie out of the bottle. In the spring of 1988 Shanker spoke at the National Press Club in Washington, D.C., discussing how many of his union members complained of local school boards that lacked a steady commitment to experimentation and school-level reform. To overcome this stultifying effect of district bureaucracy, Shanker cited Budde's idea of giving a teacher or an entire school the license to break away and break the mold. Shanker's weekly column in the *New York Times* that same week urged the creation of charter programs, such as the schools-within-a-school experiment, a direct descendant of 1960s-style alternative schools.[24] The AFT leader could not have forecast that these new schools' autonomy would mean that negotiated labor contracts, pay levels, and personnel rules—the hard-earned gains that unionists had won over the past century—would be watered down by the charter movement.

How Do Schools Win a Charter? Institutional Foundations

Neighborhood parents, teachers, private firms, and other groups, within flexible legal parameters, can petition to receive a charter from their local school board or from the state education department. These constitutive rules are set by legislatures, and they differ remarkably among the states. Since 1991 some thirty-seven states and Washington, D.C., have passed legislation enabling the creation of charter schools.

As Robin Lake and colleagues at the University of Washington point out, legislatures have delineated different policy aims in encouraging charter schools: some state laws hope to raise student achievement; some emphasize educational innovation as a good in and of itself; others celebrate the virtues of specialized curricula. Some lawmakers believe that decentralizing to the school level is the best way to exact accountability for higher performance; others argue that new charter schools will widen institutional choices for parents and children.[25] In some states, such as Arizona, local groups must petition the state school board for permission to operate and receive state funding on a per-pupil basis. In other states, including California, it is the local school board (or, if stymied there, the county office of education) that hears the request and approves a charter.

The legal charter received by the neighborhood group or private firm—granted, shall we say, by the colonial authority—does not provide total autonomy. Political theorists use the term *relative autonomy*, which is apropos in the case of charter schools. They are granted a degree of independence from the state, relative to the old regime. But autonomy is limited in two crucial ways. Schools receive public funds to operate, based on their student enrollment, and since many taxpayer dollars come in the form of categorical or "stovepipe" programs—for special education, compensatory reading, bilingual programs, and class-size reduction initiatives, to name a few—important resource dependencies vis-à-vis the state remain.

A majority of teachers in charter schools eagerly seek the freedom to innovate in their own classroom. But in California, one recent survey of the state's charter schools found that just one-fourth of all principals reported that they have "full control" over their budget.[26] And some charter schools do *not* desire complete autonomy from the school district or state board of education, since they are eager to have these more central elements of government provide liability insurance, payroll and accounting systems, and legal services. If bought on the open market, the financial burden on charter schools of such support services would prove fatal.

Most charter statutes require that each school be reviewed every three to five years before it can be rechartered. Many states require that charter schools participate in statewide testing programs, follow curricular guidelines, publish student test scores, or submit financial statements annually.[27] These requirements are important, at least symbolically, in that they signal that charter schools must be transparent: in distinct contrast to private and parochial schools, under most state statutes information on student performance and how taxpayer dollars are being spent must be available to the public. In our case studies we show how these requirements are sometimes met ritualistically by charter school leaders—call it *symbolic compliance.* Yet with the political halo that surrounds new charter schools—thanks to hopeful praise expressed by local newspapers, politicians, and reform-minded educators—schools are commonly rechartered even when hard evidence of achievement effects is entirely absent.

The issue of public accountability has flared up in several communities, especially when the organizational integrity of a school becomes questionable. Thomas Toch recently reported on the fraudulent practices of a few charter schools eager to tap into taxpayer dollars. West of Detroit, the Romulus school district established a satellite center, opening a school and enrolling 2,200 students, including many former dropouts. Families were offered a fifty-dollar signing bonus. The school qualified for $14 million in state aid, but only one-fifth of the new enrollees continued to attend the school. Toch also visited the NFL-YET Academy in Phoenix, an elementary school receiving taxpayer funding for 620 students. The school's founder, Armando Ruiz, is a former state senator. His twin brother, Fernando, is the budget director, and his younger brother is the head of "spiritual development." Armando's mother, father, and sister also are employed at the school.[28]

The Marcus Garvey charter school in Washington, D.C., made national headlines in 1996 when its principal, Mary Anigbo, physically ejected a *Washington Times* reporter from her office. The writer, Susan Ferrechio, wanted to visit the school, but the principal, who was later fired, apparently wasn't keen on gaining this kind of public attention. When Ferrechio returned with two staff members from the *Times* and two D.C. police officers, a melee erupted, and Anigbo was charged with assault.[29] These incidents also point out a problem with how "accountability" often is approached: even if salient features of the organization and its management come under scrutiny, the core teaching and learning processes typically escape notice.[30]

California taxpayers shell out about $200 million a year to for-profit companies and computer jocks who run home school charters and collect more than $6,500 per student, children that no credentialed teacher ever sees, despite recent legislation limiting such practices.[31] Furthermore, more solid charter organizations, that is, school organizations that actually have a building and teachers one can see, can act like private schools in largely nontransparent ways. The director of the Valley Charter School (see Chapter 6) bluntly told us, "If a parent with a handicapped child knocks on my door, I politely urge her to visit the next public school down the road."

We must be careful not to generalize from these bad apples. Yet they crisply illustrate how the rhetoric behind "direct market accountability" gives way to tolerance of entrepreneurs and well-meaning charter directors who are really not held to account for whether their students are learning effectively. In the absence of careful accountability and regulation—as in health care or child care—we should expect to see rip-offs and ineffective schools.

A second conception of the political charter involves the broader political legitimacy of the charter school institution. It sounds odd to use the term *institution* in discussing what typically are small and feisty schools, but these fledgling organizations have been awarded a broad political charter to operate, even when neither the letter nor the spirit of accountability is really being met. When Democrats like Gray Davis, corporate activists, and teacher union leader Bill Chase all rally around the charter school device, a high level of political legitimacy has been reached. We are far from knowing whether charter schools outperform neighborhood public schools, or the conditions under which this advantage is realized. But the political and symbolic advantages have become irresistible for politicians and school leaders.

Most charter school founders I have met are on a mission. They have grown disaffected with big, impersonal public schools; they have done battle with the downtown city schools office and become disillusioned; they see themselves as pioneers in creating more stimulating learning environments for kids and teachers alike. They are held together by the shared ideals, symbols, and connotations of the institution of charter schooling, what sociologist Emile Durkheim called "collective representations"—the symbolic building blocks of imagined communities.[32]

Similarly, if one follows the *Wall Street Journal*'s true-believer editorials on school choice one feels this missionary zeal, formed and reinforced by a set of sacred "facts" or tacit assumptions: liberating individual parents from the monopoly of public schooling; the evil, unresponsive education bureaucracy; the power of idealized market dynamics (even if played out in Catholic schools) to make public schools become more responsive or die off. At all levels—among policymakers, commentators, and leaders inside their own charter schools—the movement is becoming institutionalized, defined by sacred rites and holy assumptions.[33]

Between legistlative action by state governments and the movement's grassroots energy, growth in the number of new charter schools has been truly phenomenal over the past decade. The first officially designated charter school opened in Minnesota, following the 1991 passage of that state's pioneering legislation. By fall 2000, more than 1,600 schools were operating nationwide.

State legislation varies in how much rope is given to charter schools, and whether this line can be pulled by a transparent public authority that reviews the effectiveness of each school. States also expect varying levels of accountability. For example, Arizona law grants a charter for fifteen years, requiring a review by the state board of education every five years. In Florida, charter schools can gain a license to operate for three years before they are formally reviewed.

States also diverge in a number of key organizational domains: the extent to which charter schools must conform to salary schedules, hiring practices, and negotiated union contracts; whether public funding flows through local school boards or comes directly from the state; and whether entirely new schools can be chartered, or whether the license is awarded only to "conversion schools"—that is, public schools that break away from the system.

Taxpayer-funded networks of parents who home school their youngsters represent one of the fastest growing segments of charter schools, especially in California. School districts, for example, can enroll home-schooled children on the Web and provide curricular materials and a "learning facilitator" who may review parents' lesson plans. Full $6,500 per-pupil allocations flow from the state capital to the district or to a for-profit firm that organizes the families. One recent investigation in California found that more than 30,000 students were served through these two devices. The One2one charter company received more than $30 million in state funding during the 1998–99 school year, with about one-fourth of this revenue allocated to parents for materials and cash that they can use to enroll their youngsters in computer, music, or dance classes. Where the remaining funds go is not known, since these firms are privately owned and not subject to public disclosure laws. School districts have a strong incentive to host such schemes, since they shave off an administrative fee, even though their teachers rarely, if ever, see the students. In fact, students often live hundreds of miles from the district that participates in the virtual-school operation.[34]

What Do Charter Schools Look Like?

It's difficult to put your finger on a "typical" charter school. As comedic statisticians like to joke, "average" in this case would be like standing in a cold New England kitchen during the deep winter, sticking your head in a 450-degree oven, then calculating your mean body temperature. At the same time, many policymakers and educators are eager to wrap their arms around the universe of charter schools, as well as to advance contrasts with typical neighborhood schools. Like their predecessors—alternative and magnet schools—charters will be judged as a group of schools sharing basic organizational features. In a deeper way, educators and policy wonks should be learning about what it is inside charter schools and classrooms that may engage parents and boost student motivation, the focus of our case studies. But the first-order questions have to do with how the basic contours of charters compare to conventional public schools.

The federal government's recent descriptive study provides the most complete overview of the charter sector to date.[35] First, charter schools are quite small. Based on the almost 400 charter schools participating in the national study, enrollments average about 150 children per school. About one-third enroll fewer than 100 students. And charter schools that have opened since 1996 are about 40 percent smaller than the earliest charter schools. Whether this is a function of maturation or new schools filling even narrower market niches is not known. Over one-fourth of all charter students nationwide attend a school located in California. The next most active charter states are Arizona and Michigan, together enrolling almost 140,000 children, compared with California's enrollment of more than 120,000 in the fall of 2000.

About two-thirds of all charter schools focus on the middle or secondary grade levels. The remaining third are primary schools. This may reflect parents' greater disaffection with large, impersonal high schools, relative to their neighborhood elementary schools. Average enrollment in charter secondary schools equals just 140 students, similar to New York City's experiment with small schools. The average charter school is less than three years old.

Charter schools in some states are serving a diverse range of students, according to the U.S. Department of Education's inventory. Enrollments in all charter schools sampled included 17 percent African American, 16 percent Latino, and 5 percent Native American children in the 1996–97 school year. These proportions were very close to the ethnic composition of public school enrollments, pooling across the sixteen charter states represented in the sample. This comparison, however, masks the fact that ethnic minority families are underrepresented in three of five states with the most charter schools: Arizona, California, and Colorado. In California, 56 percent of all charter enrollment is non-Latino white, versus only 46 percent of all public school enrollment. Almost half of all charter schools serve predominantly Anglo students. One in four serves mainly students of color. One in three charter schools has a substantially lower percentage of white students than other schools in their district, reflecting preexisting residential segregation or a move by some families of color to form their own schools.

An independent assessment of charter schools in Arizona, where one in four charters nationally is located, found a widespread pattern of racial separation. Comparing the enrollments of fifty-five urban and fifty-seven rural charter schools to their neighboring public schools, the share of white enrollment in the charters averaged 20 percentage points higher. Researcher

Gene Glass also found that the charter schools primarily serving minority students resembled continuation high schools or offered non-college-track vocational programs.[36] Charters, in such cases, may be hardening the channeling of Latino and black youths into low curricular tracks.

This ethnic segregation of families and children manifests a curious irony. Many policy leaders who support wider parental choice also are pushing for uniform achievement standards that mesh tightly with a more culturally constrained, Anglocentric curriculum. The shift by some textbook writers to teach children more about multiculturalism, critical history, or a wider range of literature is anathema to these conservative supporters of choice. Yet, as will become apparent in our case study chapters, the ethnic roots of many charter communities define the boundaries of their philosophy and preferences for how children should be raised. The recent national evaluation report on one Afrocentric school notes that "the school's educational program is built on seven principles, including unity, self-determination, collective work and responsibility, cooperative economics, purpose, creativity, and faith. The underlying premise . . . is the belief that building a strong Afrocentric identity will give the youth the power and strength to succeed in life."[37]

Similarly, Luis Huerta will report on one home-school charter that is mainly comprised of fundamentalist Christian parents who mix secular curricular materials with church teachings. I am not judging this segmentation of children along ethnic or religious commitments. You will see how these shared beliefs, symbols, and convergent forms of pedagogy do strengthen the school's normative cohesion. The point is that enrollment patterns often reflect the particular cultural rules that govern a charter school's internal life and forms of learning. The book's contributors will revisit the question of whether charters are advancing the resegregation of children along ethnic and sectarian lines—including why some parents of color indeed are supportive of this trend. We also explore two charter schools that, instead, are committed to racial integration and diversity.

Finally, the national evaluation asks school directors about the major organizational and implementation problems that they currently face. The list is telling, offering a set of nitty-gritty issues that our case studies inform: lack of start-up funding and insufficient operating support, poor facilities, lack of planning time, political opposition from the local education establishment, and internal conflicts among board members and staff. These daily organizational problems can overwhelm charter directors and teachers who had believed that they would have time to think about pedagogical innovation and improvement.

Parents' Enthusiasm for Charter Schools

Other charter school assessments from several states have revealed vibrant enthusiasm among parents. This initial evidence also shows significant pent-up demand from families who have not won slots in desirable charter schools. The extent to which excess demand for charter spaces will persist, driving growth in the number and enrollment size of these schools, remains an intriguing question. As public choice options widen—including open-enrollment, magnet, and noncharter alternative schools—the intensity of demand may subside. Only so many inner-city parents have the time, resources, and wherewithal to work the educational marketplace. And surveys consistently show that many suburban parents are happy with their nearby public schools.

Parental support for charter schools has risen steadily over the past decade. Parent surveys in Colorado and Minnesota have found overwhelmingly strong parental support for their particular schools, with almost 90 percent of responding families giving their school a summative grade of A or B.[38] In California, two in five charter schools require that parents commit to at least several hours of work for the school. Authors of a report by SRI International warn that this may exclude some families, such as single or low-income parents who have much less discretionary time.[39] They also found that two-thirds of the ninety-eight charters participating in the study had more applicants than they could admit. The California legislature's 1998 decision to raise the cap on permissible charters from 100 to 250 will provide a chance to assess the level of demand for new schools. The Center for Educational Reform, a procharter advocacy group in Washington, D.C., found that more than one-third of the 300 charters surveyed in 1997 maintained waiting lists averaging 135 families in length.[40]

Do Children Learn More—or Differently—In Charter Schools?

At first glance the ability of selected charter schools to boost children's learning curves, relative to the growth typically observed for kids in neighborhood schools, appears to be encouraging. One charter school, the Community Day Charter outside Boston, has displayed impressive achievement gains: in one recent academic year, the children advanced one and one-half grade levels.[41] In Los Angeles, an evaluation team in 1998 claimed that two charters—the Fenton and Vaughn schools—were able to move student learning upward at rates significantly higher than comparison schools serving similar children.[42]

The authors of these initial studies are to be commended for attempting to focus on students' learning growth over the course of one year, rather than simply taking one-time snapshots of achievement. The Los Angeles evaluators also tried to compare learning curves for children in charters with those of similar youngsters attending neighborhood schools. Yet even these studies suffer from serious methodological flaws. Overall, the level of public and private resources being spent on charter schools is way out of proportion to the paucity of hard evidence demonstrating their effectiveness. Few competent evaluators have been able to enter the field with sufficient funding to study the long-term achievement effects of this faith-filled experiment.

Equally distressing, the groups conducting these early evaluations repeat mistakes that are well known among experienced evaluators. For example, no studies have yet to control for so-called selection bias. Like private schools, charters attempt to admit a select number of children who show promise and have parents who are committed to the mission and culture of the particular school. We know that the best shoppers for better schools are parents who are better educated or more strongly committed to education, and who watch like hawks over their children's homework and school performance. So when the learning curves of charter students look steeper than those attending neighborhood schools one must ask if this advantage is really due to the school or to the special push provided by the parents.

Student performance in Los Angeles charter schools climbed 4 percentile points between 1997 and 1998 according to a report by the San Francisco firm WestEd, double the gain observed in all schools citywide.[43] But if charter schools are working—gaining positive reputations among informed parents—they likely have attracted parents who push their children each night to get homework done and to take school seriously. That is, they attract a select group of families who adeptly play the charter school market. And these family characteristics may explain learning gains, not the schools per se. The WestEd evaluators did attempt to minimize this source of bias by selecting comparison schools that appear to serve students of similar family background, as signaled by typical measures like ethnicity or eligibility for free lunches. But if charters spur (nonrandom) migration of certain families into the charter school, then steeper average learning curves will simply indicate higher numbers of more involved parents. Indeed, school choice is engineered to spark such patterns of family migration.

It remains unclear whether charter schools can do a better job than garden-variety public schools in overcoming the effects of family poverty or disadvantageous parental practices. The much celebrated Renaissance School in Boston—praised widely for admitting a highly diverse urban student population—recently ranked in the bottom 10 percent of all schools statewide. A cofounder of Renaissance, Robert Gaudet, argued that the poor showing was not surprising, since "86 percent of the (achievement) outcome on the new test in Massachusetts can be explained by the demographics of the communities."[44] Ironically, Gaudet's claim is vociferously attacked by some charter advocates as an excuse for incompetence whenever it's put forward by public school loyalists.[45]

Another important question also should be studied: What are the shared ingredients of charter schools that contribute to steeper learning curves for children? It is understandable why government wants to know whether the overall charter school movement is yielding promising results. But don't we also want to know why effective charter schools are able to boost achievement beyond expectations based on their kids' socioeconomic characteristics? Just as with earlier forms of decentralized school governance, we know little about how charter directors are spending dollars differently or how teachers are innovating pedagogically.[46]

Initial evaluations consistently reveal that parents are very keen on placing their children in institutions that are safe, that enforce clear discipline standards, and that socialize their children according to the local norms by which their parents live. This may involve a charter school that teaches La Raza ideals, the tenets of religious fundamentalism, or the expressive virtues of the performing arts. Indeed, recent national surveys reveal that most parents are at least as concerned about socialization processes inside their children's schools as they are with standardized test scores.[47] Yet evaluators to date have focused on either parental satisfaction or student test scores, disregarding parents' keen interest in socialization outcomes.

Headless States? Charter Schools and the School Choice Movement

To understand the origins and theory of reform that underlie charter schools, we must place them in the broader political struggle over school choice. One can quickly grasp the political force of the broader movement for choice by observing children's rising rate of exit from assigned neighborhood schools. The share of students attending private schools, at family expense, has remained at just below 10 percent over the past half-century. The raw number inched upward as the overall student population grew during the 1990s, and stood at 4.6 million of the nation's 52 million elementary and secondary pupils at century's end.[48]

Enrollment in public alternative schools has climbed remarkably in recent years, moving from under 10 million to almost 14 million students who now attend magnet or charter schools or participate in cross-town transfer programs, statewide open-enrollment options, or publicly and privately funded voucher experiments. In the fall of 1999, fully one in four children no longer attended their assigned neighborhood school, a telling structural shift in the organization of schooling.[49]

Hippies Renew the Impulse to Innovate: Alternative Schools

Let's take a brief journey to explore how and why the movement for wider, more diverse school choices has grown over the past half century. I begin with the rise of alternative schools, recurring organizational experiments that have enjoyed a rich history spanning more than a century.

Urban academies such as Bronx Science, Boston Latin, and San Francisco's Lowell High School have long served families citywide, admitting new students through a competitive admissions process.[50] Yet the Progressive Era in the early twentieth century sparked an entirely new kind of alternative school aimed more at revolutionizing the mechanical form of school organization and pedagogy that had come to dominate the "one best system." One landmark effort was crafted by the Commission on the Relation of School and College, made up of leading progressive educators inspired by the pedagogical philosophy of John Dewey. In their 1930 report, a document that still sings in contemporary tones, these progressives complained of how elite universities and their narrow emphasis on test scores and academic subjects were constraining the forms of pedagogy and learning that were permitted in public high schools.

They convinced the Carnegie and Rockefeller foundations to support, over an eight-year period, thirty public and private alternative schools in the not-so-radical settings of Denver and Tulsa. The Deweyan curriculum focused on integrating subject areas, involving students in community service projects, and encouraging children's development in art, drama, and music.

The sacred Carnegie unit for awarding high school course credit (mandated by the Ivy League) was thrown out. Evaluation pioneer Ralph Tyler was hired to assess how the graduates did relative to comparable adolescents in regular schools. His team claimed that the alternative school graduates eventually outperformed the control group in college and were more active in social, political, and artistic spheres of collegiate life.[51]

Historians David Tyack and Larry Cuban offer a telling institutional footnote to this otherwise promising story: a decade after the conclusion of the experiment, in 1950, a core group of these progressives gathered to reflect on their work. Only a few traces of the schools could still be found in either city. Frederick L. Redefer, director of the Progressive Education Association, complained that the Second World War, then the cold war, had heightened resistance to progressive reforms. As he put it, "A concern for security tended to strengthen conservatism and authoritarianism . . . everything connected with progressive education was under fire." In addition, in a lesson that resonates for charter schools, Redefer reported that internal organizational stress often proved to be fatal, saying teachers became "exhausted by the demands made on them . . . challenges came too thick and fast for faculty to digest them."[52]

The 1960s bred a resurging commitment to alternative schools replete with educational ideals that flowed directly from the Progressive Era. Beyond Dewey, the heroes of the "free school" movement included A. S. Neill, director of England's Summerhill School, founded in the 1920s. Neill believed that the lockstep nature of public schools was useful in preparing factory workers but failed to build from children's innate goodness and curiosity, or to acknowledge their own pace of learning. Regular schooling also inculcated a fear of authority that ran counter to natural ways of learning. Summerhill was designed "to make the school fit the child," not vice versa.[53]

By the mid-1960s, new American thinking, largely rooted in Abraham Maslow's humanistic psychology, was presenting a serious challenge to the bureaucratic, batch-processing form of mass schooling. Ivan Illich was calling for the "deschooling" of American child rearing. Paulo Freire was urging that proper schooling must empower children and adults alike to engage the political process and pursue a more just society. The emerging counterculture demanded a form of child rearing and education that would counter the mass processing of America's youngsters. Alternative schools were to be "child centered," in constrast to the typical, "teacher centered" public schools.[54]

All this sounds like democratic nirvana if your conception of local democracy is similar to John Dewey's, in which diverse individuals come together within a shared community and work cooperatively to learn and to solve problems. This new conception of how school organizations should work—and should touch the lives of individual children—gained enormous credibility in the 1960s and 1970s. The first free schools were operated privately, often by parent collectives. Public school districts then began to open a variety of alternative schools, including "schools without walls," performing arts schools, and other theme schools that would later flow into the magnet school movement. A survey by the venerable National School Boards Association in 1975 found that one quarter of districts nationwide were operating at least one alternative school, and declared that "the concept is definitely not on the fringe of American public school activity . . . and its significance is growing."[55]

Turning to Magnet Schools and Open Enrollment

Magnet schools expanded rapidly from the early 1970s forward, energized by the struggle to voluntarily desegregate urban schools and by growing interest in sharpening the curricular focus of selected schools. Vociferous opposition to court-ordered busing aimed at desegregating schools under the Supreme Court's original *Brown v. Board of Education* decision reached violent boiling points in the late 1960s and early 1970s, in cities from Boston to Kansas City to Los Angeles. This led to enormous pressure for voluntary forms of desegregation that would stem white flight to the suburbs and enrich school quality for all urban children. Magnet school enthusiasts hoped to attract white students whose parents would otherwise head to suburban schools by creating racially integrated schools dedicated to special themes, including math-science schools, arts and drama academies, dual language and humanities programs, and later, vocationally focused career academies.

When federal courts first accepted magnet programs as one strategy for desegregating schools in 1975, just 14 such programs were operating nationwide. By 1980 there were about 140 magnet schools and programs. A decade later, more than 3,100 such programs operated in 2,400 mostly urban schools, serving 1.2 million students nationwide. In California alone, the number of students served by magnet programs almost doubled during the 1990s, now amounting to a quarter million children.[56] More than half of all magnet schools and programs are situated in elementary schools. The vast majority operate within large urban districts.[57]

Until recently very little has been known about the effectiveness of magnet schools. We do know that many are successful in achieving their basic goal of reducing racial segregation. One careful evaluation by the American Institutes of Research in Palo Alto, California, found that about half of the 615 magnet programs studied nationwide had more racially integrated student bodies than their neighboring public schools in 1993. Sixteen local studies have revealed similar results, such as in St. Louis, where 42 percent of all magnet students are nonblack, compared to just 22 percent of students in all district schools. In Cincinnati, magnet programs are similarly more racially integrated than garden-variety public schools.[58]

As with other forms of choice, a fair degree of "selection bias" does occur in terms of the kind of parents who push to gain entry for their child. Only one in eight magnet programs actually uses selective admissions procedures; some admit students through a lottery to equalize every applicant's odds of gaining access.[59] Children who gain access to magnet schools—while typically from working-class or low-income backgrounds—tend to have better-educated parents, to live in a two-parent household, and are less frequently eligible for subsidized lunch programs than other children from the same community. This fact goes back to the original purpose of magnets: to attract a range of white families who began to flee central cities with the onset of mandatory busing programs.

Do magnet programs boost children's learning curves beyond the inclines observed in typical urban schools? University of Wisconsin sociologist Adam Gamoran recently completed a national study aimed at informing this question. He found that after controlling for the effects of family background, students attending sampled magnet schools are outperforming comparable students attending typical public schools. Yet only a few important differences between magnets and regular schools could be detected. Students in magnet programs, for instance, take more core courses in math and science. But the academic climate and social ties observed in magnet schools are not significantly different from those in neighborhood schools.[60]

A more recent evaluation of New York City's vocational, or career, magnets, led by Robert Crain at Columbia University's Teachers College, found higher reading scores among their students relative to comparable city-school students.[61] Additional studies in Cincinnati, Nashville, and St. Louis have revealed that magnet school teachers are more likely to have received graduate training and to report more control over their own courses and curricula. But these differences do not consistently explain higher levels of student achievement.[62] While hopeful, these early achievement studies often lack sufficient controls for selection bias: the achievement effects attributed to a magnet school may actually stem from parental practices and students' variable home lives, which remain unobserved by most researchers.

Open-enrollment options commonly exist alongside districtwide magnet efforts in urban areas. Minnesota was the first to enact a statewide open-enrollment scheme, in 1988. Since then, sixteen state legislatures have abolished, independent of charter school bills, the old requirement that parents send their child to the nearby public school.[63] States now vary in terms of whether parents can petition to enter any school in the district or any school statewide. These two options are known as intradistrict and interdistrict choice, respectively.

Family demand for intradistrict transfer can be very high, and particularly desirable schools are often surrounded by neighborhood parents who fight to preserve access for their own children. The immense Los Angeles school district offered 5,000 open-enrollment slots in the 2000–2001 school year. In recent years more than 70,000 parents have applied annually for these openings.[64] This scarcity of slots is growing worse as states are moving to lower class size, leading to overcrowding in select schools and neighborhood parents pushing to limit the number of transfer students.

Open-enrollment initiatives vary substantially, especially in the value their architects place on ensuring all families equal access. Minnesota's statewide choice program, for instance, subsidizes transportation costs for low-income families. And schools that are successfully advancing more racially integrated student bodies do not have to open up new slots.

In contrast, the Massachusetts open-enrollment program allows market dynamics to unfold in unregulated splendor. The overwhelming majority of the 7,000 participating families are white, and they are leaving racially integrated working-class communities for predominately Anglo and wealthier suburban schools. This is a case of Robin Hood in reverse: state school dollars are pulled from already depressed districts and transferred to wealthier districts. In 1997, recognizing this severe inequity, the Massachusetts legislature approved an adjustment whereby low-wealth districts are reimbursed an amount equaling half their per-pupil spending level for every exiting student.[65]

Magnet and open-enrollment programs operating simultaneously hope to liberalize market choices while spurring creation of more distinctive school organizations. Magnets have banked heavily on the ideals contained in the decades-old "effective schools" literature, expressing faith in the power of a strong principal, a specialized curricular mission, teacher professionalism, and progressive pedagogy. Yet the extent to which these ideals are achieved is unclear. It appears that many parents choose "high-quality schools" based on incomplete signals of "quality," including a school's racial composition, cross-sectional test scores (not learning curves over time), and the appearance of school facilities. Political scientist Jeff Henig found that the most popular magnet programs in Montgomery County, Maryland, near Washington, D.C., were those offering French immersion programs—a component that yielded no particular advantage in terms of raising children's test scores over time.[66] Parents' understanding of their magnet options was strikingly correlated with their ethnicity, with Anglo parents being most knowledgeable and Latinos the least informed.

Vouchers for Private and Parochial Schools

The move to expand voucher experiments represents a hot wire of sorts, electrifying the school choice movement and occasionally jolting the education establishment. Publicly funded voucher programs still total just two in number, those in Milwaukee and Cleveland. Most recently, corporate leaders have capitalized an organization called the CEO Foundation to privately support vouchers for children from low-income and blue-collar families in several cities around the country.

Wisconsin was the first state to authorize an experiment with publicly funded vouchers. Beginning in the 1990–91 school year, Milwaukee parents could apply to receive a voucher-financed slot in one of seven nonsectarian private schools. Each participating school—they were quite small operations linked to community action organizations or preschools—received an amount equal to per-pupil financing in the public system. During the first year, 341 parents won voucher slots in these schools. Voucher enrollments rose to just under 1,000 children in 1993–94.[67]

Two years later, in 1995, the state legislature made parochial schools eligible to participate—a controversial move eventually permitted by the U.S. Supreme Court in 1998—and expanded the number of vouchers available to parents. If enrollments in the choice plan rise to the program's capped maximum of 15,000 children, the Milwaukee school system will lose at least 12 percent of its enrollment; $75 million in public financing will move to private schools. Students now enroll in 1 of 122 participating private schools, 89 of which are religious institutions.[68]

The Milwaukee experiment is carefully targeted to benefit low-income families. Eligible parents earn no more than 1.75 times the federal poverty level. During the first three years of the voucher program, just under 60 percent of all parents participating in the program were receiving cash welfare assistance. Three-quarters of parents were African American; 18 percent of the voucher parents were Latino.

Cleveland's voucher program, begun in September 1996 and the only other taxpayer-supported experiment, is closely targeted for low-income families as well. From its inception, the Cleveland effort has included parochial schools among those serving the 3,000 participating families. This has significantly benefited children who were already enrolled in Catholic or other religious schools prior to the program's inception. (Likewise, when Wisconsin made parochial schools eligible, about a third of the students who won the new vouchers were already attending a religious school.) The net effect is not to enable parents to choose but to provide tax relief for low-income families who have already found a way to exercise choice.

Family demand for these municipal voucher programs has clearly outpaced the number of available slots. But how do children attending a "choice school" fare, compared with their peers who remain behind in the neighborhood school? This has been a slippery question to answer, and initial evaluation designs have been shaken by blasts of technical criticism. The initial evaluation of the Milwaukee experiment, conducted by University of Wisconsin political scientist John Witte, found that students attending the first generation of small, private voucher schools did no better than their cohort in the Milwaukee public schools.

In a vociferous attack and reanalysis of the Witte study, Harvard professor Paul Peterson claimed that children who stayed in the voucher program for four years outperformed the control group of students in math but not reading. However, only a very small number of all participating students stayed for four straight years in these small private schools, leading to concern over exit selection bias: these children may have come from families differing from those whose children dropped out of the program.[69]

A third analysis, done by Princeton economist Cecilia Rouse, did yield more convincing evidence that Milwaukee's voucher students significantly outperformed those remaining in the public schools. The magnitude of the difference was small, however (1.5 to 2.3 percentile points), and no effect on reading performance could be detected.[70] The original evaluation design, which yielded the data on which all three studies were based, failed to gather information about families or home practices that might explain why learning curves may be a bit higher for children whose parents pushed to participate in the voucher program.

Voucher advocates—stymied by legislative defeats and lopsided losses at the ballot box in California and Colorado—are now creating privately funded voucher experiments. Financed by a handful of wealthy individuals, including Wal-Mart heir John Walton, the CEO Foundation has created voucher programs in fifteen cities around the country, programs that served 40,000 children in the fall of 1999. In the spring of the same year, Florida's governor Jeb Bush pushed through its statewide voucher program, targeted for children attending "poor performing schools." Fewer than ninety students were granted vouchers in the fall 1999 school year, and at least two private schools in the north Florida region refused to accept the voucher winners. The program faces a serious court challenge.

The young New York City voucher program is currently offering portable "scholarships" to 2,000 elementary school students, chosen by lottery, and thus offers a true (random assignment) experiment, similar to the method by which medical researchers test the effects of new drugs. It largely avoids the prior problem of selection bias, although families applying for vouchers do differ from low-income New York City parents overall.[71] Led by Harvard's Paul Peterson, analysis of the program's first-year results showed that reading and math scores were up 2 to 7 percentile points for voucher winners (who largely enrolled in parochial schools) compared with kids who didn't win the lottery and returned to the public schools. The first-year report details how the parochial schools attended by the voucher recipients had smaller classes, enrolled fewer students in total, and were staffed by more stable sets of teachers, compared with the city schools.[72] This raises the question of whether these organizational advantages, if financed throughout the public system, would yield similar results. Nor is it clear that the parochial school system would want to accept the diversity of students found in the broader population, including learning disabled students and kids with behavioral problems.

Evaluations are under way of corporate-funded voucher experiments in San Antonio and Washington, D.C., led by the unabashedly provoucher study group at Harvard's Kennedy School of Government. Findings from this research team, led by Peterson, will place hard evidence into a discourse now dominated by polemics and ideology. Yet the long-term issue, even if children from low-income families migrating to parochial schools score 2 to 5 percentile points higher, is whether these schools really want to serve a truly representative cross section of urban kids, including those with learning disabilities and troubling behavior problems. Parents applying to private voucher pilots are indeed low-income, but they are more highly educated and are willing to put up $1,000 or more in cash to supplement their voucher. Peterson has taken long methodological strides, including the move to real experiments with control groups, just like in clinical trials for new medicines. But until we have large-scale programs and we test the willingness of private and religious schools to serve a truly diverse range of children and families, we won't know whether radical market remedies yield achievement gains for a broad range of children.

Still, the early evidence on Catholic schools, in particular, suggests that there often is something about a private school's ethos, including its deep commitment to the whole child and its high expectations for all students, that may shed light on why many blue-collar kids do surprisingly well there relative to their peers in typical public schools. This suggests that tinkering with specific features of public schools enmeshed in sluggish bureaucracies may not yield the same results observed in smaller private schools.[73]

How Sold Is the Public on School Choice?

Over the past two decades Americans have come to believe that parents have the political right to select a school of their choice for their children. The old system of assigning children to the nearest elementary school or high school has lost a good deal of credibility. Yet widening support for the kind of choice options just detailed doesn't mean that parents are necessarily eager to change schools. A nationwide poll in the early 1990s found that only 23 percent of all families would leave their child's neighborhood school if awarded the freedom to do so.[74]

Importantly, voters' sentiments toward their own neighborhood school remain warm. In 1998 the Gallup poll on education found that 46 percent of those interviewed gave their own schools a grade of A or B (this rose to 62 percent among parents with older children in school), while just 18 percent awarded an A or B to the public schools in general.[75] In California, where school reform rose to the top of the political agenda again during the 1998 gubernatorial campaign, 61 percent of all respondents said that the school system needed a "major overhaul."[76]

This deepening concern over the state of public education has led many to support far-reaching reforms, including market-oriented attempts to radically decentralize the control of schools. In 1993, only 24 percent of Americans supported the idea of allowing parents to enroll their child in a public or private school of their choice at public expense; 74 percent opposed it. By 1998, 44 percent supported this choice policy and just 50 percent expressed opposition.[77] A National Public Radio (NPR) poll in 1999 put opposition to vouchers three points higher, at the edge of each survey's margin of error. Perhaps most remarkable is the finding that 59 percent of all black respondents and 52 percent of Latinos surveyed support the idea, as many are seeking options outside their neighborhood schools. Yet in a chilling finding for private educators, three-quarters of all respondents said that private schools accepting taxpayer dollars must become regulated by government and admit a more diverse set of students.[78]

One additional finding stands out from these recent polls, particularly for political candidates and state policymakers: Americans are far more supportive of seemingly strong government efforts to hold schools accountable and to equalize spending across communities than of placing all our reform eggs in the school choice basket. The NPR survey found, for example, that three out of four citizens would pay $200 more in taxes for state-led reform programs. More than half would be willing to pay $500 more in taxes. Interestingly, 83 percent said that they support equalizing school aid even if it means taking funding from wealthy school districts and giving it to poor ones.

The 1998 Gallup poll similarly revealed that more than 80 percent of respondents support congressional Democrats' focus on lowering class size and massive public investments to renovate schools. Our own 1998 PACE-Field poll of Californians (conducted by the Berkeley-Stanford institute Policy Analysis for California Education) similarly revealed overwhelming backing for strong government action: higher curricular standards, greater school accountability, and mandated summer school for low achievers. And those citizens who are most likely to vote—including suburban women and independents—remain less supportive of vouchers and decentralized policy remedies in general.[79] These public sentiments help to explain why a Republican-controlled Congress in the fall of 1999 approved the most centralized school reforms ever passed in Washington, aimed at tightening accountability of Title I funds for disadvantaged students and boosting the program's effectiveness. Efforts by House conservatives to approve Title I–funded vouchers were voted down.[80]

All this has led Democrats and born-again centrists like governors George W. Bush and Gray Davis to advance state-led reform measures that in many cases *increase centralization* to the state level. National politicians and the national media focus largely on debates swirling around the devolution of Washington's power down to state capitals. But education bureaucrats inside the beltway have never had much say about education policy. Federal funds represent less than 7 percent of public school revenues. The real story since the early 1990s is how governors and state legislatures have substantially centralized school financing, curricular control, testing, performance accountability, even how teachers teach and how students are promoted from grade to grade.

The key point is to understand that even as charter and school choice movements spread, state-led reform strategies, now backed by a wide range of governors and voters, signify a counterstrategy to radical decentralization. This leads to the provocative question: Instead of spreading market-oriented reforms, legitimated by ever more headless states, are mindful governments engineering policies that yield real effects inside local schools and classrooms? This is the dialectical tension to which we next turn.

Mindful States? School Reform Led by Governors

Giving form and force to Americans' desire for institutional change is often the political leader's first challenge, be it aimed at the reform of schooling, taking on HMOs, or trying to fix the welfare system. If one can generate a mobilizing sense of crisis, then the conditions have been set for aggressively moving ahead with policy reforms. The difficulty, of course, is that "crises," pumped up with a stiff dose of hysteria, often lead to policy remedies that don't acknowledge the constraints under which besieged institutions and their grassroots staff must work. Ironically, it was Ronald Reagan's White House staff that spawned the feeling of crisis and the sustained political energy that still powers the school reform bandwagon.

In April 1983 Reagan—with much fanfare—released *A Nation at Risk: The Imperative of Educational Reform*. In dramatic tones, the report read like an exposé, the result of investigations by a team of dissonant journalists:

> Our Nation is at risk. Our once unchallenged preeminence in commerce, industry, science and technological innovation is being overtaken by competitors throughout the world . . . The educational foundations of our society are presently being eroded by a rising tide of mediocrity that threatens

our very future as a nation and a people. If an unfriendly power had attempted to impose on America the mediocre educational performance that exists today, we might well have viewed it as an act of war . . . We have, in effect, been committing an act of unthinking, unilateral educational disarmament.[81]

This report became "the mother of all critiques of American education," in the words of researchers David Berliner and Bruce Biddle.[82]

The country was in the depths of an economic recession. President Reagan's popularity had taken a nosedive, partially due to many Americans' rising view that he was too hawkish on nuclear arms. The White House was eager to put forth a domestic issue on which Reagan would be viewed as a concerned moderate. As the report came to the Reagan cabinet, Education Secretary Terrel Bell and senior White House staff members could see the political pluses in proclaiming that America's education system was going down the drain, and that decisive public action would be required to save it. In his memoirs, Secretary Bell expresses a deep belief that "declining academic standards" were eroding school quality and that something dramatic was required to stimulate higher visibility for the education issue inside a besieged White House.[83]

An important debate would ensue over whether America's schools were truly in a crisis. Professors Berliner and Biddle show that most indicators of student achievement, going back to the 1950s, displayed no such decline.[84] While overall movement in student learning has been stagnant or modest over the past two generations across all age groups, recent work confirms that the learning gap between black and non-Latino white students actually closed significantly between 1971 and 1996, in both reading and math. The underlying causes for this narrowing remain rather mysterious, although state and federal reforms may have played a forceful role. The reduction in achievement inequities appears linked to rising school attainment levels and declining birth rates among black parents. Rising graduation requirements during the 1980s, declining average class size in the southern states where black scores rose most sharply, and rising teacher quality in many states also have been empirically attributed to student gains in black and low-income communities.[85]

Sharp critics, such as Hoover Institution economist Eric Hanushek, have attacked the revisionists—naysayers like Berliner and Biddle who insist the school crisis was exaggerated—by detailing how school spending has tripled over the past three decades. For all of this largesse, Hanushek asks, shouldn't parents and policymakers expect more than the upward inching of test scores observed over this period?[86] Should we be satisfied with merely advancing equity? Isn't there an equally broad public interest in raising average learning curves for middle-class children?

The "crisis" over public education gave voice to a host of other, deeper issues: worries that the economy's slowdown was attributable to declining educational standards, concern over the "culture wars" and intensifying ethnic and class Balkanization, not to mention the political search for a unifying issue that would capture crucial suburban swing voters—nonpartisan parents who remain deeply concerned with the state of public schools and allied family issues, like preschool and child-care options. The body politic's sustained focus on improving public education, now nearly two decades since the release of *A Nation at Risk,* demonstrates the lasting force of these underlying worries in the minds of American voters.

Ironic Affections: The Appeal of Strong State Action

Once centrally situated actors inside government highlight a problem, it becomes very difficult for politicians to remain inactive on the policy front. This was the problem facing the Reagan White House following the spring of 1983. Authors of *A Nation at Risk* recommended a renewed federal investment in education and a pay raise for teachers. But this was not going to fly within this particular Republican administration. Instead, the Reagan and Bush administrations would continue to advocate (at least during campaign seasons) abolishing the Education Department. Tuition tax credits for affluent parents who send their children to private schools would rise to the top of Reagan's domestic agenda. Conservatives, by the late 1980s, emphasized the potential magic of school vouchers and choice over the more centralized public actions urged in *A Nation at Risk.*

Yet the lasting political impact of the 1983 crusade was to legitimate action by state governments in the school reform arena. By 1989 President Bush would enthusiastically pull together all fifty of the nation's governors and nudge them to agree to a handful of ambitious national goals for education. The old conservative belief that the public schools should be run by local school boards, a quaint governance holdover from the common school's heyday, was no longer tenable. Fifty points of light had been lit—with national commissions and eager governors offering all sorts of incendiary devices. A young governor from Arkansas named Bill Clinton would lead the National Governors Association (NGA) charge on school reform during much of the 1980s. South Carolina governor Richard Reily, who would become Clinton's secretary of education in 1993, was at his side.

One of NGA's leading thinkers, Michael Cohen, published a paper in 1990 that became a blueprint for several reform-minded governors over the subsequent decade.[87] In addition to crafting strong state-level reforms, it artfully crafted a centrist map for how Democratic reformers could blend selective centralizing policies with the decentralization of power to the school level. It was Cohen—along with allied policy theorists inside the academy—who arrived at the colorless term *restructuring.* The essence of restructuring, or what some call *systemic reform,* involves tightening up the system by closing the organizational slack between the state and thousands of schools around the country. This is a century-old conception of how to rationalize the far-flung school institution, originally conceived by industrial elites who believed that schools could be managed just like networks of automobile plants.

The specific way to tighten up, according to restructuring advocates, was to set national or state-level curricular standards, reinforce academic content through standards and more intense testing, lengthen the school year (increasing the "opportunity to learn"), and provide incentives to schools that reward high-performing teachers while setting negative sanctions for the laggards. At the same time, some decision-making authority was to be moved down to the school level. In essence, then, the early restructuring proponents urged state governments to accumulate political authority to set specific standards for learning outcomes, while leaving school principals and (more professional) teachers with great control over how organizationally and pedagogically those learning objectives would be achieved. The big losers in this power struggle would be district administrators and locally elected school boards, in which few reformers held much faith.

Centrists, like White House education advisers Cohen and Mike Smith, upped the ante in 1999, borrowing strategies from Texas and North Carolina. In Bill Clinton's 1999 State of the Union address he called for an unprecedented centralized role for Washington, D.C., in tightening lines of school accountability: "All states and school districts must turn around their worst performing schools or shut them down. That is the policy established by Governor Jim Hunt in North Carolina, where test scores made the biggest gains in the nation last year." The president went on to attribute climbing test scores in Chicago to "ending social promotion and (making) summer school mandatory for those (students) who don't master the basics."[88] Clinton proposed that federal school aid be withheld from districts that did not end the automatic promotion of children from one grade level to the next. The federal government was to enforce how students were being assessed and promoted in every school across the land.

Heresy? Perhaps. But later that year the Republican Congress would inject centralized accountability regulations into the $8 billion federal Title I program. And Republican presidential candidate George W. Bush would similarly push to create centrally determined achievement standards on which the flow of federal education aid would be contingent.

Why Are Achievement Levels Inching Upward?

An intriguing mystery does bolster the promise of restructuring and, more broadly, the claim that central (state) governments can be mindful and efficacious when it comes to school reform. The mystery comes in two subplots. First, the reading scores of African American students, tested at the ages of nine and thirteen, rose significantly during the 1970s and well into the 1980s, before stagnating in recent years. Math performance for black children showed a similar gain, albeit at a slower rate, into the mid-1990s.

The second subplot is more complex. Reading and math scores remained remarkably flat for white students during this same twenty-five-year stretch, with one important exception: math skills among nine-year-olds began to rise around 1990 and have continued to inch upward. Math scores for all thirteen-year-old children rose by about 6 percent between 1990 and 1992.[89] The average math score on the SAT exam in 1997 was the highest ever recorded.[90] This was achieved despite the fact that the ethnic diversity of SAT test takers—high school students who anticipate entering college—was the most colorful ever recorded.

National Assessment of Educational Progress (NAEP) reading scores for 1998 showed another round of incremental gains for fourth- and eighth-grade children. Twelfth graders slipped a bit, relative to performance levels observed in 1992. The strongest gains were posted by black and Latino children, suggesting that some elements of urban school reform are paying off.[91] States, like Connecticut and Kentucky, that had seriously equalized school financing and pressed higher achievement standards posted significant gains in schools serving low-income children.[92] Regional disparities remain sharp across the United States: students in the South and the West scored significantly lower than children in the Northeast, partially on account of demographic differences.

A Victory for Central State Action?

Strong action by state governments—focusing on clearer curricular standards, tighter tracking of low-performing schools, and early interventions in reading—do help to explain this steady if slow rise in test scores over the past decade. The upbeat results for fourth-grade reading performance on the NAEP offer encouraging evidence of how central action can make a difference. The share of nine-year-olds judged proficient in reading climbed from 34 to 46 percent in Connecticut between 1992 and 1998. The percentage rose in Colorado from 25 to 34 percent. The share in Texas, where rates of child poverty and limited English are high, jumped from 24 to 29 percent during the same period. All three of these states had moved aggressively early in the decade down the path of state-led accountability. Connecticut has focused on raising the bar for those entering the teaching profession, upgrading training programs and credential requirements.[93]

The key questions then become: Are state-guided reforms responsible for the rising inclines in children's learning curves? Does the slow pace of progress warrant even stronger action by state and federal governments, such as instituting national exams? Or is progress so slow that we should move full steam ahead toward radical decentralization?

Many educators and a few governors have been traveling to Texas to learn how that state has dramatically boosted children's achievement. The success of the state's twelve-year-long reform effort supports the likely efficacy of restructuring. The basic facts in Texas are stunning. Between 1992 and 1996 math scores for Texas fourth and eighth graders rose almost .35 of a standard deviation, equaling a 14-percent jump, almost 50 percent higher than average state gains nationwide. Reading scores were more difficult to budge, but they did begin to rise after 1995: the average elementary school student scored 5 percentile points higher by 1997.

The state's restructuring strategy appears to have helped close the gap between white, Latino, and black children's achievement levels. In 1994, a 40-percent gap existed between the share of black students passing the Texas Assessment of Academic Skills (TAAS) relative to white students. By 1998 this gap had closed to 21 percentage points. Overall, Texas now ranks between second and fourth among the forty-two states participating in NAEP, after controlling for family characteristics such as the large number of children coming from low-income homes (one in four) and with limited English proficiency.[94]

Critics of the Texas program, such as Stanford's Linda Darling-Hammond, argue that significant numbers of poor-performing high school students are dropping out, artificially boosting mean test scores. Others argue that the TAAS is too easy and sensitive to coaching. But even if these claims were true, and the evidence is murky at best, it would not explain away the results, especially for elementary school children.

Texas undertook its restructuring initiative when policy and business leaders realized that the state's schools had reached rock bottom. In 1981 almost three in ten high school students dropped out. Only 18 percent entered college and received a degree.[95] By the late 1980s a consensus emerged—sparked by the state courts' central push to radically reform the school finance structure—to realign the public education system from top to bottom. The policy pieces that came together, energized by favorable court rulings and strong political backing by Governor Ann Richards, represented a dream come true for restructuring advocates. Preschool and kindergarten programs were expanded; the preschool enrollment rate of Texas four-year-olds is now among the highest in the nation, and the majority of children now attend full-day kindergartens, not half-day programs, the latter still being the norm in urban states like California.

Clear and concise curricular standards were crafted for which schools were then held accountable through the standards-aligned TAAS exam. The legislature capped class size at twenty-two for kindergarten through grade four. Every school had to report on several benchmarks of progress, including the change in the share of children passing the TAAS exam and the change in daily attendance and drop-out rates. The emphasis was on growth year to year, not just ranking schools each year based on a snapshot performance. Schools were pushed to move all students into core academic courses.[96] The number of Texas high school students taking Advanced Placement (AP) math and science exams rose 88 percent during the mid-1990s.

In sum, the upward creep of students' test scores is one of several indicators suggesting that central state institutions—demanding accountability and offering stronger resources for local educators—can be effective. And when the state demonstrates that it can be an efficacious institution, voters become more optimistic, expecting that government can act even more boldly.

This creates a telling dilemma for the political right—comprised as it is of interest groups that normally back radical decentralization and market remedies for public problems. "When it comes to education, nearly all the prominent Republican governors have forsaken small-government orthodoxy," writes *New Republic* senior editor Peter Beinart.[97] Instead, Republican moderates such as Bush pursue strong-state restructuring strategies that reap the political benefits of boosting children's achievement *and* parents' renewed faith in public institutions.

Paradoxically, this undercuts conservatives' habitual pleas to scale back government and advance market remedies, like school-choice policies. Within this context the mini-institution of charter schools becomes emblematic of a centrist political strategy: it retains some public oversight—allowing political leaders to accumulate political karma points with families (especially nonpartisan swing voters)—while advancing the symbols of innovation and democratic choice. The pressing empirical question, of course, is whether charters are also making a difference in what and how much kids are learning.

Questions for Decentralists

Vast public spaces in many cities remain vibrant settings—offering pathways for tranquil walks and luscious gardens, delighting our children with green fields and intriguing playgrounds. In San Francisco, Golden Gate Park features museums, aquatic sights, and those unrelenting players of African drums. The Public Garden in Boston attracts diverse families, many relaxing in the odd serenity of the swan boats. And there is the most famous of all, New York's Central Park, although it's now a public place managed by a private firm.

Proponents of radical decentralization must face the question of what happens to the large public square as we shift resources and collective power down to small, really nonpublic places, embedded in old villages or newly mobilized ethnic, regional, and religious enclaves. Perhaps our pluralistic society needs both: expansive public gardens that host a feeling of membership and potential for all, as well as neighborhood parks in which we can speak our own language and raise our kids according to our own mores.

This chapter has placed the rapid growth of charter schools—small and pluralistic public squares—within the wider political debate around school choice and the ongoing attack on the central institutions that have largely

shaped dominant forms of schooling and child rearing, and the economic resources that have funded them.

I close here by distilling the political and historical facets of school reform
into the enduring questions that would-be decentralists (and their critics)
should seriously engage. Ironically, education reformers often hold little
sense of history, on the assumption that when you're on the cutting edge
there's no sense in looking back. Nor do local reformers always consider the
wider political context in which they are both players and pawns. However,
if we fail to confront these issues, the perils of radical decentralization may
outweigh its promises.

How Can We Craft Effective Communities?

THE PARTICIPATORY IMPERATIVE   The chapters that follow demonstrate how individual charter schools, at the grassroots, are nurtured when
parents and teachers attempt to create a warmer and more fulfilling community for themselves and their children. In this sense, government can enact reforms that enable local tribes to strengthen their cohesion and attract
like-minded families and educators.

Policy talk in America—especially in the essential arena of public education—must always contain a participatory theory of action. The political limitation of state-led accountability measures is that they are largely mechanical. They signal that politicians are "getting tough" on schools, just like they
crack down on crime or drugs. But there's little discussion about how accountability or "getting the incentives right" will actually enrich parents'
and kids' immediate community. Ironically, it's conservatives now who talk
about community building. We need a progressive rendition of village republicanism. Slick mechanical models of how to jerk the strings of school
principals or teachers won't over time energize local actors or evoke symbols
of warmer, more engaging democratic communities. Public education is as
much a democratic expression of Americans' ideals and hopes for the future
as a utilitarian institution aimed simply at transmitting technical skills to our
children.

This search for human-scale civic organization—offering a crisp feeling
of community located somewhere between the family and the state—has
intensified in recent decades. But it is certainly not the first time that the
topic has arisen in America's political culture. De Tocqueville, fascinated
with the social authority of New England's town governments, made his fa-

mous tour of the fledgling states in 1831 and 1832. He wrote: "The Europeans believe that liberty is promoted by depriving the social authority of some of its rights; the Americans, by dividing its exercise . . . No trace of an administrative hierarchy perceived, either in the township or above it." Then, speaking to how the municipality helped to advance a shared commitment to social regulation and cooperation, he noted, "It was never assumed in the United States that the citizen of a free country has a right to do whatever he pleases; on the contrary, more social obligations were there imposed . . . than anywhere else. No idea was ever entertained of attacking the principle or contesting the rights of society; but the exercise of its authority was divided . . . and the community [is] at once regulated and free."[98]

But this early village republicanism, in which small communities supported their own school, consonant with local norms, even in a natural synchrony with growing and harvest seasons, could not be sustained. Big demographic and economic forces swamped the small public squares. The industrial revolution transformed American cities in the last third of the nineteenth century. Factory jobs and commercial expansion sucked young people off the farms and into urban centers, giving birth to a fledgling middle class and rising numbers of poor families. Successive waves of immigration in the nineteenth and early twentieth centuries brought diversity and cultural conflict, and served to further sharpen social-class divisions. Between 1880 and 1910 the Catholic population alone swelled from 6 to 14 million, mainly owing to the immigration of Irish, Italian, and other European families.

Civic leaders—dominated by corporate elites—entered the education sector with confidence and optimism. They had been there in the mid-eighteenth century, contesting Horace Mann's push for state-led common schooling, seeking to protect what historian Michael Katz has called "paternal volunteerism."[99] But at the turn of the century, business leaders were pushing for stronger school administrations, consolidation of little districts into big regional units (the unified school district movement), and moving their school boards to build larger, "more efficient" high schools.

The "one best system" spread across the land, seeking to flatten the uneven diversity of students and languages that was transforming schools and applying factory-style production to the public schools.[100] The idea that the village school could be a social and moral center for the community, governed and celebrated by local residents, remained a reality only in wealthy suburbs and the rural Midwest.

THE EFFECTIVENESS IMPERATIVE If participatory school reforms are full of soul, engineered reforms might be seen as mindful, yet often heartless. The rub is that we want stronger communities and we impatiently seek schools that work. If civic efforts aimed at boosting parents' participation or teachers' professional commitment to kids actually worked, there would be no dilemma between participatory and technical strategies for school reform. But as our case studies reveal, charter school founders are long on the symbols of participation and short on any real knowledge as to whether this enthusiasm is changing classrooms, pedagogy, or parents' commitment at home.

The ideals of decentralization must be translated into wide and deep forms of neighborhood participation and technical know-how in order to deliver on advocates' promises. When either thrust falls short, recentralization will almost certainly follow. We already see this in the counterreform strategy gaining steam: school accountability and state-engineered reforms. And all the national polling reveals popular support for decisive governors who champion what appears to be strong, if bitter, medicine for the public schools.

As you explore our six charter school cases, you might ask if they are meeting these two imperatives. Are their founders and believers delivering on the promise of grassroots participation? Is their particular version of Tocquevillian democracy leading to real change in how learning is structured, how teachers teach, or the values by which children are being raised?

Why Don't Classrooms Change Even after a Thousand Flowers Bloom?

Another lesson for the radical decentralists deals with the need for caution and a hard-headed understanding of how difficult it is to change classroom and pedagogical practices. In other words, is all the hope and hype emanating from these alternative schools truly resulting in effective forms of pedagogy, or somehow helping to raise our children better?

As you read our case studies, the enthusiasm and inventive approaches being taken by a subset of charter schools are quite remarkable. Amigos Charter Academy is attempting to chuck dumbed-down bilingual curricular materials. The Chelmsford Charter School has daily meetings at which students and teachers alike weigh in with their opinions and arguments in a democratic, Deweyan process. Students in the Minnesota New Country School spend relatively little time in classrooms, instead engaging in real work and prosocial projects out in their rural community.

But at the same time, the historical landscape of public education is littered with the crumbling skeletons of prior generations of reform, from progressive alternative schools to magnet schools. If the contemporary rendition of radical decentralization is to yield sustainable effects—on both the small slice of kids attending charter schools and the much larger public school system—it must reckon with two forces that make real and lasting change extremely difficult to sustain.

ENTRENCHED INSTITUTIONAL HABITS   Classrooms are enormously resilient and insular little institutions. Despite all the political rhetoric and legislated "reforms" observed over the past half-century, the underlying "grammar of schooling" remains remarkably intact. Frozen in time are, as sociologist John W. Meyer says, the "ritualized categories" of the school and classroom: kids sitting in rows, sorted by age and grade, surgically attached to written text, playing out largely passive roles as the teacher-expert didactically delivers official knowledge.[101] Teachers within this institutionalized theater called schooling attach their own loyalties to their subject area (math, PE, English) and too often remain subordinate to the principal, textbook companies, and in-service trainers who bring on one curriculum framework or pedagogical technique after another.[102]

The theory of action behind charter schools is that autonomy and entrepreneurial possibilities will render obsolete all these embedded forms of what a school must look like. But it is a most telling irony that the official governance of America's public schools has been quite decentralized for more than two centuries, officially run through thousands of village councils or local school boards, while the basic contours of schools and classrooms remain remarkably similar, homogenous, and uninventive. Throughout the 1950s the organization of schooling converged on a single model of governance and didactic teaching inside the walls of classrooms. As in other areas of institutional life, the behavior—here, of teachers, children, and parents—is highly scripted and predictable. Social roles are well understood, and the range of legitimate knowledge presented, or pedagogical approaches enacted, is constrained and normatively reproduced generation after generation.[103]

CONFLICTING MODELS OF DEMOCRATIC COMMUNITY   Insular organizations, behind high walls that comfortably envelop their members, provide fertile ground for shared stories and collectively held understandings of how things work, both inside and outside the "fortress." The best way to sustain these cultural pillars is to admit new members who are exactly like the current members.

But this conception of community directly conflicts with the democratic conception of community offered by Horace Mann and nineteenth-century common school advocates, along with that of John Dewey and progressive educators in the early twentieth century. They hoped not that parents would freely sort into like communities, but that diverse parents and community members would come together and talk out their differing models for how the democratic school should be constructed.[104] The idea that many charter schools hold to an insular set of pedagogies or an isolated theory of learning suggests that some may become stagnant, settling into an unreflective dogmatism.

Tribal Contention Requires Public Mediation

Historian Diane Ravitch highlights why central levels of government have recurrently entered the education arena over the past century and a half. Broad public interests occasionally demand that local preferences be confronted, even overturned by the state. The federal government's strong resolve was necessary to combat racial segregation in southern schools. The rise of bilingual education stemmed from a recognition on the part of the courts and Congress that local districts often ignored the problems of children with limited English proficiency.[105] The most centralized and prescriptive education reform—civil protections and highly specific procedures for serving disabled children, approved in 1975—continues to force local educators to assist in the mainstreaming of these children. It is inevitable that particular disenfranchised classes or ethnic groups will push the central state to help them move from the edge of society into the mainstream.

At the same time we feel unrelenting pressure, nurtured in the soil of America's political culture, to decenter government. Many groups have grown tired of our nation's common cultural frame. We are discovering that it was never as commonly held as cultural elites would have it. Deepening faith in the magic of markets, the recurring reification of the self-reliant American, and the growing political strength of ethnic enclaves all work in concert to shatter the old feeling of a shared public agenda.

In a sense, the likes of radical progressives Dorothy Day and Saul Alinsky are winning the battle against the concentration of public authority and economic resources in the hands of institutionalized state elites. Indeed, we observe a common lineage in the rise of community action agencies and Head Start in the 1960s, the use of tax credits and vouchers for everything from college scholarships to child-care chits, and the remarkable rise of charter schools. They all stem from a ground-up philosophy that insists that government should play a minimalist role in advancing neighborhood action and aiding the individual's ever localized choices.

I, for one, cannot help but be drawn to the "thousand points of light" strategy. As you enter the front door of the robust charter schools detailed in the following chapters, the energy and optimism of their residents will be uplifting, riveting, contagious. But keep thinking about the larger questions posed in this chapter. The recurring push by local activists to radically decentralize the state and disembowel public bureaucracy should not be simply a reactive movement. Charter advocates must have a proactive strategy for delivering human-scale schools that actually fulfill their promises—demonstrating inventive pedagogies, enlightened learning, and more potent ways of socializing youngsters. Their organization-building efforts must advance democratic participation and lead to technically effective forms of teaching and learning.

If the thousand points of light represented by charter schools illuminate only the affluent suburbs and fail to shine a light on more opportune pathways for poor families, then charter schools will simply reproduce our society's deep ruts of inequality. If charter schools fail to discover and sustain efficacious ways of boosting children's learning curves, a new generation of skeletons will mark the depressing landscape of American school reform. And, finally, if charter schools fail to address these challenges, the recentralization of school governance will most certainly follow, as we are witnessing it in state capitals and a handful of large cities across the nation.

With these questions in mind, let us take you into the neighborhoods and move inside an intriguing array of charter schools.

CHAPTER 2

We Hold on to Our Kids, We Hold on Tight: Tandem Charters in Michigan

PATTY YANCEY

Using a makeshift cup crafted from an empty Coca-Cola can, the charter school's specialist for at-risk students pours motor oil into the engine of the little yellow school bus before it embarks on its afternoon route. Much to the dismay of the driver, each minute of the delay produces a new youngster exploding out of the door of the bus to charge back into the school building to retrieve a forgotten coat or book.

El-Shabazz's second "bus"—a large passenger van on loan from the local Baptist church—is also ready to depart with a full load, but a first grader scheduled for the ride home is nowhere to be found. As Principal Ruby Helton walks out the main door of the school, the bus driver scrambles off the bus and makes a beeline toward her: "Dr. Helton, where's Precious?"

"Precious went home early. Her mom picked her up. Tell Rashaad to get back on that bus."

The school parking lot begins to fill with more parents and assorted family members coming to escort their children home. A distraught mother walks up, shaking her head, "Dr. Helton, he lost another tie. Just can't keep buying these ties."

Dr. Helton commiserates, assuring her, "I just bought two, they're in my office."

The mother keeps shaking her head. "I just can't keep buying these ties. After this I'm not buying one more tie—not one more."

Dr. Helton, now shaking her head in unison with the mother, "I know, I know—*Rashaad!* Get on that bus and *stay* on the bus."

A green 1979 Oldsmobile Cutlass cruises into the parking lot and from the open window on the driver's side, a voice carries above the commotion: "Hey, hey, Dr. Helton! How you doin'?"

Dr. Helton breaks into a big smile and calls out, "What have you been up to? How's everybody?"

Dr. Helton turns to me and tilts her head in the direction of the Olds, still chuckling to herself in a low voice, "Ummm, I had him when he was in school and he was something! Just about killed me with a headache everyday."

Dr. Helton turns toward a young woman struggling with a tired baby and grasping the hand of a reluctant kindergartner.

"Was Jasmine better today, Dr. Helton?"

Dr. Helton looks down at the kindergartner. Their eyes lock. "Jasmine did fine today. She knows what she needs to do to be able to go on that riverboat trip with me. And we know how much she wants to go, don't we?"

Jasmine nods.

Dr. Helton looks over her shoulder and points toward the bus: "Rashaad! This is the last time . . . "

Located on a grassy corner lot with plenty of shade trees and shrubs, El-Hajj Malik El-Shabazz Academy is housed in a medium-size, red brick school building that was once the property of the Lansing Public Schools. The structure has historical significance in the community because it was once the elementary school that Malcolm X attended. Now owned by the Masons, the tidy building exudes a charm reminiscent of a traditional 1950s Midwestern schoolhouse. In 1995 Dr. Ruby Helton was asked to become the principal of the charter school, after having just retired from a long career as a Lansing Public School District teacher, principal, and planning specialist.

Now in the fourth year of its charter, El-Shabazz enrolls approximately 181 children in kindergarten through sixth grade and is one of five charter schools operating in Lansing, Michigan. Ninety-eight percent of the student body is African American, with 100 percent of the children considered to be at risk of failing in school. Most of the students are from single-parent homes or foster homes, with approximately 77 percent qualifying for the free- or reduced-price lunch program.

Carrying the Muslim name of the late Malcolm X, El-Hajj Malik El-Shabazz Academy follows a traditional academic curriculum and is teacher-centered in its overall pedagogy. Except for the small school size, a surface glance at the majority of African American children who make up the student body does not necessarily distinguish the charter school from a regular, urban public school. The physical space and the organization of students also do not constitute a radical shift from the traditional public school. In explaining why Shabazz enjoys a full enrollment and is popular among the low-income African American community, Dr. Helton remarked, "Our success in the community is related to our ability to relate to the parents. They don't feel like they have to be careful with us [the staff]. Everybody knows everybody. Over half of these parents were my students when I taught. I know *their* parents and their sisters and brothers and uncles and aunts, I know exactly where they live, who they live with, where they shop for food . . ."

Dr. Helton's twenty-four-year career in the Lansing public schools and her familiarity with many members of the African American community appear to provide a foundation on which the Shabazz operation relies. Always impeccably dressed and coiffed, Dr. Helton does not mince words, cajole, or beat around the bush when making a request of a staff member or reprimanding a student. Her authority is tangible in her walk and her tone of voice, and is reflected in the respectful way school members talk to her face to face and talk about her in her absence.

However, there is also a palpable ease in how parents, staff, and students interact with Dr. Helton that reveals a sense of trust and comfort in her leadership. This was vividly illustrated one hot day after school, as she sat in her office during an interview. Children, parents, and office staff sporadically sauntered in to get a cup of water from her water cooler, ask a question, or just to say "hey." She did not seem to mind the interruptions; in fact, she routinely answered questions, offered advice, and reached out to hug a child or straighten a collar.

The word *family* is used repeatedly by staff and students in describing their school community. One teacher explained that "the kids see Dr. Helton as the grandmother" and the teachers and rest of the staff as "dads or uncles . . . aunts or big sisters." Any boundaries that do separate students and teachers, parents and staff, and administrators and teachers appear to have more to do with respect for personal authority than with professional distance or class. A statement about the El-Shabazz families that came up frequently during the interviews of the teachers, administrators, office personnel, and board members is, "We're them, they're us." It is this sense of community that marks the critical difference between Shabazz and the regular public schools and that is the reason most cited by families and staff for their choosing to be there.

This case study of El-Shabazz provides a glimpse into the opportunities and challenges faced by charter schools designed to serve the African American community. A brief look at another Lansing charter school that serves African American children is included to illustrate the diversity of educational approaches that appeal to black parents within the same local community. To situate the tradition of independent black schools in the context of U.S. education—as well as explore the changing motivations of African American educators and parents in organizing and supporting this practice—a section on the history of separate African American schools is included toward the end of the chapter.

A Painful Beginning: Divergent Views in the Black Community

An industrial giant at the turn of the century in the manufacturing of engines and automobiles, Lansing is today an aging, landlocked city struggling to combat the shift in modes of production and the migration of families out of the metropolis. In 1998 the Lansing public schools enrolled about 19,000 students, a marked decline from the 35,000 enrolled in 1974. When the charter school movement exploded on the scene, Lansing school district officials were already implementing a school-closing plan to address the declining numbers. According to one district staff member, "White flight contributed to the need for downsizing." Exacerbating a difficult financial situation was the 1994 passage of Proposition 8, which eliminated school districts' ability to finance operations through local taxes.

Distress over the Public Schools

The Parent Support Network (PSN), an African American community group, had been discussing the possibility of starting an alternative school for its children even before Michigan's charter law was passed in 1993. According to Dr. Helton, many of the PSN parents and grandparents were motivated by their disillusionment with the public schools and their fear for the physical safety of their children. The group's original plans were for El-Shabazz to be a private school, but a private operation was just not financially feasible for the low-income community. Except for the president, the majority of PSN members had no experience in starting or operating a business and were largely unfamiliar with public school mandates and regulations. Helton recalled: "These people were not school administrators or teachers, they were just community people who were really upset with the schools. They had kids who were just not being served well. If I'm not mistaken, one of the main drivers of the [charter] idea was a grandmother whose grandson had been killed, and she blamed the public schools."

Mr. Hollingsworth, Shabazz's present at-risk specialist, explained that black parents were unhappy with the large number of African American students being suspended in the regular public schools. To these parents, it appeared that school officials were choosing suspension as an easy way out of helping needy students. He contended that "the regular schools just won't take the time with at-risk, African American students. They'll suspend them in a minute. There were 800 suspensions at the school I was at before this, and 450 of those were African American kids! I even instituted a special program to work with at-risk students, but the school I was working in discontinued it."

When the Michigan charter school legislation was approved, PSN's president was directed by the group to begin researching the possibility of founding a charter school under the sponsorship of Central Michigan University (CMU). Before Dr. Helton was brought into the process, the PSN president enlisted the aid of Dr. Freya Rivers, a respected African American teacher with a fourteen-year career in the public schools, to assist in writing the charter and designing the educational program. Because the Michigan charter law allowed for private school conversions, the PSN thought it would be a good idea to begin operations as a small private school and then convert to charter status. The plan was for parents to pay whatever they could until their charter was approved later in the school year. With Dr. Rivers's help and the donation of space from a local day-care operator, the private school opened with forty students in September 1994.

Dr. Rivers, whose lifelong dream was to create an Afrocentric school, had a concrete vision of the educational program and learning environment that she wanted to institute. It became clear shortly after the interim school opened, however, that her vision did not mesh with what a number of PSN members had in mind for their community school. The parents wanted to be involved in directing the educational program as well as in daily operations, and disagreements surfaced "in a matter of weeks." According to one founding member,

> The big differences . . . what it was everybody was disagreeing about . . . I
> can't even remember now. It just [took] on a life all its own after the school
> opened. It seemed the big struggle was over power: parents versus the pro-

fessionals. The two camps just saw things differently. It wasn't that the parents didn't have good ideas—they did have some good ideas—but they couldn't express those ideas productively. Some wanted jobs here and wanted to be involved with the day to day, and they tended to focus on the little things.

Political Contention in Michigan

In addition to this internal conflict, there were plenty of external sources of worry. The PSN missed the first deadline to submit its charter petition to CMU. The second time, it was rejected because of the vagueness of the proposal. In November of that year, a county circuit judge—troubled by the substantial control that was placed "beyond the hands of the public"—ruled the state's charter law unconstitutional.[1] The implications of this ruling rippled uneasily through the national charter movement like a bad dream, but on the local level the effects were heart-stopping. Eight Michigan charter schools, with charters approved and ready for operation, were facing both eager parents and start-up loans with the very real possibility of no state aid. Other founders who were banking on receiving approval during that school year—such as the PSN—were also thrown into limbo, wondering whether to forge deeper into charter waters or to abandon ship.

By the time the Michigan legislature amended the charter law to the temporary satisfaction of the courts and CMU resumed its chartering review process later in the school year, the PSN and Dr. Rivers had decided to sever their partnership and petition for two separate charter schools. At this point, Dr. Helton was brought in to assist the PSN in the development and writing of the Shabazz charter. Under Helton's direction, the educational program shifted to a more traditional model that would be in compliance with federal and district special education regulations and therefore be eligible for special education funds. In marked contrast, the charter school that Rivers was proposing to CMU was an Afrocentric K–8 school that would not follow federal and district guidelines for special needs students and could not, therefore, use special education funding. An African focus would inform the curriculum, pedagogy, physical environment, uniforms, and organizational structure at the school, called Sankofa Shule. The two petitions were submitted to CMU for approval around the same time. El-Shabazz was granted charter status one week before Sankofa Shule's proposal was approved. Both schools began charter operations in the fall of 1995.

The parent and educator disagreements within El-Shabazz did not end with the exit of Dr. Rivers and the hiring of Dr. Helton. The educational program being put into place in the 1995–96 school year was still not what a number of PSN members wanted. They continued to involve themselves in the day-to-day decision making and, as the school's business manager recalled:

> The split between the educated folk and the PSN became even more painful. You have to understand this was a very grassroots effort. The parents didn't understand things like the bidding system, finances . . . There were so many times that we would end up wasting time in board meetings on things like buying toilet paper . . . We had to borrow $165,000 to start this operation, and there was just no understanding of how hard it was to do this and how important it was to be aware of legal procedures and rules . . . If you did understand the big picture and tried to explain or compromise, you became the enemy. I was one of them [PSN] technically, but I wasn't one of them really. Oh, it was, it was—it ended up being a very painful exercise.

As the conflict worsened over the year, various members who provided some balance on the El-Shabazz board resigned. In March, the remaining board members fired the business manager and moved not to renew Dr. Helton's contract for the following school year. Up to this point, CMU had remained largely uninvolved—"offering some advice and some hand-holding"—but as one former CMU staff member explained, "Everything was so new then and there was so much going on . . . the question of whether or not they [the charters] were even legal was being argued at that time. And we were getting our feet wet as sponsors and were just beginning to get an idea of what the whole job [as a sponsor] was really going to be."

It was not until some of the Shabazz parents and staff appealed directly to CMU for help in the spring that the university began to take a more active role, such as sending representatives to the board meetings, actively recommending individuals for the board, and interviewing all board nominees. By the end of July, the intervention of CMU had assisted in substantially altering the makeup of the Shabazz board; only four founding members remained. The new board moved immediately to rehire Dr. Helton and some of the original staff members, and Shabazz reopened in the fall with 103 students enrolled, a sharp drop from the original 165. Only two of the first-year teachers returned for the second year.

In spite of the negative stories about the school that continued to circulate in the media and via word of mouth, enrollment increased steadily over the course of that second year, and by the third school year enrollment peaked at 181. El-Shabazz was in its fourth year of operation during my fieldwork. Enrollment levels were steady, parent satisfaction appeared high, and the negative feelings that polarized the community that first year had vanished.

So far as the continued role of the sponsor is concerned, it appears that CMU maintains a distant yet supportive relationship with the school. The university holds Shabazz accountable for the budget, health and safety regulations, and student scores; it also maintains the practice of reviewing and approving board nominations. Dr. Helton reports that other than the fact that the "paperwork is terrible, they really don't bother us."

Daily Life at Shabazz

El-Shabazz occupies the rear section of the red brick building it shares with a private Christian school. The two organizations are completely autonomous and operate in opposite wings of the building, sharing use of the gymnasium/cafeteria, the parking lot, and a grassy field that serves as a playground. A plastic sign with removable letters announcing the latest Shabazz events greets traffic on the west side of the building, which borders a moderately busy street.

The Shabazz wing contains seven classrooms, a computer resource room partitioned into two separate spaces for working with students, another large room partitioned into four office spaces, the principal's office, and two small rooms used for vending and copy machines, storage, and general spillover. A common hallway connects all the rooms and leads, through double doors, to the wing that contains the gymnasium/cafeteria. Aside from two glass display cases of impressive African artifacts and assorted mounted photos and carved reliefs of the African diaspora that line about a third of the Shabazz hallway, the physical environment feels and looks like that of a traditional public school. There is only minimal student work on display on the walls outside and inside the classrooms, and classroom layouts are fairly typical in their various integrations of teacher personality and institutional norms.

A Commitment to African American Perspectives

Kiswahili language instruction is sometimes offered, along with a heavy dose of African American history. But other than this, the Shabazz educa-

tional program adheres closely to the Michigan Department of Education requirements. Arts programming is not a part of the core curriculum. Classrooms are usually single-grade; however, if a particular year's enrollment
warrants it, two grade levels are combined into a single classroom. Class
sizes average twenty-five to twenty-eight students. For the 1998–99 year
there were seven classroom teachers, six aides, and two Title I teachers.
Teachers had either full-time or part-time aides, depending on the size and
the needs of the individual classroom.

One current Shabazz board member who persevered through the founding and first-year turmoil has strong personal ties to the independent black
schools movement of the 1970s. As a young public school teacher, Dr. Willie
Davis was fired in 1975 for changing the focus of his high school American
history class to African American history. Well-known in the Lansing black
community among artists, educators, and community activists, Davis went
on to operate an independent black school in Lansing for almost a decade,
starting in the mid-1980s. So far as his involvement at Shabazz is concerned,
in addition to his board of directors duties he serves as a substitute teacher,
offers Afrocentric workshops when requested, and donates artifacts and
photographs from his private collection for the charter school's African diaspora display in the main hallway. In contrast to the founding board's tendency to involve itself in the day-to-day operation, he explains that the
present board is primarily a policymaking board: "We trust Dr. Helton to run
the school. The old board micromanaged a lot, and I'm really conscious of
this. We don't have the time to be second-guessing everything the staff does.
We meet once a month, and we have a curriculum committee, a personnel
committee, and a finance committee that each meet once a month. Dr.
Helton is an ex officio member of the committees."

Unlike many of the Shabazz community members, Davis continued a
working relationship with Rivers after she chose to separate from the founding group and start Sankofa Shule. Except for a spattering of athletic events,
the two charter schools do not collaborate in any way. Although Afrocentrism appears to be Davis's personal passion, he feels strongly that Shabazz's traditional approach works particularly well with the almost 100-per-
cent at-risk student population that it serves:

> Shabazz has at least twice the at-risk children as Sankofa, which really
> changes your flavor, your interactions . . . Rather than an African focus that
> centers around Africa, Shabazz has an African American focus that empha-

sizes the African American experience. We're a good, urban, African American school that merges the best from two systems—the public school system and the African American community . . . Dr. Helton is a great link to both of these systems or worlds. She's hired a lot of people from the community—real people from the community—which is a deliberate strategy. Parents and families that come in here need to feel—no—they need to know we're them, they're us . . . so they can trust us. At the same time Dr. Helton has her foundation in the system—years of experience in the Lansing public schools—and she has [made use of this] knowledge to help these children, some of whom are so far behind socially and academically, succeed.

Although Sankofa and some of the other charter schools in the community report a distant or oppositional relationship with the school district, Dr. Helton describes her dealings with the district as amiable. When she needs information or assistance from district personnel, she explains, "I just pick up the phone and place a call to somebody I know." Going through official channels to inquire about procedures or to negotiate things like Shabazz's lunch contract might have been difficult for an outsider, but as Helton explains, "People know me."

One Version of Democratic Leadership

Dr. Helton characterized her leadership style as "a combination of things—laissez-faire, autocratic, and democratic." According to her, this mix is important in running a charter school, because of the broad range of duties, issues, and dilemmas that surface daily. She acknowledged her "years of experience as an educator," prior to the founding of the charter school, as invaluable in her discernment of "when to let things go and when not to." The following interview excerpt reveals her personal philosophy of schooling, which underlies much of El-Shabazz's vision and program:

That saying—it takes a village? I really believe it, especially for *our* kids. With the hardships they deal with daily . . . The three critical players in our village are the church, the police, and the schools. These three have to work together . . . And with Shabazz as the school part of that village, we can make a difference. I know we can. We're not in competition with anyone but ourselves. We're out to prove that with love, affection, attention, meeting a child's basic needs, like making sure they're fed and safe, and using the

Comer model—we can make a difference in a child's life . . . We hold on to our kids, we hold on tight. [She raises her eyebrows and starts to laugh.] Sometimes that arm gets awfully short, though.

According to James Comer at Brown University, schools are ecological systems in which student behaviors, attitudes, and achievement levels reflect the school's climate. Climate is defined as "the frequency and quality of interactions among parents, teachers, students, the principal, administrators, and adjunct staff."[2] To sustain a well-functioning, caring community, a school staff and stakeholders in the Comer model are organized into three teams: the School Planning and Management Team, the Parent Team, and the Student and Staff Support Team. These teams are supposed to work collaboratively and employ a "no fault" approach in identifying problems and accepting equal responsibility for change.[3] The full implementation of Comer's school development model was not observed during my research at the charter school; however, the Comer philosophy of fostering positive relationships among the adults was apparent in the interactions between staff and parents.

A key strategy that Dr. Helton employs to create a healthy school climate is achieving a "good fit" among staff members, between staff and students, and between staff and parents. She explained that the institution of school does not prompt fond or comfortable memories for many Shabazz parents and guardians, many of whom had serious problems themselves when they were students. So it is critical that parents "feel welcome" at the school, whether they actually participate in activities or not. Parental trust in the school and parental support for school practices is the goal.

Dr. Helton uses every angle—professional connections, knowledge of the community, family contacts—to find the teachers she feels will "fit at Shabazz." Although she is known to "help people get on their feet," as one teacher explained, she is not hesitant about shifting staff members to positions where she feels they would be more productive or replacing them with new employees. Some of Dr. Helton's recruitment strategies are revealed in the following two interview excerpts. In the first, a young Michigan State graduate recalled his first encounter with Dr. Helton:

I'd been subbing for about a year and a half up north—about an hour away. I was still pretty new to everything, just being a recent graduate and all . . . I started quite late in applying for a permanent position—it was already August. I figured I would have to settle for a long-term sub job for the coming school year . . . One night, my uncle—who is a good friend of Dr. Helton's—

called and told me about Shabazz. Dr. Helton was looking for more male African American teachers . . . you know, effective role models for the kids. But I wasn't that excited because I really didn't want to work in Lansing. I like where I live and really didn't have any intentions of moving, so I didn't jump at the chance. The next thing I know the phone rings—the same night—and it's Dr. Helton asking me if I want a job. I laughed and said, 'Well, why don't I come see you.' She told me to come down to Lansing the very next day to talk to her, so I did.

Ms. Edna—a retiree from the Lansing School District after thirty-one years—was Shabazz's full-time special education teacher when I first met her. An imposing, no-nonsense, quietly commanding individual, Ms. Edna (who is white) had no intention of coming out of retirement to teach full-time. She was teaching and supervising student teachers part-time at Michigan State and enjoying her retirement "just fine" when Dr. Helton called one day:

> Ruby needed to bring the school into compliance and didn't know I had retired. I told her I would help her, but that I wouldn't teach . . . I do like teaching and I do love children, but I live twenty-five miles away and figured I would maybe volunteer . . . There is no way in the world I would be here working full-time if it weren't for Ruby. We worked together in the school district for years and have great respect for each other . . . At first we figured we could work something out, but what we worked out couldn't be done, so I said I would work full-time for a year—teach and bring the school into compliance. I wanted it to be part-time, but the kids are in such need . . . It's only out of my affection for Ruby that I agreed to do this.

The school's two newest teachers (one black, one white) mentioned at first that they were hesitant about working at a charter school because they had heard from colleagues that charters paid less than regular district schools and that benefits were marginal. The fact that Dr. Helton was offering the same starting salary as the district, a retirement plan, and comparable benefits convinced them to accept teaching positions at the school.

A Sticky Issue: How to Involve Parents?

Although the Shabazz student population is almost entirely African American, the ethnic mix of the teaching staff over a two-year period averaged 80 to 83 percent African American and 16 percent white, with one teacher of

East Indian descent. The administrative and support staff are all African American. Dr. Helton has hired a majority of residents of the immediate community for positions in the front office; for lunch, playground, and custodial duties; and for driving the school buses. These individuals, more so than the teachers, appear to have informal connections with the students' home lives; some in fact have sons, daughters, nieces, or nephews enrolled in the school.

The majority of staff accept the staff-as-family strategy, but many also cite a number of negative aspects. For example, some teachers believe that the informality results in a lack of follow-through in areas such as schoolwide communication of schedule or policy changes. Others complain of support staff walking into their classrooms and interrupting instruction for trivial reasons, or berating students for petty infractions without first asking the students the reasons for their actions. The following teacher's comments reveals some of the dilemmas teachers encounter with the school-as-family strategy:

> The kids see Dr. Helton as the grandmother, [the adult males] are the dads or uncles . . . There are problems with this, but it's good for the kids, because they know they'll be taken care of when they come here . . . But students misuse this sometimes. Like today, one student got to school thirty minutes late and then he wants to eat before getting to work . . . We also let students lie down in the office if they're sick, so everybody wants to lie down. They know they'll be cared for no matter what . . . and the parents take advantage, too. For example, now that we have a bus, everyone wants to send their kid on the bus when before they got their kid to school on their own. Oh, and with our spring show this year—last year we didn't charge money—this year we did. Some parents drove up to the school for the program and when they found out they had to pay, they drove away! Some of the parents come just because they know they'll be fed . . . and, of course, we always have food.

Even though some of the parents come to school functions only because there is food, the overwhelming staff opinion is, "If that's what it takes, so be it." According to Dr. Helton, the parents "have got to feel welcome here even if they don't come to every school activity or volunteer. The main thing we need from them is to back us up when that student is at home." Thus a lot of energy goes into schoolwide activities and celebrations. One teacher explained that the benefit of these events is not limited to strengthening the relationships with students and families:

> It seems that cliques always form among teachers wherever you work, and we're no different. We've some teachers and assistants who are still around from the first year of the school, and they seem to form a sort of a core group . . . then we have the new teachers who stick together . . . But I see us getting closer as the year winds down because of all the school activities. Thanksgiving, for instance . . . Thanksgiving at Shabazz is not like anything I've ever seen at any other school. Ms. Wilkins [the administrative assistant] doesn't play . . . she fixes enough food for the whole state of Michigan, and you better know what you're getting yourself into if you volunteer to help her [laughter].

Some parents do not agree wholeheartedly with the celebration strategy, stating that "there are too many parties" and that the school "asks for too much money for these parties." However, these same parents also say that the celebrations are a trade-off, because their children are "learning more than they were at their old school and they like to come to school now."

Although the majority of parents and guardians appear to trust the staff and support teacher authority in the home, 75 to 80 percent of parents remain largely uninvolved. The general opinion among Shabazz teachers is that "not every parent is cooperative or involved at the level we'd like, but they do care." Parents seem to view the school staff favorably, too. In talking to random parents who were picking up children after school, I found that the majority made statements such as: "The teachers are good" and "I trust the teachers and Dr. Helton to take care of [my child]." As one father explained: "My boy likes it here, which is good. He's just like me cause he really never took to school . . . Yeah, yeah, Dr. Helton remembers me!" His voice rises; he laughs and shakes his head back and forth. "I was always getting in trouble just like him. But [my son] likes—really likes it here. He's made a lot of nice friends, and he seems to listen better."

A large majority of the comments from parents revealed satisfaction with the charter school and support at home for the teacher's role, but no interest or time for volunteering or becoming more involved:

> My wife and I can't be up here all the time checking on every little thing. We work and . . . well, [my son] is doing fine. They know they can call us if they need to. He's doing better in reading than he was, and he's more aware

of what's going on around him than before. He's making a lot of progress in this school.

I work three to eleven and have three other kids, so it's hard to come for programs and after-school things . . . [My daughter] shows me her homework in the morning before school. She likes her teacher, and her cousins are here and some of the kids on our block . . . My sister comes in to volunteer, I think . . . or she used to. She could do that type of thing because she didn't work, but she got a job about a month ago, so I don't know if she can still do it.

They have my number and I come down as soon as they call me, or his grandmother comes . . . The teachers are good here, so I don't get called a lot.

In asking parents how they found out about Shabazz or why they enrolled, the overwhelming majority mentioned that they learned about the school through word of mouth:

My sister's neighbor told her, and she told me. We thought our kids would do better if we could get them back together in the same school. They grew up together, and when my sister moved 'cross town, we had to separate them, and then they had to go to different schools and they just about had a fit. Now they're together and happy.

We were talking at choir practice and I heard about it. I knew Dr. Helton and I know she's good, so I thought we would try it out.

Dr. Helton called me up.

In instances where the child attended another school prior to Shabazz, the parents all reported that they were more satisfied with Shabazz than with the previous school. The following themes were echoed repeatedly:

His old teachers didn't tell me he couldn't read. Now his third-grade teacher tells me he can't read—in third grade! Yeah, they could [not] have cared less . . .

They [Shabazz staff] know how to handle our kids. [Our other school] didn't get after the kids enough. I'd go up to school and all these kids would be running around the halls talking bad and loud and disrespectful. They wouldn't stand for that here.

I don't think they [the prior school] really cared about whether the students learned how to act nice or be nice to each other. I think [my son's] last teacher was afraid of black kids [because] she wouldn't be hard on them, make them act right . . . Even [my son] told me it was too noisy and too much nonsense going on all the time, so I had to get him out of there.

Teachers in the lower grades reported more readiness on the part of their students' parents to be actively supportive of the teacher's role, especially the parents and guardians of kindergartners. Two white teachers, both of whom taught kindergarten at some point during their tenure at Shabazz, were the only teachers who spoke positively about the level of parental participation:

My fiancée's sister works at a school in a poor neighborhood and warned me that her parents just don't seem to care. So when I came here I was prepared for this kind of thing . . . but I was so surprised! It's not that way at all—I have a *lot* of supportive parents. One mother came up to me the first day and put her number in my pocket and said she wanted me to call her if [her son] acted up. I have and she's been right there . . . It does help with behavior.

I have many grandmothers raising children. One in particular took a consequence workshop and learned about consequences—things to motivate her child, what privileges or things should be taken away. She comes in to volunteer, and I can see her using the information she learned . . . She was so excited [after the workshop] and said she learned so many helpful ways to deal with her boys instead of yelling at them . . . We talk a lot. She said it's important this generation grows up right because we lost the first generation . . . I think she could be a wonderful peer teacher for other parents.

Nevertheless, the majority of teachers and staff reported that overall involvement is minimal and "more parent involvement would be helpful for the staff." Turnout for after-school parent programs (computer classes, parenting classes, and the like) is usually very low, and parent surveys distributed in the 1997–98 school year were largely unreturned. Attendance at parent-teacher conferences also dropped from a 95-percent showing in spring 1997 to 85 percent in spring 1998.

Although there was a policy outlining the importance of parent involvement, there did not appear to be a schoolwide strategy in place to boost involvement numbers. There was evidence of a variety of tactics—in addition to serving food at school activities—employed by individual teachers and administrators to boost face-to-face contact, but the effort was not collaborative. Encouragement and reminders for parents to attend events or volunteer appear in school-to-home written communications delivered via students or by mail. Note the following excerpt from the monthly newsletter:

> Our last parent meeting was held on November 10, 1997 a [sic] 6:00 P.M. 6 parents attended the meeting. With a total enrollment of 178 students, this amounts to only 1 percent of our parent population. The next parent meeting will be held on Monday January 12, 1998 at 6:00 P.M. This is an extremely important meeting. Especially for those parents who have children who ride the bus. During this meeting we will be developing some strategies to *improve* our busing program. Part of this revitalization will be to have *re-registration* for busing students. *Non-attendance* at this meeting will *clearly indicate* that your child no longer needs transportation to and from school. You must be present at this meeting to register. *No phone registrations* will be excepted.

At the parent meeting that was held after the mailing of this newsletter, thirty parents attended. The at-risk specialist reported that this turnout was only because of the threat of losing bus privileges and that attendance declined again in subsequent meetings.

Student Voices

There is a student uniform code at Shabazz of black pants or skirt, a white shirt, and a vest of red, green, and yellow African patterned cloth. Boys wear black ties on special occasions. Dr. Helton contracts with a local seamstress for the special vests, and parents have the option to buy them or not. The uniform rule does not appear to be strictly enforced, but every now and then Shabazz's at-risk specialist will randomly reward students who are wearing their uniform with a "red ticket" that is redeemable for a piece of candy or gum at lunchtime.

Several teachers report that student absenteeism is extremely low. Some students who live close to the school often stay late and have to be encouraged to go home. In talking to students about Shabazz, all were positive in their comments about attending the charter school. They also reported that their parents were very satisfied with the charter school. The following student quotes contain themes that surfaced repeatedly in their comments about "what they liked most about Shabazz":

- A second grader: "We have a nice principal and all my sisters and brothers go here . . . My mom thinks the principal is nicer than the principal in my old school."
- A fifth grader: "It can be fun when you don't have people mad at you. You get to play in Kiswahili, and we do geographic games, and I like the spelling tests. I like recess, too."
- A sixth grader: "I like it because of the parties when Ms. Wilkins cooks. I like my teacher. [At this point some of the other sixth-grade students moaned and laughed. The student I was addressing quickly responded to their protests.] He isn't strict *all* the time!"
- A first grader: "I like my teacher."
- A sixth grader: "My mom thinks I'm learning more. I go home and talk to her about what I learned, and she likes that."

One student made a point of telling me that her reason for liking Shabazz was that it was "all black." Later, she elaborated on what she meant by all black: "Everyone is nice, and I learn a lot. I have a lot of friends, and we have fun . . . The teacher and the principal are mean sometime, but only when we're bad like when [somebody] fights on the bus or if we say a bad word . . . and Ms. Wilkins cooks all the time, and we never had anything like that in my old school."

The students' major complaint was that they had to share the building and playground with the neighboring private school. With classmates excitedly voicing their agreement with his opinion, one student explained, "It's how they treat us. It's not that we don't like them; they don't like us. They don't want us to use their drinking fountain, and they look at us like we're retarded or something." Other than this, student complaints centered around such things as the wearing of uniforms and the long name of the charter school. They were often teased by other children about "the funny name" and because of the ridicule, wished their school had a different name. The historical significance of El-Hajj Malik El-Shabazz appeared to have little impact on student opinion.

Students' academic skills are "more than often way below average" when students enter Shabazz, according to Helton. Although teachers and aides report progress academically and behaviorally in those students who return year after year, each September a new group of students enter "who seem even rougher and more behind than the kids the years before." Some members of the playground and lunch program staff remarked in the first month of the new school (1998–99) year that the difference in behavior between the new students and the returning students was "unbelievable." One commented: "Ooooooh, we have some new ones that are just, well, I just can't begin to tell you. [She points to some students on the playground.] Just look at how hard they play and how loud they are compared to the others. The girls, too! Oh my. And let me tell you they don't listen, no, they don't listen when you try to tell them something . . . But the other children help in telling them when they're wrong or what they can't do here, so they'll come around after awhile."

Student Performance Inches Upward

Students' performance on the Michigan Educational Assessment Program (MEAP) tests concur with teachers' individual assessments of student skills and academic performance. Students enter Shabazz demonstrating extremely low levels of proficiency on standardized tests in all subject areas. MEAP scores in 1995 revealed that 39 percent of Shabazz students were performing in the low range in math, 39 percent in the moderate range, and only 22 percent in the satisfactory range. Scores rose significantly in 1998, with 17 percent performing in the low range, 29 percent in the moderate range; and 54 percent in the satisfactory range. Students who have been at Shabazz for three years demonstrate the most improvement, with all students achieving scores in the moderate (49 percent) or satisfactory (51 percent) range in math.

Shabazz reading levels have not revealed the same progress as those demonstrated in math. Reading scores in 1995 demonstrated that 52 percent of the students were operating in the low range, 35 percent in the moderate range, and only 13 percent of students in the satisfactory range. In 1998, 46 percent of students scored in the low range, 42 percent in the moderate range, and 12 percent in the satisfactory range. Reading scores for those students who have been enrolled for three years reveal 33 percent still performing in the low range, 44 percent in the moderate range, and only 23 percent in the satisfactory range. This was an improvement over their second-year scores, when 50 percent of the students were still performing in the low range, 33 percent in the moderate range, and only 17 percent in the satisfactory range. Shabazz had its greatest success in fifth graders' achievement in writing, with 67 percent of fifth-grade students scoring in the proficient category in 1998 compared with only 25 percent demonstrating proficiency in 1996. Their 1998 scores were above the state proficiency average of 64.3 percent.

Dr. Helton closely monitors student academic progress on standardized tests and uses the results to shape the schoolwide educational program. For example, because of the low reading scores, students at the start of the 1998–99 year were tested to target their individual reading level and then placed in mixed-age reading groups. Groups meet every day to read and receive instruction. Tutors from the Michigan State graduate and undergraduate programs have been recruited as volunteers, and a retiree from the local school district staff has been retained to tutor students on a weekly basis.

Teachers and Their Work

I noted in my classroom observations that teacher-centered instruction was the norm and that classroom rules were often rigid and uncompromising. Those teachers who appeared to be the most successful in terms of establishing and maintaining a positive classroom learning environment rarely raised their voice but were still very stern in their overall manner with the students. Classroom rules were explicit. The less successful teachers were not employing instructional strategies that appeared significantly different from those of the more successful teachers, yet their individual classrooms did not impart the feeling of a learning environment. During the observation periods in these particular classrooms, I found that students appeared disconnected and uninterested in their work, and the teachers spent the majority of class time trying to control behavior. Overall, the curriculum and pedagogy were traditional and unremarkable; in fact, they substantially mirrored the rote teaching practices widely associated with public schools in inner-city neighborhoods.

One of the most successful teachers in terms of spurring on academic and behavioral improvement is Mr. Dixon, an African American teacher who has worked at Shabazz since its conversion to charter status. He serves as acting principal when Dr. Helton is not on site. It was his fifth graders who scored above the state average in the MEAP writing test in 1997–98. The majority of those students had been with him since their third-grade year. In their second year with Dixon, as fourth graders, they demonstrated a 40-percent improvement in math on the MEAP. It was Dixon's personal decision to remain with his students from the third grade until they graduate from Shabazz.

A young, fit, and soft-spoken individual, Dixon maintains a quiet, orderly classroom and employs a teacher-centered instructional approach. Often appearing deep in thought, Dixon discussed his fifth-sixth grade students:

> I've had a lot of my fifth graders since third grade. [Smiling] They're my babies. It was my decision to stay with them . . . I had to stay with them. It just would have made no sense to let them go after one year. It's like they were bleeding and I was the Band-Aid. I just couldn't let them go . . . Quite a few new sixth graders who joined the class this year make it difficult because they are so far behind—still learning cursive, don't know how to borrow . . . But we've come a long way because we work well together inside the classroom.
>
> My old students help me manage everything, and everyone has an understanding of their role and others' roles, which is critical to the environment. It actually didn't take too long to achieve this year—my fifth graders helped a lot, and the new students could see clearly how the classroom is run. Everyday they can see the routine. I always repeat: "This is how we do this."

After this group of students graduated, Dixon faced the challenge of a whole new classroom of third graders the following year. In asking around Shabazz about the changes the new school year had brought, office and support staff mentioned repeatedly that "Mr. Dixon has a real rough bunch this time." In accompanying Dixon to his classroom to observe the new group, I asked him how things were going compared with last year. He shook his head and laughed, "Well, you have to deal with what you get and just keep smiling . . . yeah, you have to just keep on smiling."

Comparing classroom observations from the previous year with this particular year, it struck me that Dixon exercised a much tighter rein on his new third graders. With his fifth-sixth class in the late spring (twenty-seven students; fourteen girls, thirteen boys), Dixon would explain in more detail why it was important for them as individuals in the world at large to "read more often," "have favorite books," or "pay attention to directions." Dixon sat at his desk as he talked to the students; students appeared to be working independently and on task. With his new third graders the following fall (twenty-two students; eleven boys and eleven girls), the classroom atmosphere felt more electric; Dixon was on his feet more, pacing and looking around the room at students. As soon as the noise level rose above a certain point and student attention began to wander, Dixon immediately restored order with a look or a verbal reminder.

As he stood before the third-grade class reviewing test questions for an upcoming quiz, students appeared to be having fun and were noticeably pleased with themselves when they answered a question correctly. The boys would quietly rejoice, smiling or clenching their fists and mouthing the word "yes." The routine went something like this:

Mr. Dixon [*in front of the chalkboard, pacing back and forth, with a slight frown on his face*]: What's a compound word? [*About half the class raise their hand. Dixon stops pacing and faces the class.*] All hands should be up. You should know this. [*The rest of the hands go up. Dixon calls on a student, who mumbles an answer. At this, Mr. Dixon resumes pacing.*] I can't hear you.

Student [*still mumbling*]: It's a word made . . . up . . . of two . . . words.

Mr. Dixon [*stops pacing, looks at the student, and tilts his head forward*]: Okay. Now sit up straight and tell me again. [*With eyes on Dixon, the student sits up and repeats his answer more clearly.*] Good. Give me an example. . . . [*The student sighs and his shoulders slump. The rest of the class starts fidgeting; noise level rises slightly. Dixon looks around the classroom and the fidgeting stops. He then turns to the student he was previously addressing and tilts his head slightly.*]

Student [*looks at Dixon, straightens up in his chair*]: Homework.

Mr. Dixon: Very good. Who can tell me the two words that make up this compound word? And . . . [*his voice rises and he pauses dramatically*] what do they mean?
[*The majority of hands shoot up, and students gesture and squirm to be called on—including the boy who had just answered.*]

After about twenty minutes of reviewing grammar, Mr. Dixon asked his class to "switch their brains" to review for their Friday social studies test. The students, especially the boys, enjoyed pantomiming their own individual interpretation of "switching their brains" as Mr. Dixon prepared. During the brief transition, he repeatedly reminded students to "use your think time" or "take care of your business." During the social studies review of the seven continents, Mr. Dixon integrated the previous grammar lesson into the activity. The entire class had their eyes on him and appeared to be paying close attention. Fifteen of the twenty-two students were actively participating. After about twenty minutes, Mr. Dixon congratulated the students on their work, paused, and then noticeably accelerated the pace of questions and the integration of other subject matter. The students appeared prepared for the shift in gears as the classroom quickly adopted a more spontaneous attitude. Although still reviewing social studies test questions, the exercise became more gamelike, with students gesturing and answering questions as if they were competing for a prize. At one point during the session, Mr. Dixon invited fourth graders from another classroom to join the question and answer session. His third graders noticeably relished the opportunity to see if their older schoolmates "were as smart" as they were. The fourth graders were very willing to join the "game" and did not appear flustered or embarrassed if they missed some of the questions.

As is apparent, Dixon's instructional strategy does not differ significantly from the traditional public school norm. His teaching methods, often consisting of drill and question and answer, are far from progressive. Nevertheless, the majority of the students in his classroom participated enthusiastically in the lesson; and the larger part of class time observed was spent on instruction, not on discipline. Unlike many of the other classes observed at Shabazz, Dixon's students did not need more than one or two reminders to rein in their behavior if they strayed off task. If Dixon left the room for any reason, students continued to work in a disciplined fashion. What is it about Dixon that contributes to his effectiveness with the same students who were observed "acting out" in other teachers' classrooms? Dixon credits, among other things, insight into both his students and himself:

> I think you have to understand and accept yourself before you can work well with this population of students. That probably goes for working with any students . . . You have to instill a value of oneself. The students need to learn responsibility . . . and they may not get this from other schools or from home, so it is important that they learn this from you. And you also have to get to know them—a big part of which is wanting to get to know them. Instead of yelling at them to stop talking, you sometimes need to find out why they're talking. Once I establish my rules and I know they've got them, I can let some things slide—let the petty stuff go . . . When I entered into teaching I had this mission—to get it done no matter what, to do whatever it takes to help the kids. The charter school thing fits with—feeds this personal philosophy.

The Student Discipline Problem

One white teacher who appeared less successful in maintaining classroom behavior talked thoughtfully and at length about her problems with discipline and how she felt her work in this area could be improved:

> I don't have a full-time aide, and I really need one. It's disappointing because I can't individualize things as much as I would like . . . and they need so much individual attention. I have problems because my kids don't fear me. I feel it's necessary to teach them self-control, but they're used to fear as the controller. They see my kindness as weakness . . . It's difficult for me because I've never been a strict person with children, and I know I have to be stricter. This is hard for me because I have such warmth for them . . . but I've learned that I have to keep my distance, and I have to be serious and strict.

The primary disciplinary tactics used after teachers reached the limit of their own classroom management abilities were sending students to the office, calling parents, and time-outs in another teacher's classroom. The time-out was usually spent with a teacher who was known among students as "mean" or "hard." Students would have to complete a written assignment while they were in time-out and would then be escorted back to their own classroom after talking with Hollingsworth, the at-risk specialist. If behavior was particularly problematic and a parent was home during the day, a student would sometimes be escorted home immediately for a three-way conference. Hollingsworth explained that Shabazz has "enough parents who are at home" for this strategy to be employed and that "just the threat of this is sometimes all that's needed" to curb a student's behavior. Although these methods were schoolwide policies, teachers complained that there was no system at work that dictated when particular tactics were to be used.

Helton says that she recognizes classroom management as an area that is always in need of improvement and uses the professional development funds available to send teachers to outside conferences and workshops focusing on this topic. For example, she recently enrolled a young white teacher who was having difficulties with classroom management in a Detroit conference given by African American educators that focused on working with at-risk students. In addition to off-site professional development, Helton explained, "We have mini-in-services, usually on Thursdays. About an hour or so. There's also a week we have before school starts where we have a series of workshops. Last year we had sessions on reading, computers, Afrocentric principles."

Teachers agreed that Helton is generous in her allowance of individual teacher time for outside conferences, but some teachers asserted that a more systematic approach to in-service development needed to be instituted. According to one teacher, the students "can be extremely difficult and demanding and can really tire you out after awhile, even if you know what you're doing." As the 1997–98 school year was drawing to a close, a more seasoned teacher talked about how exhausted the staff was and made the connection to professional development: "We have a Thursday hour where we get together and throw ideas at each other, but I don't think this is enough. Teacher collaboration is our weakness . . . I think professional development and knowing how to collaborate with each other could help us not end up as mentally tired at the end of the year as we are now."

Seeking Both Autonomy and Camaraderie

One of the novice teachers also expressed the desire for more collaboration and structured peer consultation. She explained that she "likes the autonomy" but would also like to have more opportunities to talk through classroom strategies and dilemmas with other teachers. Although teachers from other classrooms and Helton drop in to assist a struggling teacher when student behavior gets out of hand, some teachers complained about the lack of consistency in the area of discipline. Another experienced teacher added that "there's a lack of collaboration among teachers about how to deal with problem students. It's exhausting to not be consistent. Just keeping a positive attitude while doing the work we do is sometimes hard, and if we don't have a positive attitude, how do we instill this in our students? . . . We need a schoolwide discipline policy so that we're all on the same page. I think parents cry out for this, too. I see them struggling to figure out how to cope and how to react to their child."

When I asked Helton what short-term and long-term plans were in the works for Shabazz, she said she was aware of the need for more development in the areas the teachers mentioned. She also revealed an understanding of the "big picture" and her particular vantage point as the chief administrator:

We're finally in a position where we can work on mastering what we're doing now. There's been talk about expanding, but we have plenty of work to do on what we're doing now. We've made a lot of progress, but we can do better. A letter came today congratulating us for getting out of our budget deficit. Our special ed services are in place, every child is in a reading group, we have male role models for the kids . . . What's next? Dealing with discipline better, instituting a time-out room, a full-time aide per classroom, long-term subs for continuity so that teachers can plan . . . Don't get me started [laughing] . . . Oh, but I look around me and I can just see how far we've come. From that first year with all the political problems to now where we are. Everything you see in here, we put it in here: desks, pictures, curtains, shelves . . . We have a lot to be thankful for. Yes, indeed, we have a lot to be thankful for.

Ethnic Empowerment or Resegregation?

Although early predictions were that charter schools would further "cream" middle-class white families from the district schools, the five charter schools in Lansing enroll a combined student population that is more than 60 percent African American. Whites make up only approximately 30 percent of the district's charter school enrollment. In contrast, the rest of the Lansing public schools serve a student population that is 34 percent black and 47 percent white. Approximately 60 percent of Lansing district students are eligible for the free or reduced-price lunch program. Across Michigan at the beginning of the 1997–98 school year, minority students made up 53 percent of the state's charter school enrollment, compared with a 22-percent figure for all Michigan public schools.[4] Slightly more than 40 percent of these minority students were African American.[5]

As public schools, charter schools cannot employ discriminatory practices in enrollment or hiring; however, they can adopt or create educational and cultural programs that attract or appeal to specific populations (blacks, Latinos, drop-outs, home schoolers, at-risk students) rather than a broadly diverse constituency. Who the founders and staff are, the physical location, and whether or not transportation is provided are additional factors that further influence the makeup of a charter school's student population.

A two-day series of newspaper articles in the *Lansing State Journal* sporting the banner *"Resegregation in Lansing Schools"* explored the debate over voluntary segregation in the city's charter schools. Although the majority of articles reported a cross-section of opinion on the phenomenon, the *Journal*'s editorial stated strongly that this "resegregation" through charters was a "backslide": "No one knows if the trend will continue. But if it does, it is a disturbing portent of a society that may be giving up on the benefits of school integration."[6]

El-Shabazz's at-risk specialist, Mr. Hollingsworth, responded to the editorial by writing an op-ed piece protesting the use of the word *resegregation* to describe the charter school practice of serving students who are underserved by the regular public schools. The following is an excerpt from his op-ed, which appeared in the *State Journal* two weeks later:

> Racial segregation means to be excluded, to bar or prevent someone from a right or privilege that is inherently owed to them. Therefore to conclude that the highly Black populated charter schools such as El-Hajj Malik El-Shabazz Academy and Sankofa Shule were developed with the evils of racial segregation is highly inaccurate. These schools are not practicing exclusion, but simply offering more choices . . .
>
> We are catering to our clientele. This is a reality. This is the school of the future—the school we never had, a school for the community. This is why many Blacks have flocked to these schools because children who seem to have no place have now found a place and are beginning to excel holistically.

Mr. Hollingsworth believes strongly that the loss of black students from the Lansing school district to charter schools can be directly related to district practices. He characterized the regular public schools as "suspension specialists" when it came to dealing with African American children. He added that the key to why African Americans would choose an all–African American school is the "family feel," and that this feeling of family is instrumental in the academic and behavioral improvement of the at-risk student. According to him, "We [at Shabazz] don't believe in suspension as a way of controlling kids. If a kid gets really out of line, we call home or drive them home immediately and talk to the parents. We couldn't do that and get the results we do if parents didn't know us or trust us or think that we care about their kids . . . We don't give up on them [the students] that easy."[7]

In contrast, there are some members of the Shabazz staff who struggle with the implications of forging a separate educational community for African American children. Although these staff members are positive about

Shabazz's effect on the students' academic performance and behavior, they still questioned the phenomenon. One black teacher commented: "My chief beef is our school is not multicultural. I've worked in the public school system and in multicultural groups, and you get a better understanding of other cultures when you work together and go to school together. Are we being hypocrites? Are we doing what the public schools are doing with their tracking and their supposedly covert tactics of separation?

A white teacher linked her concern about "resegregation" to past struggles to desegregate schools and the larger society. She expressed her disappointment that charter schools appear to be "segregating" voluntarily, but also voiced an understanding of why a school like Shabazz can "make a difference":

> I'm concerned that so many of the charter schools are segregated. When you look back to the people that gave their lives in the 60s to change things—it just doesn't seem right. I think a lot of people who are all for this just don't know their history. But I'm not blind—I see how important the feeling of ownership is. I can *see* what happens when there's the feeling that this is *our* school. This type of investment really makes a difference. A little school like this can truly help in returning a balance to children's lives.

This sense of "ownership of Shabazz" or "belonging to the school" does appear to be the critical element that distinguishes Shabazz from the regular public schools. The school's predominantly African American membership does contribute greatly to the sense of community, and Dr. Helton's statement that "we hold on to our kids, we hold on tight" deepens one's understanding of why the parents trust the staff and why students want to be at the school.

Although some teachers wrestled with the dilemmas of a separate school for African American at-risk students, they repeatedly returned to the positive effects that Shabazz was having on children whom they believed would be "shunned, lost, or suspended" if they had remained in the regular public schools.

The Afrocentric Competition

Located within a quick four-minute drive, Sankofa Shule—El-Shabazz's Afrocentric sister school founded by Dr. Rivers—is also enjoying a full enrollment and a high satisfaction rating among parents. Afrocentrism informs the curriculum, pedagogy, physical environment, uniforms, and organizational structure at Sankofa. Although individuals and quite varied, all Sankofa students and teachers wear ethnic African dress or clothing made with traditional African patterns.

The physical layout of the school is based on a "living museum" model, with preschool through second grade sharing a large, open, common space. Beautifully framed prints of African and African American art and historical posters line this common room as well as the hallways. The K–2 area in the main room is divided into subject areas: math, language arts, foreign language (French, Spanish, Japanese, Kiswahili), and science. Along an adjoining hallway there are four separate, multigrade classrooms for kindergarten through eighth grade, divided according to subject area. Behavior determines when students graduate from the K–2 common room to these classrooms. The Afrocentric curriculum is aligned with the Michigan Department of Education's standards and is supplemented by Sankofa's foreign language requirement and technology studies. All students rotate between subject areas every ninety minutes. "Learning by doing" and travel are key to the educational and professional development programs. For example, students traced and traveled along the route of the Underground Railroad last summer, and as a part of Sankofa's professional development teachers have traveled to Egypt and Ghana.

In addition to their marked program differences, the two charter schools' student populations are also different. Shabazz's enrollment is considered almost 100-percent at-risk; Sankofa's at-risk population is estimated at just under half. Shabazz receives special education funds for qualifying children and follows federal and district regulations in their programming for these students. Sankofa has elected not to receive special education funding or to follow the traditional guidelines for special needs students. Although they do serve students who would qualify for the funding, Sankofa uses its own individualized approach to serving this population.

Independent and Black Roots

Looking back into the history of African American schooling in the United States, one can see that the educational programs of both El-Shabazz and Sankofa Shule have roots in the tradition of privately financed independent black schools. The first officially recorded independent African American school was in Boston in 1798. A Revolutionary War veteran placed numerous petitions before his town council for public funding of black schools, arguing that separate schools were necessary because of the constant harassment of black youths by white students in the regular town schools. His petitions were repeatedly denied before he opted to open a private operation in his son's home.[8] Separate African American schools also existed in the South in the 1700s, but they were largely clandestine operations until the Reconstruction period.[9]

According to scholar I. D. Ratteray, the vast majority of the early African American schools closely followed the Eurocentric approach in both curriculum and pedagogy. Their primary sources of financial support were African American churches, sororities, social clubs, and fraternal orders, with churches providing the most systematic funding. These neighborhood schools were pivotal in the preparation of black students for higher education, until the 1954 desegregation ruling appeared to obliterate the chief reason for the existence of a separate network of schools.[10]

The civil rights and black power movements of the 1960s and 1970s spawned a rebirth of private African American schools, and these schools often added an African-centered curricular and pedagogical focus to their educational vision.[11] This resurgence of private schools may be attributed to the shared belief among community activists and some African American parents that there were academic, cultural, and political gaps in the public education being offered to African American students in integrated schools.[12] Lack of cultural relevance in curriculum, limited numbers of black teachers and administrators, and dissonance between parents and school personnel were some of the specific complaints cited by researchers as motivating organizers to push for separate schooling.

The term *independent black institution* (IBI) was coined during this era and is still in use today to identify those schools developed by black educators for African American children.[13] The Council of Independent Black Institutions (CIBI) has been a source of continuity for the schools since 1975, offering seminars on how to develop and sustain the organizations and how to train teachers in African-centered pedagogy and curricula.[14] According to researcher Carol D. Lee, "The linking of content knowledge in subject areas to philosophical and social principles is a critical element of African centered pedagogy."[15] Afrocentric schools incorporate a strong value system that lies at the heart of their educational programming, organizational structure, and governance. The elements of this value system are unity, determination, collective work and responsibility, cooperative economics, creativity, purpose, and faith in self, family, and one's people.[16]

There is some difference among researchers as to the boundaries of the term IBI. Some restrict it to African-centered or Afrocentric schools; others use IBI broadly to include those community schools located in urban, predominantly African American neighborhoods that do not choose to adopt Afrocentrism as a curricular and pedagogical focus.[17] These community schools have also been referred to as "independent neighborhood schools" or "Black independent schools."[18] While Sankofa closely follows the Afrocentric tradition, Shabazz appears to be more in line with the "independent neighborhood school" tradition.

The Dilemma of Ethnic Community Building

The fact that some state charter laws allow the formation of schools that aim to serve one particular ethnic group is certainly not without controversy. Although the numbers are still relatively small, the loss of these students to charter schools is troubling for public school officials. For large urban districts, the effects are limited; however, for small cities with declining public school enrollments, such as the Lansing School District, the loss of students of color to charter schools is financially problematic.[19]

It is interesting to note that El-Shabazz is not offering a particularly distinctive curriculum or employing a radically progressive pedagogy such as that of its Afrocentric neighbor, Sankofa Shule. Both charter schools' educational programs are rooted in the tradition of independent black schools in the United States, and both are experiencing full enrollment rosters and high ratings from parents. For the IBI movement, decentralization and market-driven educational reform have opened the door to a stable funding base for black alternative schools, and thus a means for serving low-income African American children, through charters.

The academic gains that Shabazz students are making are slow, and the effectiveness of individual teachers varies. It is not unusual to witness adults at the school raising their voice and scolding students for infractions. Not enough teacher collaboration, lack of an effective schoolwide discipline policy, and lack of parent involvement are all common complaints voiced by teachers—the same kinds of complaints expressed by teachers in traditional public schools. So what is the difference between Shabazz and other Lansing public schools? Why is enrollment at capacity and why are parents "more satisfied" with the charter school? Why do students report that they "want to come to school" and that "they like this school more than their other school"?

It appears that the answers lie in the predominantly black staff and the leadership of an African American educator who is known, trusted, and well respected throughout the community. Parents, students, teachers, and administrators clearly had little interest in progressive curricula and cutting edge instructional methods. Instead, what attracted them to the school was the powerful "feeling of family." And although this informal, family atmosphere is not a panacea for working with at-risk students, all Shabazz teachers echoed the belief that "the [family] atmosphere is more important for the kids' academic and behavioral improvement." Helton remains emphatic in her belief that a strong feeling of community and the sense of belonging are key to being successful with her at-risk students, and that the charter school framework enabled her to build this intriguing community.

CHAPTER 3

An Empowering Spirit Is Not Enough: A Latino Charter School Struggles over Leadership

EDWARD WEXLER

LUIS A. HUERTA

Early in the 1997 school year, the Amigos Charter Academy celebrated its fifth birthday by hosting an open house and potluck dinner. The nearly two hundred celebrating parents, board members, and teachers stood on a patch of dirt outside the school's office bungalow. Another dozen mothers huddled on the only three benches, placed neatly in the barren courtyard. All were facing a makeshift stage that usually serves as the entrance ramp to the principal's office—a trailer perched on slim stilts. Most parents were dressed in jeans, T-shirts, and sneakers or work boots. While awaiting the beginning of the festivities, some conversed with each other in Spanish, others seemed content standing alone. Most teachers were actively welcoming new and familiar parents. Students were running around, playing football, or just hanging out in the adjoining field.

The congenial if somewhat chaotic celebration unfolded under the banner: *Quienes Somos*—Who We Are. No need for a question mark. This was a close, affectionate community: a ragtag collection of dissident teachers, escapees from the public schools, and parents who knew what they stood for. Amigos' fourth principal in three years approached the microphone and introduced herself to the crowd. Robin Daniels first spoke nervously in English, often raising her voice over the noises of trucks and cranes working nearby in the loud industrial park in which the school is located. She then read from her notes in Spanish. Her choppy sentences and uncertain pauses served to punctuate the distracting noises coming from just twenty feet behind the audience, and the small crowd grew visibly bored. Most simply couldn't understand Robin's attempts at Spanish. A local musician next took center stage, leading sixth-grade students through a medley of Spanish songs. Parents, hands cupped around ears to capture the sounds from the stage, smiled proudly as they watched their children perform.

A seventh-grade student then captured the crowd's attention by reciting a poem she had written for history class:

> We are proud Mexican American people.
> We come from Jalisco, México
> Our heroes are Cesar Chavez, Frida Kahlo, Dolores Huerta, and Pancho Villa.
> We are Mexican American people.
>
> We feel sad about the Chicano farmworkers because they work hard for their families, and they work in the fields in the heat without being paid well.
> We worry about good poor people trying to get across *la frontera* for better opportunities in this life.
> We cry because good helpless poor people, Latinos, are dying while they cross *la frontera*, for better lives, and a better situation for their families.
> We are Mexican American people.
>
> We understand the truth about helpless people who have many crises because of money.
> We believe in happiness and that by having one another we're rich people.
> We dream that one day people will stop being greedy and cruel.
> We hope that poor helpless people one day become rich, and have rights like everybody else, to say things about laws just like rich people can.
> We are a strong, proud Mexican American family.

Amigos Charter Academy is foremost an expression of Latino community, a heartfelt effort to reinforce a broad and caring commitment to *educación*. Not simply a search for higher test scores, *educación* emphasizes family, morality, and manners as much, if not more, than the mastery of subject matter. Children are expected to respect their elders and abide by school rules; adults are expected to discipline and nurture.[1] Amigos has fostered these values, creating a familial spirit that ultimately enabled it to overcome a fuzzy academic mission and recurring periods of organizational chaos.

Amigos is a small school centered around a shared set of aims and cultural symbols and meanings. The school's first principal, known as the "founding mother," referred to students as "*mis hijitos pequeños*—my little children," and to parents as "our *mamas*." Classroom walls exhibit pictures of Cesar Chavez and paintings by Diego Rivera. Students learn to dance salsa in gym class, and they study the Mexican-American War from the perspective of Vera Cruz peasants. The majority of formal instruction occurs in English, but teachers often speak Spanish when underscoring a lesson on morality or disciplining a misbehaving student. In these ways, the school, explicitly and with distinct pride, reinforces the culture and priorities of the community.

The open house was, in fact, unique only in its details, as community members frequently congregate at the school for various activities. Every other Saturday, dubbed "Sabado Gigante," parents volunteer their services by picking up trash, trimming hedges, fixing leaks, and carrying out other activities to help maintain school facilities. They also coordinate and oversee recreational events such as coed soccer tournaments, in which teams compete during the lunch recess. Amigos' staff and parents have successfully developed a school in which this working-class community expresses an enthusiastic commitment to a human-scale organization that they see as their own. Two former Amigos students eloquently described their school's close-knit culture:

> [Amigos Charter Academy] was just really like a community setting. It was like we were learning at home or something, with a bunch of our friends. They had really nice teachers, who were, you know, mostly Chicano and Chicana . . . We could relate to them . . . The teachers seemed to care a whole lot more about the students . . . The parents were a lot more involved. It just seemed like a more community-type setting.

> They know your culture, your background . . . the way they encourage you, you know, they talk to your parents . . . And your parents trust them, and it's like a family . . . My parents hardly know my teachers now.

The family feeling, however, could not completely stem a rising tide of discontent; just six months prior to the open house, the members of Amigos had been struggling to prevent their organization from falling apart. Confidence in the once highly touted principal had plummeted. The board had continually failed to present an adequate budget, garner essential resources from the private sector, or fulfill many of its other responsibilities. Teachers were bickering with one another and felt overworked. One teacher explained: "The problem with working at a school that's so small, in which we have so much decision-making power relative to other places and so much personal connection, is that the personal and professional become hard to separate. Sometimes the school is so much like a bunch of teenagers and little cliques—*chismiando*—and business is conducted during backdoor meetings with people's friends instead of out in the open."

The small teaching staff scheduled an emergency meeting. In her agenda for the meeting, the principal candidly admitted that "the school community recognizes that individuals have experienced conflict and/or lack of clarity in regard to roles and responsibilities in school governance and decision making." The goals of the meeting were "to seek understanding, not blame; to reduce stress from conflict; to practice good communication and share responsibility." But it was too little too late; the principal had already lost the confidence of her staff. Two weeks later, as the principal's legitimacy continued to wane, the school board and teachers asked for her resignation. With its mission drifting and a breakdown in decision making, Amigos was looking for a strong and charismatic leader—the kind of leader the school had enjoyed in its initial years.

Amigos Charter Academy enrolled 170 adolescents in grades six through eight for the 1997–98 school year. This is in stark contrast to the other three public middle schools in the district, which serve an average of 850 students each.[2] Nearly all of Amigos' students are first-generation Mexicans or of Latin American descent. More than 90 percent of them are eligible for the free or reduced-cost lunch program. Most hold limited proficiency in spoken and written English, and many are at least three years below grade level on measures of academic performance. Ten teachers, one principal, one counselor, one part-time secretary, and a resource specialist make up the staff. A substantial majority of the staff, but not all, see themselves as Chicano or Latino, and nearly everyone speaks Spanish fluently. In each of the three years we conducted fieldwork, one-third to one-half of the teaching staff left at year's end.

Amigos does not look like a typical school. Instead of having a library, a book mobile visits them every two weeks, lending books to unimpressed students and frustrated teachers alike. In lieu of a cafeteria, the familiar "taco truck" provides daily lunches. Teachers and students share and clean the only bathroom on the premises. Because there are no custodial services, parents volunteer time to help maintain the facilities. Still, while the water-stained walls and cracked ceilings betray aesthetic sensibilities, they do little to dampen the enthusiasm that, despite the recurring staff breakdowns, still pervades the school community. The parents have, by and large, attained what they had long hoped for—a safe, familial school.

But whether this unifying and participatory spirit is enough to sustain an institution over the long haul remains to be seen. Amigos' parents and teachers have founded a new form of community, crafted in counterpoint to the large, impersonal public middle schools that they feared. But this seemingly empowered, close-knit community has been unable to devise an organizational structure that retains enthusiastic teachers or concretely raises student performance.

In its first couple of years, Amigos directed all of its efforts toward securing and equipping a school site, fostering a strong sense of community and culture, and promoting a safe environment. The founders overlooked many of the "nuts and bolts" involved in building an educationally rigorous institution. They thought that if students were disciplined and well cared for, and parents empowered to assume an active role in running the school, all would fall into place. The fact that this did not occur, that Amigos has in fact continually struggled with the challenge of institution building, raises questions about charters that develop their identity around shared community symbols and rituals while neglecting the necessary work of solidifying an organization that energizes effective teachers. Will charters founded on cultural identity be able to develop long-term institutional strengths based on solid planning and administrative stability? Will parents who are under a great deal of economic stress, with minimal education themselves, be able to assume the numerous administrative responsibilities that, in the public schools, fall under the purview of state agencies? Will such schools, with a weak articulation of purpose, be able to endure the internal conflicts that challenge their sense of community spirit?

By taking an analytical lens to the telling events at Amigos, we can see how it has succeeded in affirming culture and values regarding *educación*. But we also observe that Amigos has floundered in terms of fulfilling its curricular and core learning objectives. After five years, for example, the faculty had yet to agree on discrete benchmarks for gauging students' learning. This gulf between the school's ability to create a community and its relative inability to craft the nitty-gritty elements of an effective school is the issue on which we focus.

The Founding of Amigos: Breaking Away from a Troubled Urban School District

Amigos Charter Academy opened its doors in the fall of 1993, coming out of a backlash against Oakland, California's junior high schools. Parents in Amigos Academy's working-class Latino neighborhood had long been alarmed by the prospect of sending their children to schools many perceived as dangerous and chaotic. The district schools are, in fact, among the worst in California along measures of dropout, student achievement, and large class size.[3] Stories of children who graduated from their local elementary school only to join gangs, use drugs, and drop out during their tenure in junior high are well known throughout the community. According to one parent, "I don't want my child to go to one of those schools . . . If the charter didn't exist, I'd have to pay for a private school." Parents desperately wanted to buffer their children from such influences by creating a familial school where students would be nurtured and protected in a supportive learning environment. According to one parent who was actively involved in mobilizing support for the charter:

> Our children are too small to attend a junior high school with all the problems that there are in those schools. We became aware of all the problems: gang problems, academic and discipline problems. I would worry, and a lot of parents would worry about our small children attending that school . . . I liked the idea that as parents we would get more involved, that we would be more attentive to the children. And above all, [we worried] about the problem that [our children] would get involved with other types of people that would be bad influences for them . . . We started to see what was happening. Where are the children going to go? How are they going to get there? Then we decided to support [the charter]. We decided to support [a school] where the children would be more protected, where the children would be safer. And it was initiated. We supported all aspects of the school, and it was created. The children enrolled soon after.

When we asked parents why they chose Amigos over the district school, their responses were strikingly similar: "We learned that it's a safe school where the children don't use drugs nor weapons of any type." "Because the children are not scared to go to this school," another parent commented.

Parents desired a school that resembled Lakeville, their neighborhood elementary school, where many members of the Amigos community had first become acquainted. At Lakeville, their children received an education in an environment sensitive to bilingualism and other aspects of their Latino heritage. The founders hoped to further this tradition by cultivating in Amigos a climate similar to that of an idealized Mexican school, in which *educación* so blends academic achievement and moral development that the two goals cannot easily be disentangled. One parent explained: "You see, the academic and the social always go together, because if you're a good student, you're not going to be misbehaving in the classroom. Education is all about respect; our children must always obey the adults, teachers, or whoever, and try to learn as much as they can."

Julia Perez, a former counselor at Lakeville and a founding staff member of Amigos, relayed an anecdote—with tongue in cheek—that also reflects many parents' commitment to a Mexican *educación:* "Parents want strict! I developed the discipline point system, meaning the last line of intervention is the point system. We had parents saying, 'Give them a point,' and I'd have to say, 'No, no, no; we got to give kids a chance.' For the most part, our parents wanted a very traditional Mexican school. I mean, we could have thrown some nuns in and it probably would have helped; parents would have been happy, you know, if we gave the nuns some sticks."

To be sure, concerns about safety provided the impetus for breaking away from the district, but parents also were alarmed by the distressingly low performance of their largely Spanish-speaking children. Indeed, few groups of students fare more poorly in U.S. schools than children of Spanish-language backgrounds. Latinos, who form the majority of immigrant students both in California and across the nation, have the highest dropout rates of any group; currently, only 56 percent of all Latino youths eighteen to twenty-four years old have completed high school. California schools now serve approximately one million Spanish-speaking children. Like other Latino parents, those at Amigos undoubtedly felt that their kids had been trapped in a large urban school district that just wasn't addressing their needs.

Even before the idea of forming a charter school surfaced, a group of parents had attempted to reform the junior high schools through traditional channels, by pleading with the school board. A founding parent described the experience: "When we went to the school district for [board] meetings, sometimes we would stay there until midnight, waiting for someone to listen to us. But they didn't want to listen to us."

Frustrated with remote and seemingly indifferent school officials, the original founding parents decided to build Amigos on a shared commitment to parent and community involvement. According to their charter, "Empowerment of staff, students, and parents will be a visible reality. Active and meaningful participation of parents and students, along with leadership roles taken by all staff, will result in a school where everyone has a voice and a contribution to make in the development of this middle school."

Several policies were enacted pursuant to this commitment to spark parent involvement when the school was first established. Parents were to hold a majority representation on the board so they could play a central role in on-going policy decisions and fund-raising activities. They were required to sign a contract before enrolling their children in Amigos, committing themselves to at least four hours of volunteer work each month. Parents attended staff and board meetings, assisted in classrooms, even watered a modest garden that lies between two classroom trailers. One parent summarized the mission succinctly: "That is the goal of the charter school: that the parents get involved and pay more attention to the children."

Key to this grassroots effort was Margarita Ortíz, who had been the principal of the Lakeville Elementary School before she left to lead the campaign for the charter. Neighborhood parents had the utmost respect for Ortíz and knew that she shared many of their concerns about the district schools. She grew increasingly disenchanted by the number of students who, after graduating from Lakeville, became alienated in what she called "Mickey Mouse" English as a Second Language (ESL) courses in middle school. Whereas parents' foremost concerns centered around safety, Ortíz wanted to pursue broader aims, building from the socialization goals to include a more rigorous academic program: "We need to get these kids into a place where they can compete, get them into the middle class." From the beginning, she promoted a cultural agenda primarily as a way of providing a strong social and academic foundation for her middle school students.

When the state legislature approved California's charter bill in 1992, Ortíz and two of her colleagues saw their opening. They quickly informed parents at Lakeville that they were going to put together a proposal for a new charter school. Ortíz was by all accounts the leader of the movement. She solicited the help of a nonprofit community organization, which not only assisted with public relations strategies in the beginning but also provided much-needed financial support. She also gathered written endorsements from key city officials, the local parish priest, and California's state schools chief, Delaine Eastin, who ultimately wrote letters to the local school board in support of Amigos' charter bid. The district board resisted Amigos' petition, so Ortíz pulled an end run. Under California law, the county office of education can approve a charter. In September 1993, Amigos Charter Academy—having successfully petitioned its county office of education—opened its doors to students and parents alike.

The Struggle for Resources

Ratification of Amigos' charter represented a milestone in a difficult journey. It was an uphill but inspiring climb for all involved, especially for those parents whose earlier efforts to reform the system from within had failed. But the challenges were far from over. The first task was to find a suitable and affordable location. A temporary answer was found when a branch of the Roman Catholic diocese generously offered to lease Amigos space in its community park, for the sum of one dollar per year for two years. Five weeks were needed to prepare the portable classrooms, during which time Amigos held classes in various locations, including two private schools and a local university. As Ortíz put it, "We were homeless." Two years later, in the fall of 1995, Amigos put an end to its nomadic ways and relocated to its current site. Euphemistically referred to as a "business park," the shoddy space features a small plot of dirt and barbed wire fences and on one side is shaded by ten stories of modular containers that await shipping from the local port. On the opposite side of the little cluster of dingy brown portable buildings, grass and weeds grow three feet high. For an annual cost of $40,000 for the following three years, Amigos had finally found a home.

Shortly after Amigos settled into its industrial site, the school's fiscal crunch began to take its toll. Outlays were needed to purchase and equip the aluminum-sided bungalows. Electricity and water bills ran overdue. In its third year, 1995–96, the school operated without electricity for more than three months. One teacher explained: "This community wanted a school so badly that they were willing to have their classes in these crappy portables, with no running water, no electricity, and no bathrooms; they had to take kids to people's houses to go pee in between classes."

Like all charter schools in California, Amigos receives the same base-level per-pupil funding as any conventional public school. As a start-up school, however—in contrast to preexisting public schools that convert to charter schools—Amigos had expenditures beyond those of traditional schools. It had to figure out how to pay for and renovate a site, manage cash flow, dole out money for administrative expenses, and adhere to state tax codes and mandates. To alleviate some of these costs, many charters negotiate agreements with their sponsoring district under which the city schools office provides administrative assistance in exchange for a small fee. Amigos founders adamantly opposed any such agreement because of the district's initial political opposition. And this feisty independent stance also meant forgoing thousands of dollars in bilingual and special-education funds.

Margarita Ortíz's pursuit of unconditional autonomy proved costly, leaving Amigos with little to no district support and numerous economic and administrative problems. One telling story centered around liability insurance. Since districts normally provide student insurance for schools, they receive discounted rates, which are then passed on to individual schools. Amigos opted to pass on a $3-per-student deal offered by its sponsoring district, which would have translated to a $400 total for the entire Amigos student body. Instead, because Ortíz refused to jeopardize the charter's hard-earned independence, Amigos incurred a $10,000 insurance bill.

After essentially cutting itself off from the district, Amigos lost access to both state funds and local resources. When students entered Amigos, the district literally dropped them from its central files. Districts use these files to track students along a variety of statistics, including measures of English proficiency and family income. This information is then used to determine how much money a district receives from the state or federal government via categorical programs like bilingual education and Title I. But since the district stopped accounting for Amigos students, most of whom qualified for compensatory services, the district received less money from the state. The result: Amigos did not obtain funds to which it was entitled. Nor did Amigos receive access to district-sponsored services and events, such as staff development and resource drives. One teacher explained: "They do not invite us [to staff development activities]. We are technically invited, but they do not send us an invitation. So if we happen to find out about something, and if there happens to be room, then we can participate. But since they won't include us in their mail route—you know, we have this whole interschool mail thing, but we do not have a box downtown—they won't deliver to us. Their warehouse is just up the street here, like it would be such a big deal, but they don't include us." Another teacher offered a political explanation for the district's failure to support Amigos:

> The teachers at this school have to do so much work, but I don't see that
> level of district-school cooperation here to support these teachers and these

kids . . . Other schools have a lot of books, computers, a building, and most of the stuff is just collecting dust, and I find that [this] is a disadvantage to the spirit of education. The [district] institution is very separatist, racist, intolerant, and that speaks to the nature of the problems of this community anyway. They should be glad to help a school in our predicament. We don't . have a blue card here so we can't get the stuff from the district.

To stave off insolvency, Ortíz appealed to a local community organization for help, enlisted the support of local businesses, and successfully petitioned the state for financial assistance. Through her relentless commitment, Amigos managed to stay afloat. "Margarita was a workhorse," said the lead teacher. "She has lived, breathed, done everything with the charter school. She worked twelve, fourteen, sixteen hours a day, digging ditches, cleaning bathrooms; it was not above her to do anything."

Ortíz's efforts provided Amigos with short-term financial stability, but little to no money remained for educational supplies. Teachers made do without the most basic necessities, including books, paper, and chalk. Of course, they had no "luxuries" either—such things as a library, microscopes, Bunsen burners, and computers were beyond the realm of possibility. One teacher said she considered the scarcity of resources her "nemesis." Certainly the scarcity placed a difficult burden on the teachers, who tended to have an extremely short tenure rate: eight of ten Amigos' original teachers left in the initial years, burned out by the lack of resources and lack of consensus on the vital issue of how to build a more efficacious instructional program.

A Charismatic Leader Is Not Enough

Just running the school from one day to the next proved an enormous challenge, undermining efforts at achieving long-term objectives such as formalizing a clear curriculum, devising student assessment policies, and setting up budgeting and attendance systems. The overworked staff ultimately left the majority of these issues unresolved, forcing teachers to address them in subsequent years.

Amigos did enjoy some success under Margarita Ortíz, whose charisma and resourcefulness provided teachers and parents with a unifying vision and fragile organizational stability. The school began to make inroads on some key organizational and educational objectives. By 1995 it had successfully lowered the class size to approximately twenty-four students, and

Amigos' dropout rate (or student exit from the community) was well below the district average. Newly arrived immigrants attending the school received content instruction in Spanish, and classes in core subjects lasted two hours.

Teachers often pointed to the size of the school and the accompanying smaller class size as the key advantages of working at Amigos. They claimed that it led to deeper relationships between teachers and students, contributing to the safe, familial feeling of the school. One teacher said, "We pay more attention to the students. At other schools, because they're a minority, [Latino students] get lost, but not here. We do our best to keep them engaged." Many teachers mentioned that they have a greater awareness of the students' interests and backgrounds, and that they use such knowledge to develop more effective lesson plans and motivational strategies than they could in other schools. Another teacher championed the school's small size, arguing that it precluded Amigos from offering students electives at the expense of academic courses, thus helping to ensure that students will get access to college-track classes in high school. Echoing advocates of an academic core curriculum, this teacher summarized: "Who cares if they get music?"

The staff experienced some growing pains in the attempts to implement a fairly participatory process for school decision making, as teachers often held different and competing ideas of how things should get done. Staff members, especially the younger teachers, were quite political. On one occasion teachers debated the ethics of accepting donations from a company that opposed bilingual instruction; on another, they disagreed about whether they should risk bankruptcy to partake in a teachers' strike unfolding in the district.

Yet Ortíz attempted to limit teacher participation in schoolwide decisions, explicitly recognizing that they needed sufficient time to focus on teaching. She understood the need to strike a balance between teacher involvement in democratic governance and her own strong leadership, so that teachers could devote most of their energy to instruction. Without a decisive founding leader, Amigos undoubtedly would have been bogged down at the start by process, politics, and cynicism during its episodes of distressing uncertainty. Ortíz's ability to walk an organizational tightrope—to be both a decisive leader and a skilled collaborator—is reflected in the following two teachers' descriptions of her leadership style:

When Margarita was here, the staff made the decisions. There were some times when it just didn't happen like that, but only once or twice, when she said she didn't think the staff's way would work, and she did it her way. She was right both times. But this happened rarely. She really deferred a lot to the teachers because the teachers often knew what they were talking about.

Margarita was a superhuman person who basically took care of everything. She would either do it herself or delegate responsibilities to other people, and those people knew exactly what they needed to do. Margarita took care of everything, and the school was running sometimes on the chaotic side because there was a lot of work to do, always too much work for one person to do, but eventually things would get done.

Robust Parental Participation in the First Years

In addition to Ortíz's leadership, parent participation enabled Amigos to persevere during the difficult early times. Parents were especially active in the first years, during which they organized support for the charter, developed the school site, and took the lead on a few policy issues. In the time leading up to the charter proposal, at least ten parents actively campaigned for the creation of the school, lobbying the district school board and circulating petitions throughout the community. Later, nearly the entire community joined the effort. Julia Perez provided a summary of events: "When it came down to the vote, at the board meeting, when they voted seven to zero after saying they would never do it, we had a couple hundred parents there; it was at least two hundred, but I heard estimates of four hundred. It was Lakeville parents, it was us, the staff and parents. Parents were really buying in, in a very active way, to the point that by the time we got a school, we had many many parents really buy in, taking the risk of sending their kids to us . . . And it was very exciting."

The initial enthusiasm that led to the charter's ratification also fueled the development of the school in the early years. Parents spent evenings and weekends connecting electrical equipment, installing air conditioning units, helping with carpentry, and in general building the school site. Parent board members also enacted schoolwide policies during this time. They voted unanimously in favor of a strict discipline system in which students who exceeded a predetermined number of points would face expulsion; a school uniform policy requiring khaki pants and white-collar shirts, aimed at preventing exhibitions of gang-affiliated clothing; and a closed campus to ensure that students were supervised throughout the entire day.

The beginning years marked the apex of parent involvement. Parents participated in all sorts of committees, attended board meetings, in droves, and made a real effort to provide assistance any way they could. According to one parent, "We'd pick out the problems at the meetings, and we all participated in trying to figure them out, to decide what was the best thing for the school." These parent founders had worked together for many years, from their days at Lakeville through the early years of Amigos, and so they understood the importance of investing time and energy in the school. Perez spoke of the role of parents during the school's first three years: "In the beginning parents were much more involved in all elements. And I think that has to do with how strong the buy-in was the first couple of years, how strong that buy-in was from these parents and how long we've known these parents—we've known these parents forever. There were a couple of things that really helped that along, and it seemed like a natural thing to continue to work together, 'cause these parents were also very active at Lakeville. So when their kids graduated, they came with us, they continued."

Still, most parents seemed more confident attending to facilities than developing school policy. Perez explained that the teachers had always held more "broad-based objectives" for the educational program, whereas parents just wanted "safe." Through the school's first five years, debate continued among teachers and school community members over just what kind of role parents should assume at Amigos. But while the founding parents may not always have felt comfortable as policymakers, they did hold a steadfast commitment to the shared mission, and they knew that they had to remain actively involved if the school was to succeed. Of course, like their children, they too would soon graduate, leaving the responsibility of sustaining Amigos to a new generation of parents.

Changing of the Guard: Replacing the Founding Mother Proves Difficult

During one of our routine site visits in the winter of 1997, Amigos' fourth year, we arrived minutes before lunchtime recess for a scheduled interview. The teacher we were to interview explained that there was yet another emergency staff meeting. We would have to reschedule. Although the staff refused our request to attend, when the meeting adjourned, their angry faces reflected the frustration and hostility that had been building up for the past several months. We talked with one exasperated teacher who had this to say: "There's no respect here anymore. How do we expect to get anything done when people can't even look at each other when we're in the same room. There's a real ill feeling around here. I feel ill."

Burned out and beset by family problems, Margarita Ortíz had left Amigos at the end of the previous school year to pursue her doctoral studies, and a leadership void had quickly emerged in the young organization. In only its third year of existence, Amigos now confronted the challenge of replacing its founding mother. Perez and Ortíz had searched for a skilled veteran to step in. Specifically, they looked for a Spanish-speaking educator who had worked with them before, who knew the community, and who understood the shared mission. The job had been offered to Elena Sanchez, a veteran principal recruited from a neighboring district.

From the outset, however, Sanchez seemed both unclear about her own responsibilities as principal and unaware of the priorities of the parents. One teacher explained, "I noticed that Elena was overwhelmed and a lot of things were not getting done, in terms of budgeting, reporting to staff, in regard to attendance and procedures." She failed to submit on time the documentation that determines school funding, nearly shutting down Amigos entirely. She addressed student discipline problems in a remarkably permissive fashion, given the parents' emphasis on rules. "The whole attitude of the school was like being sent to the principal meant nothing," said another teacher. For the first time, Amigos faced a graffiti problem; students defaced the bathroom walls with spray paint and markers, and as one teacher put it, "It was disgusting to go in there." Staff often complained or expressed bewilderment about how little time Sanchez spent at Amigos, and no one seemed to know where she was or what she was doing during her absences. One confided: "Last year we knew how invested Margarita was in the school, so no one worried that things were being done. Everyone saw her here working her butt off constantly, and there was no doubt that she was giving her all and that she had a lot of talent to make contacts and raise money, which is so vital at a place like this. But this year, well, it's difficult for anyone to fill her shoes, but I get the sense that there is really little confidence in what Elena is doing. She's barely ever here."

Amigos appeared to be falling apart. Students wandered into classrooms late and often seemed indifferent to learning when they arrived. One teacher told us that "classes are more chaotic than in a regular school," and a student mentioned that "it is easier." Frequent midday staff meetings interrupted the flow of the school day and interfered with teaching time. "We get to class late, and it is really difficult even to see all the ways that it is getting in the way and really affecting the kids," one teacher said. "The emotional stress is taking its toll." Sanchez could not unite the staff or help advance many of their organizational and educational objectives. Teachers could not arrive at a clear policy for deciding when to expel students who just were not responding. Amigos' spirit was flagging.

Amigos still had not implemented a bilingual curricular program, nor had teachers reached a consensus about what such a program should be like. The school also lacked a formal curricular sequence: instruction was not linked across subject areas, and teachers rarely found time to collaborate. Teachers struggled to adopt coherent policies regarding peer review, staff development, and assessment. According to the lead teacher, "We act like we are in our infancy even though it's our fourth year."

The extent to which the staff struggled with developing the formal aspects of the school well into its fourth year suggested deeper problems within the organization than just failing leadership. After all, even during the first years of Ortíz's generally productive tenure Amigos struggled with the nuts and bolts of forming an efficient and academically rigorous organization. The leadership vacuum was not the sole cause of the problems, but it exacerbated those that had always pervaded the school. "It's not just the leadership, this has been a recurring issue," said the lead teacher. The turmoil surrounding Principal Sanchez was in fact a symptom of a larger issue: the pressure associated with governing democratically at a school with few institutional routines and little focus on curricular or pedagogical improvements. The lead teacher gave us her interpretation of these deep-seated ills:

> I think that part of the problem that we have had here historically is that we were a start-up school. You know, we have to deal a lot with survival issues; it's basic survival. And I think that has been what has sort of gotten in the way of improving and creating a school that we want to see. You know, Maslow's hierarchy, and we are stuck at the basic level. And so, I do not think there has been the kind of emphasis that I would like to see on really changing the structure and curriculum of the school. We have got to get our organizational act together if we are going to be successful. By organization I'm not just talking about teachers, I'm talking about the school board.

How to Sustain Human-Scale Democracy?

When the founders created Amigos, they thought that parents would be eager to participate in the governance of the school. Therefore, the founders established the board as a mechanism through which parents could shape the direction of the school. Most of the board members were parents; the remaining few were members of the broader community. The idea was that the parents would advance school policies and programs built on thoughtful, long-term planning. The school's nine teachers already had more responsibilities than they could fulfill, as did the part-time secretary, the principal, and the counselor. It was up to the parent-dominated school board, then, to make a substantive contribution.

By year four, however, the nature of parent involvement began to change and diminish and, as Julia Perez explained, "We could have lost the entire school because we not only didn't have good leadership, but we graduated our founding parents." Attendance at committee and board meetings decreased significantly. The board itself included slightly fewer parents then it had before, though parents still managed to retain majority representation until the following year. Perez realized that the founders' original intention of empowering parents as real partners in the education of their children "in terms of policy decisions, school direction, running of the school, homework clubs . . ." never reached fruition.

One first-year teacher described the difference between her expectations of the roles parents would assume and the reality: "I guess I had thought, based on the stated mission, that parents would volunteer in lots of different ways. And what I found out is that really what they do is either clerical stuff or, you know, sort of janitorial work. So we have all these parents, like, cleaning and vacuuming, but I didn't realize it would be like this. I thought there would be parents helping in my classroom all the time."

To be sure, teachers and staff valued the fact that parents compensated for the lack of janitorial services by cleaning up the school. "It's not peripheral, cleanliness is a really big thing for us," Perez said. "They come and do my floors, and that's of value to the community." Although we rarely observed parents in classrooms—much less assisting teachers directly with instruction—most appeared comfortable working with teachers in other capacities. One mentioned that "I go to watch behavior." Another claimed that "certain teachers lack authority, so it's good to have the parents in the room." All of the parents with whom we spoke expressed enthusiasm about Amigos Charter Academy and their relationship to it: "It was a dream to have a school where we could participate," said one parent. Another added, "We just want to be involved in the school, seeing how the students behave, seeing them respect teachers and adults." Parents who once felt disenfranchised and helpless in the traditional school system now felt more empowered.

Competing Cultural Models of Participation

But the founding of Amigos had centered on a different model—an ideal model—of parent involvement. Parents were not only to attend to the facilities and be a visible presence in the school, they were also expected to play an intricate role in the running of the school. Consequently, some teachers even raised questions about the ethics of allowing parents to assume custodial jobs. From their perspective, parents were not empowered but exploited when they fulfilled their contractual requirements through maintenance-type work: "We are treating them as slaves," said one such teacher. Those who subscribed to this point of view acknowledged that Amigos could not afford an alternative arrangement and thus understood that their expectations for parent involvement conflicted with the reality of their being dependent on parents for school upkeep. But as one teacher noted, "Every year we've talked about wanting parents to do more for the school than just maintenance; we want the parents to be involved in policy, in governance, in the classrooms, helping teachers and students as opposed to just being out in the field."

The problem was that the expectations teachers had for parents were, at best, disconnected from those the parents had for themselves and, at worst, unrealistic. Each group held a tacit understanding of what parental participation means, and the competing conceptions were rarely confronted. Parents were content to leave education decisions to the educators while they focused their energies on maintaining school facilities, doing clerical work, and ensuring that students are respecting their elders and abiding by school rules. So long as parents felt confident that the staff was committed to enforcing the strict rules on which the founders had agreed, Amigos parents did in fact feel empowered.

Moreover, expecting parents to assume an active role in the school and classrooms presumes that parents have the time and wherewithal to do so. As one parent explained, "There are parents who don't have time to study the issue because, economically, a mother and father who are working can't . . . It's impossible, because sometimes it's more important to bring home money than it is to attend a meeting." The majority of Amigos parents possessed little formal education and spoke little if any English; consequently, most did not feel comfortable assisting teachers with academics in the class-room. Said one parent, "How can I watch a lesson given by a teacher who speaks English? What can I do? I can't help at all."

In previous years, such concerns over the nature and amount of parent involvement were mitigated because parents not only spent time maintain-ing the facilities but also attended board and committee meetings. Still, de-spite the fact that parent attendance did indeed drop off, the truth is that parents had never really participated as actively in these school meetings or wielded as much influence over policy matters as the founders had envi-sioned—even when meetings were routinely conducted in both Spanish and English. According to one teacher, "The problem is that parents don't have levels of participation in decision making that teachers have or that they are supposed to have according to the charter. It's difficult for them to get used to becoming part of the school. They can't make time, and in terms of running the school and meetings, they are not as savvy."

Even during board meetings of years past, when parents attended and participated in greater numbers, Perez explained, "they used to tell these long overdrawn stories that weren't really appropriate at the board level, but they were there!" The parents had always been less involved with gover-nance and more preoccupied with other matters. Listen to one founding parent's memory of her experience on the board: "I was on the school board since the inception, and every parent would go and say, 'I will help with this, I can go and help in the yard, or I can go during recess and help with super-vision of the children and make sure everything is alright; that children are playing properly.'"

The fact that parents often spent time at the school caring for facilities, helping in the office, and monitoring student behavior set Amigos apart from its public school counterparts in the district. Their presence, in and of itself, undeniably improved the school in immeasurable ways. When par-ents were around, whether in the classroom or outside during lunchtime, the students rarely misbehaved. Because the teachers and parents knew each other well, their interactions were more meaningful and comfortable. One former student summed it up well when he rightly pointed out that "the parents go a lot to see, check up on their child, and I think seeing the parents get involved a lot helps the teachers." There is no doubt that the climate of the school was made more familial and secure because of the amount of time parents spent at the school.

Still, the ways in which parents helped did not directly advance the organizational or academic goals that were of most importance to Amigos teachers. Although the founders had hoped parents would alleviate the burden placed on staff members, who were expected to both teach and administrate, this did not occur. Without support from the downtown district office, Amigos had counted on parent board members to, among other things, develop educational programs, budget short- and long-term expenditures, and garner additional outside resources. But none of this had taken place, as the lead teacher explained while describing the organizational "nightmare" Amigos faced: "Clearly the school board has got to define its roles and responsibilities; it has to present quality to the members of the staff and really start moving toward their governance responsibilities, which I feel have sort of gone by the wayside this year. There are, you know, only three or four people on the board who probably understand it, and I would say the rest really don't. And I'm very aware of the board's lack of goals and systems and, well, purpose."

Over time Amigos had begun to depart from the founders' original model of parent involvement—and that trend only accelerated. By year five, the 1997–98 school year, Amigos' organizational structure looked more like that of a traditional school than that of an "innovator," as championed by proponents of charter schools. That year, while under the tenure of the school's first and only Anglo principal, Amigos board meetings were no longer conducted in Spanish, precluding most parents from getting involved in governance issues even if they wanted to. The composition of the board underwent a radical transformation as well: only two parents with children at Amigos remained. The other members, Perez explained, were professionals from in and around the community: "a rich white lawyer," "a Ph.D. with maybe the right racial mixture but who never lived in this type of context," "a social worker who at least has Spanish language skills," and "a director of a private school." Moreover, the board began to seem as detached from Amigos as many central administrators in urban districts are from public schools. As one teacher noted of the attitudinal change, "It is bizarre because the board and the staff don't even know each other."

Crafting Organizational Routines and Stability

In terms of governance, Amigos still struggled with many issues that radical decentralization is supposed to resolve. By its fourth year of operation, beset by a poorly functioning school board, Amigos was in some trouble. Teachers were beginning to feel overworked, overwhelmed, and burned out. They continually faced the challenge of addressing the minutiae of daily school operation and negotiating school politics while trying to develop long-term institutional strengths. "We are always dealing with immediate crisis intervention and daily business stuff, so we never set anything up for long-term running," explained one teacher. The energy teachers expended to address tasks normally performed by the state, school boards, superintendents, and principals were taking their toll in the classroom. Another teacher lamented, "I would honestly say that this year I have probably spent 80 percent of my time on administrative duties and only 20 percent on teaching."

In an effort to get administrative and organizational assistance, Amigos began to move closer to its sponsoring district. District officials began to keep track of Amigos students in its central files, to determine the amount of categorical funds Amigos should receive from the state, and to pay for a resource specialist so Amigos could comply with special education codes.

Nevertheless, the school remained in disarray. Every Wednesday, Amigos held a meeting intended for staff to discuss substantive educational matters, but the enormity of trying to keep the school going in the most basic operational sense made this difficult and sometimes impossible. As one teacher commented:

> There are so many mundane tasks, and they end up being so important because we spend two or three hours at so many meetings, and nothing is getting resolved. It is so frustrating and ridiculous; there are so many things that we should be doing, and we end up doing nothing. What has happened is, faculty meetings—which are supposed to be about curriculum—have gone on and on and on, and all we have dealt with are other issues. You know, whether it be school policy, or attendance issues, or who is doing what and when. We have focused so little on curriculum. You know, it has taken away from our main job! So, that's frustrating and [it has] created some tension between staff.

Inability to Forge a Consensus

Our observations of staff and committee meetings revealed deep-seated differences among staff members, even though teachers had chosen colleagues who ostensibly shared the school's mission. One example centered on discipline policy. If an Amigos student accumulated more than twenty-five disciplinary points or was caught fighting repeatedly, he or she was sup-posed to be expelled. While punitive, the policy stemmed from parental fears that Amigos would become as dangerous as its public-school counter-parts. Therefore, from the very beginning the measure had been widely sup-ported by parents and educators alike. On one occasion, a seventh-grade boy exceeded the twenty-five-point cap. He was promptly suspended until the parent-led Discipline Committee could deliberate his case. The commit-tee ultimately gave teachers the final decision, but the teachers could not reach a consensus. Veteran teachers argued that the school must stick to its policy, fearing that any concessions would leave the school vulnerable to similar disputes in the future and undermine the original priorities of par-ents. Other teachers questioned the utility of expulsion, believing that in-creasing parent involvement and implementing a conflict resolution pro-gram could prove to be more constructive.

The teachers never did have to render a verdict; the mother withdrew her son and returned to Mexico after learning that he had become involved in a neighborhood gang. But this discipline incident portended future debates, as staff frequently became polarized along lines of seniority and individuals' connections to the founding of the school. One teacher described meetings as "really volatile in terms of people feeling the threat to the mission, the vi-sion being changed, the school being taken away from the people who had fought for it and created it." Senior teachers felt their voice should carry more weight, whereas younger teachers wondered whether the school was truly democratic: "When I was first hired it was presented to me as 'This is our school, we're empowered to make decisions,' but that's really not the case." Another teacher spoke of the challenges of governing democratically and creating a shared culture:

> The decision-making process may be democratic, but it tends to be over-powered by those who have been here longer. Because of the way this school started, by the blood, sweat and tears of people in this community, their investment in this school and feelings about their ownership of it are very different from someone who was just hired on. When it comes to dis-cussing certain issues which are particularly sensitive to the people who have the most ownership, it's the kind of thing where you're committing some big social-fall-from-grace by acting like everything is open to discus-sion. The running of the school becomes so superpoliticized and personal-ized, and it comes at the expense of professionalism and participation.

Casting Outside for Lifelines

Advocates of charter school reform presume that schools unencumbered by
district bureaucracies and state regulations will form around common objectives and advance novel forms of administration. But this did not occur
at Amigos. Rather than being innovative or genuinely democratic, the decision-making process at Amigos more closely resembled the institutional
habits of traditional public schools. The principal and select members of the
board dealt with issues of finance and employment, whereas the staff pre-
sided over what one teacher considered "more mundane, everyday matters,
like whether we should have an honors ceremony for kids who are doing
well." With few systems or processes to facilitate the governing of the
school, coupled with a dysfunctional board and ongoing school politics,
Amigos staff could not promote long-term administrative stability.

In 1996, as the school threatened to dissolve into chaos, the Coalition for
Essential Schools—a national organization developed by reformer Theodore
Sizer to provide technical assistance for restructuring schools—approached
the staff. While Amigos teachers recognized the need for outside help, they
were reluctant to accept the Coalition's services and jeopardize their carefully constructed, if increasingly fragile, sense of community. Some teachers
felt that the Coalition did not sufficiently address issues of race and class and
therefore had no business working at a Latino-centered school. One teacher
recounted the dilemma:

> The Coalition approached us, and I was very skeptical. They took us to one
> of their networking functions, and the only people of color were from our
> school. It's like, what do I have to learn from having a dialogue with these
> people? The Coalition itself probably sees us as a feather in their cap, that's
> why they're courting us, they want Latinos. I mean, we are already do-
> ing what the Coalition professes: they want smaller class sizes and small
> schools, site-based management . . . So sure, now they have a school of
> color to show that they are diverse. What we need is authentic coalitions
> with other schools that are our peers.

Despite such reservations, Amigos did decide to accept the Coalition's support. The Coalition provided Amigos with a "school coach" to operate as
critical friend, facilitator, and organizational therapist. The coach primarily
helped staff with facilitating meetings, building consensus, and ensuring
that at least some time is spent on curriculum. In addition, the Coalition

sponsored a summer retreat for Amigos teachers to learn about the history of their school and to develop communication skills that they hoped would prevent another year of organizational disarray. The investment paid dividends in the long run: several teachers acknowledged that the Coalition had been helpful, and by the end of year five, the organization would begin to show signs of improvement.

But not even the Coalition could ameliorate all the discord and organizational problems that pervaded Amigos during year four. The principal, Elena Sanchez, ultimately bore most of the blame, and by the spring of 1997 a petition to remove her had gained widespread support. So Amigos turned once again to its founding mother to get the organization back on track.

Perez notified Margarita Ortíz of the school's problems and convinced her to withdraw from graduate school and resume her role as principal of Amigos. Sanchez and Ortíz agreed to share the leadership responsibilities and serve as coprincipals for the two months remaining in the school year. But under substantial pressure from board members, the counselor, and teachers, Sanchez instead resigned.

When Ortíz returned, the staff anticipated that life at Amigos would significantly improve—especially Perez, who had lobbied most actively for her return. Unfortunately, things did not improve. Perez noted that "Margarita came back and it was awful, she came in with another agenda, on this technology thing, which was really odd for all of us; she wanted us to look like we were in the twenty-first century." Although teachers voiced concerns over the new direction of the school, Ortíz refused to listen and "took it as disloyal" when they objected. So Amigos spent thousands of dollars on computer-related equipment, which Perez said they "never used." Ortíz wanted the school to appear modern, to look and feel like a typical "progressive" school. She, too, had apparently grown detached from the original mission.

The fourth year ended much like the first three. Three-quarters of the staff left to pursue teaching positions at other schools, and Amigos was forced to start over yet again. As mentioned, the fifth year, 1997–98, brought a variety of other changes as well, such as the hiring of the school's first Anglo principal, a closer relationship with the district, a reconfigured school board, and more modest expectations of parent involvement. Most significantly, however, Amigos began to take steps to defend its charter, which was up for renewal in late winter. Despite five difficult years, Amigos still enjoyed the unconditional support of parents in the community. Having creating a small school in which children felt protected and secure, Amigos still had a chance to develop both academically and socially under a broad and caring commitment to *educación*. Amigos believed that it had achieved what mattered most to parents. In the end, the district school board agreed and voted unanimously to approve the charter for another five years.

Spirit, Chaos, and the Absence of Pedagogical Reform

It's difficult to issue a summary statement about the Amigos dilemma. Clearly the warm spirit of this small-scale institution continues to sustain a very fragile organization—one that has yet, five years after its founding, to focus on pedagogical innovation and curricular cohesion. From the very beginning, the impetus behind the creation of Amigos Charter Academy was not a desire to advance a common set of academic principles or an organizational mission. The school emerged, rather, as a backlash against what it did not want to be. During its original chartering bid, Amigos never presented itself as a beacon of innovation or a laboratory for school reform. The educators and parents who founded Amigos had simply felt alienated and disenfranchised by a system of public education they perceived as unequal, dangerous, and unresponsive to the particular needs of Latino children. They wanted a familial, neighborhood school—one that celebrated their culture and reaffirmed the traditional values of their community. The founders thought that they could cultivate an organization with long-term institutional strengths, without the assistance of any public agency, by promoting a safe and nurturing environment and encouraging parents to play a central role in running the school.

But as the founders set out to build such a place, they continually struggled with the nuts and bolts of developing a school from scratch. Parents never really participated in the governance of the school as actively as the founders had hoped, nor was the board able to garner sufficient resources from the private sector. Teachers shouldered most of the administrative burden and struggled in their attempts to implement an efficient site-based management system.

After the initial growing pains subsided and Amigos still fell short of fulfilling its objectives, the school's organizational structure began to change from what the founders had originally envisioned. Resource and administrative needs gradually forced Amigos to move closer to the district. In so doing, some of the burden placed on teachers was alleviated. Amigos also reconfigured the composition of its school board, and professionals in the community replaced working-class parents. As a consequence, the board was decoupled from the school, much like the current arrangement found in the traditional system. The Coalition of Essential Schools provided insight and technical assistance, as it does with other restructuring schools. Over time, the outer shell of Amigos started to resemble its conventional public-school counterparts. But this has proven to be a strategic accommodation to the status quo, as Amigos received a ringing endorsement from its sponsoring district when its charter was renewed with few penetrating questions asked about life and learning inside.

CHAPTER 4

Selling Air: New England Parents Spark a New Revolution

KATE ZERNIKE

"Please hold the questions. First, there'll be an exercise."

As a dozen parents of prospective students enter her classroom at the Chelmsford Public Charter School one evening after work, Lori Strand instructs them to stand on a piece of fabric barely big enough to hold them all. This, she tells them, is Planet D-5. Planet D-5—the fabric on which they stand—will self-destruct, destroying them with it, unless they can turn it over while still standing on it. Anyone whose foot steps off, Strand says, smiling, "dies."

The parents stand with arms at their sides, looking half-embarrassed, half-annoyed, as if thinking she might stop this nonsense if they just wait her out. A few on one corner shuffle to one side, trying to create a little room to flip the fabric, then realize there isn't room, and shuffle back.

"Is this a solvable problem?" asks one father.

"What if we invent a new fabric?" asks a mother, smiling a bit too hard.

Strand ignores them. "You've been working five minutes," she says firmly. "Most kids can do this in six."

"Six?" the father asks. He looks at the corner of fabric beneath his loafer, then carefully bends down and turns it over, then turns it back.

"What about twisting it?" one woman suggests. The man twists over a corner of the fabric, then smooths out a piece of the other side. He continues, moving the twist along the length of the fabric and smoothing out the flipped side. The other parents watch intently, and then, hoisting suit legs and denim skirts, begin to jump over the twist to the flipped side he has smoothed out, until the twist has moved along the entire length of the fabric. Soon they are finished, and they are even laughing.

Strand then goes to the blackboard and gets the parents to work out the percentage of survivors; with four "dead" out of twelve participants, they did just a little worse than the average sixth-grade class. She explains that this is the way fifth and sixth graders would begin their unit on "outer space" at the school, learning teamwork and improvisation as well as concepts like percentages. Sensing some purpose to the evening, the parents begin to listen attentively.

Not an average parents night, they admit. But then, this is not the average school, as they and about a hundred other parents discover as they move among the classrooms located off two narrow corridors of an office building a mile from the white-steepled center of Chelmsford, Massachusetts. There are no tests here, the young teachers tell them, no grades, no textbooks. There will be no memorization of vocabulary words. Kids can wear hats and chew gum in class.

At the end of the evening, the parents crowd into the school's common room to fire questions at the principal:

"What about spelling, grammar?"

"What about discipline?"

"What about the SAT?"

To the last, Linn Murdoch, one of the parent founders of the school, responds, "I'm hoping my child is prepared for more than the SAT. Here, my child is being prepared for life."

At this, a mother in the crowd nods enthusiastically—the first obvious sign that any of this is making any sense at all to the visitors. But there has been a more subtle shift taking place all evening. The parents are clearly intrigued, even excited, about a school so clearly different from anything they have seen before.

This isn't the school they had envisioned when they bought homes in this comfortable wooded suburb of 30,000. About thirty-five miles north of Boston, the birthplace of the nation's first public school, this is still very much the cradle of American tradition. And these parents had something a little more traditional in mind. A red brick school building, perhaps. Tests, grades. But then, the traditional public schools hadn't turned out to be what they had expected, either.

So as they go back out into the cold evening at the end of the question-and-answer session, the parents aren't talking about the oddities of this new middle school. They seem to have forgotten the annoyance of the exercise with the blanket. Instead, with the pitch of their chatter rising, they are calculating the odds of securing their children places at the school, which, going into its second year, already has more applicants than it can accept.

"We moved here because the public schools had this reputation, but where is that reputation?" says Mike Lawrence, the parent of twin fourth graders. "The public schools are resting on their laurels."

"These are young, energetic teachers with a mission," says Diane Cusano, the mother of a fourth-grade girl. "Maybe that energy will fade, but it sounds like it won't."

Dissident Suburban Parents

These might seem like the last parents in the world to be interested in any kind of alternative education. After all, the schools in this town aren't crumbling, understaffed, or overcrowded. Seventy percent of the classrooms have Internet access. SAT scores are consistently above the state and national averages. The attendance rate is 95 percent, and 25 percent of high school students—twice the state average—take Advanced Placement classes. The social problems that have confounded other schools have barely brushed Chelmsford: fewer than 5 percent of students qualify for free or reduced-cost lunch, fewer than 1 percent are non-native English speakers.

The parents who founded the school didn't start out looking for a particularly innovative school, either. They moved here expecting to find what most parents expect to find when they move to the suburbs: good schools.

But what they got was the status quo. Their children came home complaining of boredom, and looking at the assignments, parents could understand why. Lessons involved too much rote memory, were too rooted in textbooks. Teachers, parents complained, had been in the system for more than two decades, and lacked energy and enthusiasm. Many were still teaching from the same lesson plans they taught twenty-five years ago. The area around Chelmsford has come to be defined by the high-tech beltway of Route 128. Many of the parents got to the suburbs by working for the companies that began there as scrappy start-ups. They know that succeeding in the new economy means adapting quickly, and that for their children it will likely mean changing jobs not once but several times in their lifetime. The parents believed that if their children were to achieve the same success they have attained, they would need an education that taught them flexibility, to think on their feet. But their schools seemed like slide rules in a semiconductor world.

The parents clung almost stubbornly to their belief in the public schools. They responded to their own concerns by becoming the very models of parent involvement. Forming a group in 1992 called the Chelmsford Alliance for Education, they invited nationally known educators to give lectures to parents and teachers, matched high school students with mentors in a range of high-powered professions, raised money to pay for professional development for teachers. They wrote newsletters, joined school improvement councils, and drafted action plans with teachers and principals.

The result? "Nothing happened," complains Arlene Parquette, one of the charter school's founding parents. Platitudes about parent involvement aside, the system didn't seem to want their input.

Finally, in 1995, the parents went in frustration to the town's superintendent of schools and presented him with a list of goals still unmet in the action plans. What could they do to help achieve them? they asked. Nothing, he replied. "He said it wasn't our place," Parquette says. "They told us to be patient, that these things took five to ten years. Meanwhile, here was a whole group of kids getting lost."

The Creation of Chelmsford Charter

Massachusetts was among the earliest states to pass a law allowing charter schools. The law was a compromise squeezed into a sweeping $8 billion education reform act in 1993; the state's strong teachers' union agreed to allow the establishment of twenty-five charter schools so long as reform-minded legislators abandoned a bid to abolish tenure.

Massachusetts ended up with one of the most liberal charter school laws in the nation. The basic idea was simple: the state would give any parents, teachers, or group with a cogent idea on how to run a school the same per-pupil tax dollars that go to the public schools in that community—in Chelmsford, about $5,400 in 1998. The law set the charter schools free from control of the local school boards—which must approve the hiring of teachers in Massachusetts public schools. It released them from union regulations as well as most other restrictions, too, save safety codes and federal special education laws. The state gave each school a renewable charter; each had five years to prove that it could succeed as well or better than the traditional public schools.

Judged on popular appeal, the charter school provision was one of the greatest successes of the education reform act. The first charter schools opened their doors in September 1995. Three years later, the first twenty-five schools were up and running, with almost 6,000 students. The state legislature, under pressure from parents pushing for more of the schools, soon doubled the number of charters allowed.

The Chelmsford parents thought winning one of the first twenty-five charters was a long shot. Conventional wisdom, after all, was that the crisis in education was contained within the urban public schools, not in quiet suburbs like this, where parents coach soccer, drive minivans, and keep food on the table and books on the shelves.

They worked hard to counter that cliché in an inch-thick charter application, which they bound in the kind of cardboard cover their children used for book reports.

"Middle-class communities such as Chelmsford do not recognize their own need for educational reform," they wrote. "In communities where it is widely accepted that public schools have failed, wholesale change is readily accepted and embraced. In established systems where the crisis is not as apparent, due to reputations built in the past, risk taking and experimentation are difficult to justify to the public."

The state application asked, "Why is there a need for this school?" It also asked applicants to try to avoid answering by merely criticizing the existing public schools. This was hard, considering that the desire for the new school was motivated almost entirely by frustration with the existing Chelmsford schools. The parents acknowledged that the town's public schools maintain a good reputation. But that reputation, they said, was based mostly on the successes felt long ago. They cited budget constraints brought on by a 1980 law limiting property tax increases to 2.5 percent a year. The school system was too large, with 5,000 students, and that meant a large bureaucracy. The administration paid mere "lip service," they said, to the need for change: "Goals and objectives stated by the school administration nearly three years ago have gone largely unmet." A strong teachers' union seemed resistant to change; most of the teachers had been in their jobs twenty years or more.

"A small school, like a small company, can respond to change better, can reassess itself more often and can switch gears more readily when it finds that its current methods are not completely effective," they argued.

Where the application asked about broad academic objectives, the parents talked about children learning to ask better questions and coming up with "more creative, more global" answers. They talked about the need to keep up with current technology, to cross disciplines, to understand strategies for problem solving. They wanted a school that would prepare students for life as well as for work.

"It is evident that public schools are falling short due to continued emphasis on memorization of isolated facts without practical application," they wrote. "We believe the school children of today will have jobs that we cannot even imagine in the future. We need to prepare them for the twenty-first century with an education that works to understand the complex world in which we live. This education should give them the tools to understand and interpret the interrelated nature of our world."

There was no particular ideological, religious, ethnic, or cultural point of view bringing these parents together. The parents were united, rather, by a sense that school could be a more interesting, engaging place. This was their moral imperative, holding direct pedagogical implications. Their application spoke repeatedly of challenge, hands-on learning, parental involvement, enthusiasm.

One Victory, Many Questions

To their own surprise, they won a charter. The parents had done an informal survey suggesting there was some interest in town for a "student-centered school." But that interest soon proved overwhelming: within weeks, there were 400 students vying for 154 spots, and 900 teachers for 9 positions—all for a school without a principal, a track record, or even a place to hold classes.

"We sold air," marvels Brian Hagopian, a parent founder.

What they lacked in specifics, the founders made up in energy, devoting evenings, weekends, and vacations to making sure that their new creation would open on time, just after Labor Day in 1996. Three years in, that energy is still impressive, almost palpable when you walk in the door of the school.

Without denying that energy, Chelmsford raises larger questions about the purpose of charter schools. Certainly, the enthusiasm here shows how deep dissatisfaction with existing public schools runs—not merely in abandoned urban centers but in suburbs like this, too, where good schools are part of the real estate package, where urban parents are supposed to dream about sending their kids. But is dissatisfaction enough of a reason to start an entirely new school? Given how many parents can find complaints with their schools, and given that public money is limited, how do you decide when there is "enough" dissatisfaction to merit a new school? To what degree does the state have to respond to, even indulge, parents who insist that something is not right with their schools—especially when objective measures suggest things are pretty good?

Everyone agrees that charter schools strive to do more than sell air—they have to show results. But what is a good enough result? Is it enough for these schools to be popular with parents, or do they also have to improve on what exists? Furthermore, charter schools like Chelmsford are supposed to contribute something to the larger debate about how to make our schools better. But even their heartiest supporters admit that may be a false hope.

Early Obstacles

Perhaps not surprisingly, the parents who founded this school weren't so concerned with the larger picture in the months after they won their charter. They had nitty-gritty problems to worry about, like how to turn air into an actual school in less than six months. The biggest obstacle—hardly unusual for a new charter—was finding a suitable building for the new school. Traditional public schools have public buildings, no matter how antiquated they may be. But new charter schools soon discover that there aren't many available spaces readily adaptable to classroom life, especially spaces that also meet regulations on access for people with disabilities (some of the few regulations from which the charter schools don't get an exemption.)

Consequently, new charters have settled in some pretty unusual places. One school south of Boston opened in a motel, moved to a restaurant, then landed in an abandoned aquarium. Some have used empty Catholic schools (being careful to remove crosses). And on a decommissioned army base west of here, noted reform guru Theodore Sizer has become headmaster of a school housed in a windowless building once used to train spies.

The Chelmsford parents searched for months, and even considered delaying opening a year, because it seemed that every building was too small or needed too many improvements. Finding one a building inspector would declare fit for 154 middle school students was proving far more difficult than they had imagined. Cost was a big consideration, too: the charter school got only $5,389 per student—the per-pupil spending for students in Chelmsford. And that money had to be used for many things besides a new building.

Two months before school was to open, the parents leased two ground-floor wings of a two-story building in an office park. They knocked down walls to make classrooms out of lawyers' offices and put up walls for a small principal's office off the foyer. The shingles on the main office building remain the original gray-blue, but the parents painted the wing of the charter school a brick red.

Improvisation is everything. Even three years later, the limitations on staff and space require it. In the foyer, receptionist Barbara Giordani opens a metal cash box from which she dispenses an asthma inhaler to a student. She is the school's only support staff, serving as both nurse and receptionist. The principal, Sue Jamback, also does double duty. Dodging students, she returns to the principal's office after her weekly stint as an art teacher, wiping her paint-washed hands on her denim jumper. For the first year there was no lunchroom, making the noon hour an odd display of students strewn about the hallways munching out of brown paper bags. There is still no gymnasium, much less any athletic field or playground equipment, so exercise takes the form of a football game on the concrete parking lot. Signs outside order visitors not to park there during school hours, and violators risk having their minivan used as a goalpost. Inside the school, after lunch, a hair-swishing group of eighth-grade girls squeezes into the common room to make up dances to Spice Girls music blaring from a boombox.

A New Educational Approach

The kids look and act like typical middle school students, average suburban kids, and they are. The students here look much like their counterparts in the town's other public middle school in terms of race and income. The student body is mostly white, and fewer than 10 percent are eligible for free or reduced-price lunch, the federal measure of low income. Both schools have the same percentage of students in special education. A survey done by the charter school found 83 percent of students coming from homes with two parents; 87 percent come to the charter from a public rather than a parochial or private school. Asked to name their interests, the largest number—30 percent—said "sports"; 13 percent said "computers." Only one child cited "learning" as an interest. The most frequent response to the question, "Why did you want to attend?" was simply, "It sounds like fun."

Their parents are striking in one respect: 89 percent of them told the school they are eager to be involved in their children's education. Their most frequently cited goals for the new school were that it teach organizational skills and develop self-confidence in their children. The primary reasons they cited for sending their children to the charter school were the small class size and the idea of a hands-on education. Relatively few cited the school's philosophy as the central reason.

Nevertheless, the founders insist that it is the philosophy of their school that sets it apart from the town's public middle school. At Chelmsford, it is "systems thinking," an idea advanced at the Massachusetts Institute of Technology. More often applied to the workplace than to a school, systems thinking is based on the belief that existing notions need to be challenged—like the one that says a school has to look like a school, with its traditional grade levels, subjects, and departments.

Systems thinking teaches students and teachers to see everything and everyone as interdependent, part of an integrated system. It encourages students to look at a problem, evaluate the larger causes and implications, and then create a model for understanding how the problem develops and ripples out to cause other problems. Students are then encouraged to think of how the same model applies to other situations and problems. They don't simply memorize facts for a test; they are encouraged to see broad patterns.

The founding parents chose this framework because they believed it would give their children a more effective way to interpret the changing world around them. To quote from the 1994 book that adapted systems thinking from the workplace to schools, "By focusing on a common teachable core of broadly applicable concepts, we can now visualize an integrated, systemic, educational process that is more efficient, more appropriate to a world of increasing complexity and more supportive of unity in life . . . Systems thinking cannot be acquired as a spectator sport . . . Hands-on involvement is essential to internalizing the ideas and establishing them in one's own mental models."[1]

In their work with the Chelmsford Alliance for Education, searching out reform strategies and consulting experts, the parents had become somewhat expert themselves—or at least they could speak the experts' language. Discussions of how students learn at Chelmsford quickly become an amalgam of education bywords: student-centered classrooms, hands-on learning, project-based education. The mission statement incorporated into the school's charter is the height of jargon: "To provide students with a challenging interdisciplinary education that will prepare them for the twenty-first century through an emphasis on holistic learning, higher order and critical thinking skills and practical application and integration of curriculum areas."

But if such a mission statement sounds trite, perhaps a caricature of progressive ideals, it emerged from the parents' very real concerns over how the traditional public schools were teaching their children. They were dismayed by the "drill and kill," the "chalk and talk." In their disdain for the rote

teaching of the traditional public schools, everything was up for revision—
what teachers taught, even how the traditional school day was structured.
One of the first casualties was the century-old division of the school day into
forty-five-minute periods. At Chelmsford, teachers decide how much time
they want to spend on a topic; in some cases, the students make that decision.

Students do not learn from textbooks but from projects that demand a
combination of skills. One project, for example, focused on how to rid a
nearby quarry of graffiti. The project became part geology class, part research and writing, and part community relations as the students eventually
took their proposals to Town Hall.

At Chelmsford, students learn algebra, but they learn it through problem
solving or projects like building a pendulum for a grandfather clock. They
learn Spanish, but they learn it from a Venezuelan man who has lived in
this country for less than five years. They learn grammar and spelling, but
through daily writers' workshops in which students might work on a short
story, a weekly letter to parents, a memoir, or a manual for a science project.

Many of the graduation requirements, drawn up together by teachers
and the parent board, are geared toward ensuring that students become re-
flective, productive citizens. Eighth graders must be able to demonstrate that
they can work with public documents and analyze arguments and statistics
used in newspapers. They must also be able to write a letter to an editor in
response to an article on a national issue.

The students are divided not into different grades but into seven teams of
twenty-two students and two teachers each. Each team comprises students
of different ages across the spectrum of grades five through eight. In class,
the students don't sit in rows. Their desks, which were salvaged from a
school undergoing renovation in a neighboring town and refurbished with
bright finger paints, are arranged in haphazard clusters.

Rather than being given letter grades in isolated subjects, students are
evaluated on long checklists that consider everything from how well they
project their voice and maintain audience interest during an oral presentation to how well they have researched and argued their position in a
research paper. They receive ratings from "master" to "novice," not from
A to F.

This is not to say that Chelmsford Charter eschews all traditional methods.
Principal Jamback notes that there are quizzes in math, and that the students take the same standardized tests that students in other public schools

statewide take. In fact, the school's goals declare that 75 percent of the students will score above the 75th percentile on the Metropolitan Achievement Test, a common measure used by schools across the country.

But the teachers and parents place more emphasis on the student project portfolios, which may include the books students have written or the grandfather clock they have built. Each spring, a panel of local writers and scientists evaluates students' presentations—a sort of junior version of defending a dissertation.

Jamback, a tall, thin woman whose soft voice belies a firm manner, has spent twenty-five years as a principal and a teacher in public schools in New Hampshire and Connecticut. She has seen education trends come and go and come again. But what goes on in Chelmsford Charter, she insists, is no gimmick. "Other schools go a mile wide and an inch deep," she says. "We go an inch wide and a mile deep."

Democratic Participation, New England Style

Sergeant Pepper had escaped. Now twenty-two fifth and sixth graders, sitting in a loose circle on the linoleum floor of the charter school's common room, are earnestly discussing how to deal with the consequences.

Pepper is the pet rabbit in Peg Ecclesine's classroom. The police had responded to a burglar alarm at the school twice the previous Wednesday night; on their second visit, just after midnight, they discovered that the black and beady-eyed creature had escaped from his cage and set off the motion detector.

A teacher who lives nearby, and then one of the school's parent founders, responded to police calls. The incident resulted in a forty-dollar fine and annoyance all around. Now, in the morning meeting that begins every day at the Chelmsford Public Charter School, Ecclesine's students are trying to find a way to pay the fine—and to keep the rabbit from outwitting the latch on his cage. The only person allowed to speak is the student holding the Koosh, a soft, palm-size ball made of fuschia rubber tendrils. One student serves as the facilitator: he or she makes sure everyone participates, resolves disputes over who called for the Koosh, and keeps the meeting moving.

"When I had Pepper at my house over vacation, I put my lock on his latch at night, and I wanted to know if you think that's a good idea," one girl says.

"I realize this happened Wednesday night, and I was the last one to be there," a boy says. "I just want to say that when I left, the cage was latched. So we may have a very clever rabbit."

"I have a cat taxi we could use," another boy says. "It has a really strong latch."

Rebecca Coakley, a sixth grader, shoots up her hand to demand the Koosh. "Look," she says, her voice as firm as her catch. "The facilitator told us we should figure out how to pay the fine, so we should be talking about that."

They rule out asking their parents for the money, then decide they should give the rabbit to one student to take home until they earn back, in literal dollars and cents, the right to have him in the class. But how to raise money? They decide to poll students at the all-school meeting later in the day to see how many would buy neon and silver shoelaces from them. And there's always the old school standby: a bake sale.

"Rebecca, what do you think?" one boy finally asks.

"Well," Rebecca mumbles. She looks uneasily at her neighbor; she doesn't have the Koosh. "Should I just answer?" she whispers.

Meetings like this are perhaps what most distinguish the Chelmsford Charter School from traditional public schools. Whole-school meetings start and finish the week, while individual classroom meetings start each day. Although the word *meeting* might imply "tedious," Chelmsford's are enlivening and sometimes even feisty. And they convey the sense that there is serious work going on here, that these are people—right down to the fifth graders—who care deeply about the quality of education. Unlike many charter schools, Chelmsford has fused human-scale participation with its pedagogical practices.

Considering the fact that the school was largely founded on the premise that parents should have a powerful voice in determining school policy, the spirit of inclusiveness is not surprising. When the school board chose a sex education program, for instance, it first held meetings to discuss the kinds of programs parents wanted, with follow-up discussions at its regular monthly meeting (open to the public, with notice of date and time posted at Town Hall). The school nurse investigated programs, then reported back to the board, which sent out a memo to parents outlining them. Finally, as the parents considered choosing a particular program, they held another meeting to discuss the course outline and meet the program instructors. After deciding that hot topics like AIDS would be taught after school, a program was adopted. A committee of parents still meets, however, to review how the program is working.

Even on some holidays, the teachers—all certified, most younger than 30—are in school at 8:30 A.M. for a meeting on what students should be required to include in their portfolio and how the portfolios will be judged. When the meeting is over, they linger in their classrooms, making improvements and plans. Certainly they are not doing this for the money. The starting salary is $18,000, compared with a state average of $26,000, and all the most veteran teachers earn is $42,000. What draws the teachers to the school is an ethos of both personal and professional involvement.

The school encourages the taxpaying public to be involved, too. Each student is trained to give a guided tour of the school on demand. In a newsletter that went out to the community, Jamback invited citizens to drop in at any time: "We believe that good schools are accountable ones, and should be viewed at any time by interested parties."

Learning through Trust

At Chelmsford Charter, students are accorded rare trust and privileges. On the most superficial level, this means that students can wear hats and chew gum in class, a point the students make in tours to the public. But to Jamback and the teachers, the trust and privileges are about boosting students' investment in their school.

To solve the problem of having no gymnasium, for instance, the students formed a committee to come up with ideas for activities that wouldn't require indoor space or playing fields. And when a football tournament was scheduled for one of the winter's coldest days, Jamback refrained from canceling it. Instead, she sent the student tournament organizer out to the parking lot for ten minutes to see if he thought spectators could stand the cold. He returned in two and told his peers the tournament was off.

"We've always had rules to restrict kids, the argument being we can't just let them loose," Jamback says. "I believe kids are highly competent individuals, and if we train them to handle meetings, handle decisions, they can do anything." Tones of local democracy, New England style.

Of course, the Chelmsford students are still children, and there are still problems. With the bloom of spring weather and budding adolescent crushes, algebra class deteriorates into note passing and elbow jabs. Toss the Koosh out of the circle during a meeting, and the gathering can dissolve into giggles. Eight students were given in-school suspension the second year of school for physical aggression or defiance. Two were suspended for carrying small knives.

But in dealing with even the most serious problems, the emphasis isn't on discipline—it's on getting students to think about the school as a community for which they are responsible. Students sign an agreement on acceptable conduct. Those who don't pay attention at a weekly school meeting, for instance, are chosen to lead the following week's meeting, to show them how difficult it is to control a crowd of 160 people. And students say the fact that they have worked together to make so many decisions means fewer typical middle school problems.

"There's not anyone who's left out. There isn't a cool group or a nerdy group," says Jacqui Bryant, a bright-eyed fifth grader. "We're all just, like, friends."

Among 100 outside visitors to the school in its second year were 9 school superintendents from Pennsylvania. Immediately after the eight-hour bus ride home, one sat down and wrote Jamback: "Your philosophy permeates every fiber of the program. Everyone is empowered and a necessary player in your educational community. I was most impressed with your students, their independence and ability to articulate the mission of your school and the various goals."

Lingering Doubts

But not everyone is so impressed with Chelmsford Charter School. Twenty students left at the end of the first year, and another twenty left at the end of the second. A few had moved away, but most had chosen to attend a private school or special-education day school instead. A few simply missed their friends. Some parents thought the meetings were symptomatic of the school's giving too much attention to what students wanted and not enough attention to what they needed. David and Beverly Klick pulled their son from the school after three months, decrying it as the "chatter school."

"We view it as a laboratory where educational theorists test trendy catch phrases with our children as guinea pigs," they wrote in a letter. "'Group dynamics for student-directed problem solving'? Picture endless, rambling bull sessions so stupefying that our son made sure he carried an extra sweatshirt for a pillow. 'Yak 'n' snack' so crowded out education that, in three months, his class read only one book, performed only one science experiment, and appeared to regress in math. For a variety of reasons (low standards, lax discipline, general time wasting), our son learned very little."

Test scores would seem to bear out the Klicks' concerns. Fewer then 20 percent of students scored above the seventy-fifth percentile on the Metropolitan Achievement Test—the school's own standard of success.

Jamback seems unconcerned about the departures. To her, a charter school must have a defined mission. It is unrealistic, she says, to expect that mission to suit every student. Where public schools have failed, she says, is in trying to be everything to everyone; it is better to do some things well than everything half-well. This illustrates a tough problem facing other charter schools: by design, they are not inclusive organizations.

The school regularly polls parents regarding their attitudes toward the school. There is at least some degree of candor about what the school can and can't do well. After the first year, for instance, Jamback and the board realized that they were not the ones to manage the budget and chose to hire Beacon Management, a private firm based in Pennsylvania, to handle payroll and other financial tasks.

Most parents who remain with Chelmsford Charter do rate the school a success in terms of how it meets its established goals. On a scale of 1 to 4, they rated communication between parents and teachers an average of 3.6. For its ability to promote rigor and initiative in students, the parents gave the school an average of 3.2. In most polls, of course, parents tend to say they are satisfied with their public schools, even if they think "public education" is in trouble. Still, given the Chelmsford parents' admitted discontent with the traditional public schools, the satisfaction on the surveys says something.

Is Popularity a True Measure of Success?

As Massachusetts has signed on enthusiastically for more and more charter schools, the schools' boosters have repeated, mantralike, that these are the "most accountable public schools." The equation is simple, they argue: if the schools don't succeed, they lose their charter; they go out of business. And while most founders wouldn't wish it on their own school, some, like Jamback, say they hope some charters do fail and lose their license. Then, they say, charter school advocates could turn around and demand to shut down the public schools that have failed for years.

For that rather bold avowal, the moment of truth has now arrived. By 2001, the Massachusetts State Department of Education must decide whether to renew the charters for Chelmsford and the twenty-four other inaugural charter schools. This means deciding what accountability looks like, as well as what defines success. Whatever standard is used for the first set of schools will become the criteria used to judge those that follow.

The state board of education has said the education department decides

whether to renew charters based on three questions: Is the academic program a success? Is the school a viable organization? Has the school been
faithful to the terms of its charter?

The most important measure of academic success is supposed to be the
state test given each spring to students in the fourth, eighth, and tenth
grades at all public schools, including the charters. The tests, known as the
Massachusetts Comprehensive Assessment System, or MCAS, tests, were
aligned with new statewide guidelines for what students need to know, and
they emphasize essay writing and critical thinking as well as more basic facts
and equations. By 2003, students who don't pass these high-stakes tests in
grade ten will not be able to graduate from high school. Schools where a significant portion of students fall below "proficiency" levels will be declared
underperforming and threatened with state takeover.

Even the statewide tests, though, have been fraught with controversy.
Parents and teachers have complained they are too long—they take almost
seventeen hours total over a week—and don't have anything to do with
what is being taught in the schools. Even state officials say they are still iron-
ing out the kinks, and that it will take a few years for the new curriculum
guidelines to be fully integrated into classrooms.

Given all of their flaws, it becomes easier to argue that the tests should not
be the only measure of success for a charter school—and charter school supporters insist that no standardized test is a complete enough measure of the
quality of an education. Critics worry, then, that popularity will come to define success. With a loud political constituency cheering on charters, they
say, state officials will balk at actually shutting down any schools. And indeed, in the absence of a wider range of test scores, charter school proponents tend to cite high demand as evidence of the schools' success.

The state commissioner of education began the process of renewing the
charters by saying he didn't see any reason—absent strenuous objections
from parents—why they should not all be renewed. The state announced in
April 1999 that the first ten schools would be evaluated for renewal of their
charters. By July, a mere three months later, the evaluations were complete
and all ten were renewed. Only one school was given any kind of condi-
tional approval, and that was only after a state audit found that the school's
chairman of trustees had billed the state for children who did not actually attend the school. Even that was not enough to decertify the school; the state
was satisfied so long as he stepped down from the board. "We've seen
enough. They're working," said Commissioner David Driscoll. "They have

waiting lists and strong curriculums, longer days, greater parental involvement. I think they've shown themselves to be very effective."

Much depends on politics, as well as popularity. No one was terribly surprised that the charters were so easily renewed, given that the head of the state board of education was also the head of the Pioneer Institute, a libertarian advocacy group that is the state's most strident advocate for more charter schools in Massachusetts.

There is no question that the schools are popular. A Pioneer Institute study found that 94 percent of the students attending charter schools in Massachusetts in the spring of 1999 planned to return in the fall. Eighty-five percent of parents rated the overall experience of charter schools as "good" or "excellent," according to the study. Other more objective measures speak to their popularity, too. The Department of Education counts five thousand children on waiting lists for charter schools in Massachusetts. And this year, again, there were twice as many applicants for the Chelmsford Public Charter School as there were seats available. High demand was enough to convince the legislature to lift the cap the original Education Reform Act had imposed on the number of charters, doubling them statewide, and the entire state board of education has endorsed tripling that number, to 150.

It may be that these figures represent dissatisfaction with traditional public schools more than satisfaction with the charters—parents are voting with their feet against the traditional schools. This is even more reason, critics say, that popularity should not be seen as some indication of how well the charter schools are doing. And until it is matched by evidence of academic gain, they add, popularity is no argument for more charter schools.

Will Chelmsford Charter Change the Local Public Schools?

There are some signs, certainly, that Chelmsford students are doing well academically. In the first "graduating" class of eighteen students, fifteen went on to the local high school and between ten and thirteen were on the high school honor roll each academic quarter. Although the school has not yet met its own goal of 75 percent of students reading at the seventy-fifth percentile or higher on the Metropolitan Achievement Test, the number of students in that percentile doubled, to 17 percent, in the school's second year. The statewide test results, released in the fall of 1998, were something of a mixed bag: the Chelmsford students performed no worse than their eighth grade counterparts in the traditional Chelmsford middle schools. But they didn't perform any better, either.

Yet even if charter schools do end up providing a first-rate education, supporters and critics alike agree that the charter movement won't meet its goal unless it has a broader effect on traditional public schools. After all, the charter schools account for only about six thousand public school students in Massachusetts, and no matter how well those individual schools perform, there are still nearly a million other students.

The founders of the Chelmsford charter school smiled among themselves this year when what is now the "other" public middle school in town—the one most students attended before there was a charter school—for the first time held its own open house for parents of prospective students. To the founders, the town middle school's becoming more parent-friendly is evidence that the charter school is working in at least one sense: worried about losing students and state money to the charter school, the traditional public school is fighting to keep students. The middle school also split into two smaller schools—one of the original goals set out in the action plan created by the parents who later left the middle school to start the charter.

Supporters cite anecdotes like this to argue that charter schools have caused market competition—and, ultimately, will lead to improvement in the wider educational product. The most often cited example of such competition is the Boston pilot schools. Created as a result of negotiations with the city's teachers' union in the first year of the charter schools, the pilot schools have been freed from many union rules, allowing them to hire and fire whomever they want. But there isn't much other hard evidence of this kind of competitive change, and even if there were, the effect would be limited to the forty or so communities where charter schools are located.

When charter schools were included in the Education Reform Act, they were envisioned as laboratories for innovation—places where new kinds of teaching would be tested and modeled before export to the public school classrooms. So far, though, there has been only limited exchange between the charter schools and the traditional public schools. Some of this has to do with initial jealousy on the part of traditional public school administrators, who worried charters were stealing away money and students, and that hostility may well ease over time. In its second year, the Chelmsford Charter School's board finally got to meet with the town school committee. They could agree only that teachers from the two schools could communicate— though none actually have. Still, said Linn Murdoch, the board's chairwoman, this "was a start."

But even the charter schools admit that, in most cases, they are employing teaching methods already used to some degree in traditional public schools.

While innovation runs deeper at Chelmsford Charter, skeptics say there are elements of it in many traditional public schools, as well, where teachers teach math through projects, and weave together English and social studies. In fact, on the charter school's visitors' night, one prospective parent listened to a student describe a science project, then whispered to her daughter, "You did that *last* year!"

Administrators in public schools complain that they can't be expected to compete when they don't have the same advantages the charter schools have: parents and children who are motivated enough to seek out a particular kind of school, and a staff that subscribes to—and is enthusiastic about—a central educational philosophy. What works in a school of 154 students is hard to scale up to a school of 600, the size of the middle school in Chelmsford. Looking back on her years in public schools, even Jamback agrees that it is wrong to think of charter schools like hers in Chelmsford as laboratory schools, for few teachers from other schools will reshape their own methods based on what they learn from a few visits there.

"There are exemplary, marvelous things happening in public schools," Jamback says. "If they need models of good teaching, the public schools don't need to come here; they can find those in their own buildings. But if we look at the evidence, that's not how we've had change. The changes never get beyond a core group of teachers."

So what, then, is the purpose of charter schools, if the academic achievement is only about as good as that of traditional public schools, and if charters are not really serving as models? Is it to meet the demands of any parents who don't get what they want from the school administration? Is it enough to open a school simply because the children say "it sounds like fun"? Certainly, the parents' dissatisfaction is very real to them—it would be hard for anyone, much less a state legislator concerned about votes, to deny parents' fears that a child is falling behind. Still, at what point does dissatisfaction become a compelling state interest? If charter school proponents themselves are admitting that their schools aren't labs, then maybe their schools look much like what critics dismiss them as: "boutique education."

The parents in Chelmsford argue, fairly, that it is not right to punish them and their children simply because the quality of education in the town's traditional schools is not at the same "crisis" level as in the cities. Rather than limit the number of charters, they argue, why not extend the privileges that charters get to all schools, to "make every school a charter" by loosening rules on hiring and transfers, allowing principals to shape their own staff of teachers. The truth, though, is that in a state with a strong teachers' union, those proposals are unlikely to get very far.

Still, there is the energy. The sheer exuberance within the walls of the charter schools must be worth something to the larger system. There must be something to learn from the parents who call weekly to see if their child is off the charter school waiting list, the teachers who fight by the hundreds for a single job opening in a charter school, the large numbers of both parents and teachers willing to risk so much on something unproved and largely undefined.

To Jamback, the energy is the lesson, a lesson about the importance of defining a mission, of working hard to get everyone on board behind change. "For there to be real change, the whole school has to change," she says. "The entire school has to have a shared vision, the entire school has to come together and say, 'What is our vision?' That's what the public schools can learn from what we've done here. That's what's unique to charter schools."

CHAPTER 5

Diversity and Inequality:
Montera Charter High School

AMY STUART WELLS
JENNIFER JELLISON HOLME
ASH VASUDEVA

In the midst of an evening meeting of Montera Charter School's governance council, principal Peter McCann explained to the teachers, parents, and staff members who made up the council why Montera had to abide by a settlement agreement between the school district and a civil rights organization. The agreement regulated teacher hiring across the district in an effort to place more experienced teachers in impoverished schools. Montera, located in a wealthy and mostly white community on the edge of this large and mostly nonwhite school district, was in compliance with the agreement. Still, there was the issue of whether or not Montera, as a charter school, *needed* to comply.

Some parents from the local community had argued that Montera should not worry about this or any other district agreement, since a charter school is technically autonomous from its district. McCann, on the other hand, argued that the school should comply. As a long-time employee of the district who had worked in schools in poor communities before coming to Montera, McCann still saw his school as part of the larger school district. In fact, even after it was converted into a charter school, Montera continued to receive most of its services from the downtown district office, including payroll, legal counsel, and transportation for the hundreds of students who lived in other communities and traveled daily to the school. Furthermore, McCann had been advised by the district's lawyers that Montera had to comply with the settlement agreement.

The issue at hand was whether or not Montera was still part of a larger public entity or an entity unto itself. At the heart of Montera's struggle to define what it means to be a charter school was the tension between those who viewed the school as a public institution still responsive to the district as a whole and those who wanted to see the school become more responsive to the particular demands of its immediate community. This tension between broader public purposes and more localized private demands permeates the story of Montera Charter High School and illustrates both the promises and threats in what charter school reform could mean to the future of public education. On the one hand, Montera's story is the story of a dying public high school that was revitalized via charter school reform. On the other hand, it is a tale of how charter status aided the school's effort to become more like a private school.

In this chapter we describe the multifaceted relationship between charter school reform and Montera, a former comprehensive high school that was on the verge of being shut down by the district because of dwindling enrollment before it went charter. After converting into a charter school, Montera lured students from prestigious private schools back into the public system while maintaining a diverse student body along racial and social-class lines. At the same time, the staff implemented challenging curricular reforms, secured additional support for its programs, and involved more parents in governance and decision making. On these counts, Montera was a very successful public charter school and a model for this very popular reform movement.

Looking at Montera through another lens, however, we see a high school that was in many ways losing its public school character by selectively recruiting particular students and finding ways to get rid of those students who did not fit the new Montera image of a diverse school for highly motivated students. At the same time, Montera had become more heavily dependent on private as opposed to public resources and thus increasingly responsive to the demands and interests of wealthy people, including a relatively small number of powerful parents. Through this lens, we see in Montera many of the concerns raised by opponents of charter school reform—namely that it will allow people to create quasi-private schools with public funds.

That both of these phenomena occurred within one school is a tribute to the complexity of charter school reform as it interacts with a socially, politically, and economically stratified society. The story of Montera Charter High School helps to explain why simple questions about whether or not charter schools are "working," how they are affecting the public educational system, and which students are best served via charter school reform cannot be easily answered. Montera simultaneously represents the revitalization and the privatization of public education. It is both a nurturing place for a select group of students of color from across the city (the "transfer" students) and a school where the most powerful and wealthy white parents from the local community generally get their way. In this way, Montera embodies both the ideal of the diverse common school and the effort on the part of some parents to create special, uncommon schools.

Meanwhile, much of what this charter school has accomplished is attributed to a strong principal, a leader who walked a tightrope between the different, often competing forces at the school while trying to keep Montera connected to the larger public system. In fact, Montera faced huge obstacles in trying to be both a public high school serving a racially diverse student body and a quasi-private school that could lure more of the wealthy neighborhood students back from their elite private schools.

No one—not even the principal—was certain how much of the change the school had gone through was related to its charter status. When questioned about whether or not they could be doing what they were doing at Montera if it weren't a charter school, most of the educators and parents we spoke to said they were not sure. While their ability to shape the student enrollment was more certainly tied to their greater autonomy as a charter school, many of the educational reforms they had instituted can also be found at other schools across the state. They did note, however, that the charter had given them the belief that they could make these changes and that sometimes that was all they needed. It is also true that the enrollment changes gave the school a new, more positive and prestigious image, which in turn energized the faculty and parents to take chances and try new programs and approaches.

While we realize that each charter school is unique in many respects, we find the story of Montera Charter High School illustrative of larger issues related to charter school reform and public education in general. To highlight the broader implications of Montera's story, we have organized this chapter into the following sections: a brief discussion of our methodology and an overview of the school, a description of the way in which Montera educators have been able to create the student body they want, a description of the curricular reforms taking place at Montera and a discussion of who benefits from them, and finally, a section on parent and community voice at Montera. We conclude with a discussion of some of the policy implications of this case study.

The Context of Montera Charter High

Montera Charter High School was one of seventeen charter schools we studied as we conducted case studies of ten school districts in California.[1] This study allowed us to examine charter schools not as isolated institutions but rather as schools that exist within and interact with a broader social context, including their school district and the state law governing charter schools.

We spent four weeks in the spring of 1998 collecting data at Montera Charter High School. During that time we interviewed thirty-five people at the school site, including five administrators (some more than once), twenty teachers, and eight parents. We observed classrooms, meetings, and after-school tutoring sessions. We also collected numerous documents describing Montera and its policies. These more recent data were added to data collected at the school three years earlier, when it first became a charter school. Our school-level data collection was in addition to more than twenty interviews with district administrators and other educators in this urban district. Through these sources, we came to know Montera as a school that embodied many of the critical themes of charter school reform.

During the days we spent at Montera, we became very familiar with the sprawling campus, which includes a large athletic stadium, two-story classroom buildings, a plush lawn, and an impressive library and auditorium. In fact, Montera looks as much like a small college as a large public high school. Its spacious, suburban-style campus belies Montera's membership in one of the largest and poorest school districts in the nation. Built in the early 1960s to serve the exclusive Montera section of this southern California city and nearby neighborhoods, Montera is surrounded by mostly large and hugely expensive houses—some costing over a million dollars. Except for those who occupy the handful of apartment buildings in the area, only people on the highest rung of the income bracket can afford to live there. The streets and the local car wash are crowded with Mercedeses, Range Rovers, and Jaguars. The vast majority of the families here can afford the tuition of the expensive private schools nearby, and since the 1980s, most of them have made that choice.

According to many of the people we interviewed, historically Montera High School had a reputation in the district as a high-quality school. As one staff member noted, people wanted to send their children to Montera "because it was almost certain that if your kids worked they could get off to college—and prestigious and good ones at that."

But in the 1980s, as the district's student integration program was implemented and more African American and Latino students transferred to Montera, white families began to flee the public system in general and Montera specifically. By 1992, Montera enrolled only 1,600 students in a facility built for more than 2,000 students. At that time, the student body was a mixture of white students from the surrounding wealthy community and African American students from outside the community who came to the school one of two ways: they chose to enroll via a voluntary-transfer desegregation program, or they were reassigned to Montera by the school district owing to overcrowding in their neighborhood high school. By this time, the number of white families from the Montera neighborhood who chose to send their children to the local high school had shrunk significantly. As local housing prices skyrocketed, the percentage of families with school-age children shrank, and more and more of those families began opting for private schools. Thus by 1992, only 30 percent, or about 500, of the students enrolled in Montera lived in the local community.

While the number and percentage of local students dwindled, the number of transfer students who could come to the school from other neighborhoods was limited by the district's desegregation guidelines. This policy of limiting the number of transfer students had two results: it sent enrollment into a spiraling decline, and it prevented Montera from becoming a completely nonwhite school in the midst of the whitest community in the city. It also meant that the district was considering simply closing down Montera because of its low enrollment.

Becoming a Charter School: Montera Is Saved

Peter McCann was hired as Montera's new principal in the fall of 1992, the same year that California passed its charter school legislation. He came to Montera from an inner-city school, and when he arrived on the plush campus he reported being struck by the lack of vitality and the adversarial relationships between administrators and teachers. His first task, as he saw it, was to change the climate of the school. Pointing to the declining enrollment numbers, McCann told his faculty that if they didn't do something, in a year or two the district would just fold up the school and send the neighborhood students to a high school a few miles away. He asked his staff to consider why the district needed a high school on such an expensive piece of real estate.

At the same time, a group of very involved parents from Montera High

School and its feeder schools began to explore charter school reform as a way to gain greater local control over their schools. McCann was soon involved in the local movement to charter all the public schools in the community, and a group of parents and educators wrote the charter and submitted it to the school board downtown. The proposal initially faced opposition from advocacy groups concerned that the Montera community wanted to use its charter status to turn the school into an all-white, wealthy enclave. The Montera parents and educators managed to convince the school board that while they did hope to bring back many of the local white students from private schools, they also wanted to maintain racial diversity in their schools, and their proposal was approved.

According to a Montera counselor who helped work on the charter application:

> It was a way that we thought that we could improve the schools here and bring back in a lot of the local community kids who had gone off to private schools. That was something that we were looking at doing, not that we did not want the [transfer] students who were coming here to come. We just wanted to bring more of the community kids back, in part so that we would have a large enough campus that we could really give the kids a lot of diversity in terms of subjects and programs that we have to offer them. Because when your campus is very small it just limits your offerings to the kids.

Thus, the original impetus for the charter was mainly to save the high school and other schools in the community from closure by using charter status to lure back more local families. Yet the charter application was also about the return of local control. A parent from the Montera community who was involved in the charter application process noted some of the reasons for the support and enthusiasm among educators and parents for going charter: "We needed to have control over who came to the school, and the ability to set our own curriculum. And being able to choose which teachers would [teach]. Teachers had to be willing to buy into our program."

By the 1997–98 school year, total enrollment at Montera Charter High School had grown to 2,500, and 35 percent, or 875 students, were from the nearby community. Thus, the number of local students attending the school had nearly doubled in five years. The other 65 percent of the student body came from all over the city. In fact, when we collected data at Montera we found that the students lived in 107 different zip codes and came from homes in which forty-nine different languages were spoken. The student population was 30 percent African American, 25 percent Latino, about 35 percent white, and about 10 percent Asian. There was a waiting list of 800 students trying to get into the school.

To accommodate the growth in enrollment and a wave of teacher retirements, seventy new teachers were hired between 1992 and 1997. Thus, only twenty-eight out of ninety-eight teachers in 1997–98 had been at the school since before it became a charter school. Many of the newly hired teachers were young or at least new to teaching—they came right out of teacher education programs and were generally excited about implementing reforms.

One teacher who had been at the school since long before it became a charter school commented on the changing face of the teaching force: "I think it is a better school than it ever has been before . . . a significant number of our teachers have been here for less than five years. They are young and energetic new teachers that really want to teach, whereas before, this used to be seen as a retirement school. I mean, you put in for a transfer to this school, and if you were lucky, you got here and then you just waited out your retirement here."

In addition to the enrollment and staffing changes, the governance and decision-making processes also changed after Montera became a charter school. Although Montera had always enjoyed a high level of parent involvement, after it became a charter school, the local, affluent parents were even more intimately involved in important decisions. For instance, the school's governance council, which included several parent representatives, oversaw the work of subcommittees on everything from curriculum to budgets. Some of this effort to decentralize governance and decision making at Montera would have occurred anyway—even without charter school status—because of a districtwide reform designed to give individual schools more control over budgets and hiring. But for many of the people at Montera, the school's charter has enhanced their ability to decide their own future.

Yet for all the talk of autonomy and the freedom Montera enjoyed, this particular charter school remained closely tied to its host district when it came to resources and support. On the spectrum of autonomy that California charter schools have in their local school district, Montera sat on the more dependent, or less autonomous, end. As we mentioned above, the downtown district office continued to handle all of Montera's payroll and legal support, as well as benefits, insurance, and retirement plans. The employees of Montera were still employees of the school district and members of their respective unions. And—perhaps the largest perk of all for a high school that was on the verge of being closed down due to lack of enrollment—the district provided free transportation, through its desegregation budget, for more than four hundred of the students who came to Montera from other communities. The district provided this transportation in part because Montera housed one of its coveted magnet school programs and in part because sending transfer students to Montera helped to keep the highly segregated school district more racially balanced.

In the following sections of this chapter, we discuss what we see as the three major school-level changes at Montera since it became a charter school. Each of these changes—in student enrollment, curriculum, and parent voice and involvement—reflect larger salient themes, mainly the tension between revitalization and privatization and the struggle within the school to meet the educational needs of the transfer students while also meeting the intense and sometimes conflicting demands of local parents and students. In other words, these changes as they occurred at the school reflected the pressures on Montera to serve both a larger public purpose and a narrower set of private interests. How much of this change was directly attributable to charter status is not always clear. But what is clear is that Montera helps to illustrate what happens when charter school reform interacts with the highly unequal social, economic, and political conditions within which schools like Montera must operate and thrive.

Engineering Diversity

More often than not, the most salient issue for Montera educators and some of the parents we interviewed about the benefits of becoming a charter school was how it had changed the student body. As one English teacher noted, "The biggest single way that the school has changed has been that we have gone from about 1,200 students to 2,500. The size of the school has doubled and this is because we can recruit students from all over [the city]."

But the critical distinction was not so much the number of students as the type of students who were enrolling in Montera. The school had successfully attracted more nearby community students as well as a "different" type of transfer student—students whom it actively recruited and who chose to come, as opposed to those who were sent to the school to relieve overcrowding in other parts of the district.

Nearly everyone we spoke to referred to the "diversity" of the students on the campus in terms of race and occasionally in terms of social class. Indeed, Montera was one of the most, if not *the* most, racially and economically diverse schools in the district. Yet at the same time, people we interviewed talked about the relative uniformity of the students in regard to their motivation to succeed in school. To assure this greater homogeneity in terms of student motivation, the school implemented attendance and discipline policies that allowed it to suspend and eventually expel the students who did not fit in. In addition, despite the racial diversity of the school, Latino students, the city's largest ethnic group, were vastly underrepresented at Montera. Furthermore, the percentage of students at Montera who were eligible for free or reduced-price lunches—about 15 percent—was much smaller than the districtwide average of 75 percent. These data suggest that student diversity was not as great when examined in the context of the school district as a whole.

Still, the change in the student body was the most consistently cited benefit of "going charter" for Montera, and it has become one of the school's main selling points.

Targeted Recruitment: Geography and Motivation Matter

As we mentioned earlier, before Montera became a charter school it enrolled many African American and some Latino transfer students from overcrowded high schools across town. Through the school district's enrollment adjustment program, or EAP, every year thousands of students were sent from the crowded neighborhood schools in the poorest and most densely populated areas of the city to underenrolled schools in wealthier communities such as Montera. Usually, the students who were reassigned under this program were those who were the last to try to enroll in their neighborhood school; thus, they tended to be the most transient students, or perhaps those who were least enthusiastic about returning to school.

In 1992, as Montera was writing its charter proposal, the majority of its transfer students came to the school through the EAP. Because Montera was so dramatically underenrolled, with only 500 students from the local community attending a school built for more than 2,000 students, the administration had no choice but to accept every "involuntary transfer" student who arrived on its doorstep. But the Montera faculty, parents, and administrators complained that too many of these students did not want to be at the school (or at any school, for that matter), were not motivated to learn, created discipline problems, and negatively affected the school culture and climate. All of these issues, they noted, made it more and more difficult for the school to attract the local community students back to their neighborhood school.

One teacher who had been at the school for many years described the decline of the school in the late 1980s and early 1990s:

> The school was used as a place where students who showed up late to their
> . . . schools were sent involuntarily because of overcrowding, and a lot of
> these students were minority students and they were not minority students
> who were highly motivated . . . obviously a student who shows up two or
> three days [after] classes start at an overcrowded high school and is told
> there is no more room is not the most motivated student. And so they
> wound up out here, and these students caused a downward spiral. And
> then the local parents and students decided that they would not want [to
> go] to school with these other students.

But charter school status changed all that, because it allowed Montera educators and parents to begin actively recruiting students from anywhere in the district or state to come to their school. As one administrator noted in response to a question about why the school had converted to charter, "It was a way in which we could improve the population of students . . . which was really needed at the time." In their efforts to "improve" the student population, the educators and parents at Montera drew on existing relationships with other communities in the city and also worked to establish some new ones. In both cases, the transfer students who chose to come to Montera tended to be less poor and easier to educate than many students from the same racial/ethnic groups in the city. This enabled Montera to maintain its diversity while also attracting and enrolling some of the most motivated and highest achieving transfer students.

In drawing on existing relationships, Montera turned to the wealthier African American communities in the city. Even in the lowest enrollment years of the early 1990s, some of the transfer students were not part of EAP but were attending Montera through a voluntary desegregation program in which schools serving mostly African American and Latino students were paired with schools in predominantly white communities. This pairing program allowed some African American and Latino students to choose to transfer voluntarily from their neighborhood schools to those in the white, partner communities.

Administrators and teachers at Montera were proud of the fact that their school was one of the first schools to jump on board with this voluntary desegregation program when it started in the late 1970s. Instead of dragging its feet and resisting any integration of their white and wealthy schools, the Montera community had actively sought out minority communities to pair up with for transfer students. In taking this proactive stance, Montera High and its feeder middle and elementary schools were able to establish a relationship with some of the more middle- and upper-middle-class African American areas of the city. Thus, before Montera was forced to enroll so many students due to overcrowding, through EAP, the school had been receiving African American and Latino transfer students through the voluntary school desegregation program. Strategically, Montera High School and its feeder schools had established transfer relationships with higher-status minority communities; these relationships continued to serve the school well when it became a charter school, as students from these relatively well-off "sending communities" were given admissions priority along with students graduating from the local middle schools

In addition to these on-going voluntary transfer relationships, the Montera administration fostered new relationships with schools and communities across the city. Interestingly enough, some of these new relationships were also with relatively well-off communities in the city. For instance, members of the Montera administration set out actively to recruit Asian students to their school. As we mentioned earlier, the percentage of Asian students who attended the school increased from less than 2 percent in 1992 to 10 percent by 1998.

One of Montera's English teachers described this selective recruitment process:

> It happened over a couple of years, and we went out and recruited, and that is one of the reasons that I stopped . . . being active . . . because it required long, long hours . . . One example is, when we first started, we had just a handful of Korean students at the school. Well, McCann and I, we knew where the Korean students were. We knew that they were going to . . . other schools . . . and we were not getting our share, so we went down and recruited Korean students and said you know that we are within a half hour, by bus . . . and they were spending much more time getting out to

[other high schools], and that we had an outstanding program here. And the result was that Korean students started coming here in huge numbers. We now have about, I would imagine about three hundred, and many of them every year wind up on the honor roll. They are some of our best students.

Montera's staff also actively recruited Eastern European immigrants from a particular area of town. The changing transfer student population was a topic that virtually everyone we spoke to noted as the most important improvement to the school since it was chartered. "Motivated" and "committed" were the types of words most commonly used to describe the students who were being selectively recruited to come to the school. According to one counselor at Montera:

So [with] the charter, by being able to draw in kids who want to be here, there is a certain motivational level, even from your less academic kids. They do tend to try, and they do go to class, and for the most part they behave the way they should. It's cut down on those kinds of problems for us— you know, disciplinary, vandalism—those kinds of problems that we experienced much more of a few years ago. And I think it makes it safer because, again, the kids that come here know that if they don't follow what they're supposed to do, they're not going to be able to stay because they could ultimately maybe have to go back to their home school if they really caused some major kind of problem.

One highly involved parent from the local community noted that since Montera had become a charter school, few of the white and wealthy parents complained about students being bused in from other communities, since the newer transfer students came because they wanted to and not because it was the school of last resort. She explained that one of the things that drove them to become a charter school was that, as a charter, they could accept students by application only. Not only were the students selectively recruited, but also they applied for admission directly to the school instead of applying to the district office. Thus the school had gained complete control over who got in, as opposed to the past, when the district office assigned students to Montera through EAP and voluntary transfers.

While Montera's success in recruiting more motivated students was good news for this school, it may have been problematic for other schools in the district that enrolled the more "difficult" students who would have gone to

Montera prior to its becoming a selective charter. Still, Montera educators were quick to claim that they were not selecting students for the school based on their prior academic achievement, and that they still enrolled some ninth graders who were reading well below grade level. Thus, motivation and commitment continued to be the defining characteristics of the transfer students who enrolled in and remained in Montera. Of course, these characteristics often, but not always, correlate with high-achieving students. As one teacher said, since the school had become a charter school and parents and students were asked to fill out applications, "I'm seeing a bigger population of students who come prepared to learn."

In addition to motivated students, Montera attracted motivated parents as well—or at least parents who had the means and the time to help their children succeed in a school that was far from their home. Due to cutbacks in the district's transportation budget, along with the fact that charter students in California are not guaranteed transportation to school, many of the parents of the new transfer students often had to transport their children to and from school. After-school or extracurricular activities demanded particular effort. As the mother of a transfer student told us: "So if they're going to participate [in extracurricular activities] you have to encourage them to participate, and when they do, you can't just say, take a bus home. So you have to go and get them. *You* have to participate."

This lack of transportation—and Montera still had much more student transportation provided through its school district than most charter schools—was clearly the result of the way in which the charter school law was written and not the fault of individual charter schools. For instance, a very involved parent from the local Montera community noted that the parents and educators at the school were highly committed to maintaining a racially diverse student body, but that the district has not cooperated with the school in terms of providing more transportation.

Attracting motivated transfer students from other public schools in the district was only one way in which Montera boosted its enrollment. Staff at Montera also recruited area students from nearby private schools. In fact, much of the increase in the number of white students enrolled in the school—up to nearly nine hundred from about five hundred in 1992—was due to the school's efforts to recruit local white and wealthy students back into the high school.

Principal McCann told us about his experience attending recruitment meetings at some of the private schools in the area. He noted that when he first went to these meetings in the early 1990s, interest in Montera High School was low, and few students or parents would come talk to him. In later years, however, Montera began drawing large numbers of these students. By 1997, he said, he was speaking to packed audiences of prospective students at these meetings, and half of the eighth-grade class from a nearby private school enrolled in Montera.

The number of applicants for the ninth-grade class had increased from about 280 the first year of the charter to 1,000 applicants in subsequent years. McCann estimated that about 180 students in a recent ninth-grade class had come to Montera from private schools.

Discipline Policies: Getting Rid of Troublesome Students

Beyond selective recruitment, Montera had also instituted strict discipline policies that enabled administrators to push out or kick out students who were not succeeding. Thus, once the more motivated students had been admitted, the school established a set of policies to assure that students who somehow became less motivated were asked to leave. For instance, when students filled out the Montera application they had to agree to maintain a certain level of achievement. On the application, the policy stated that students with three or four failing grades were placed on academic probation, and students with five or six failing grades could be "moved out" if they did not show improvement in the next grading period.

According to the administrator in charge of discipline, many of the failing grades were attributable to the school's attendance policy, which stated that if a student missed more than fifteen classes, he or she received an automatic F in the class. She added that some of the educators at Montera would like to change the policy so that students who missed ten classes would receive a failing grade.

Montera also instituted a dress code banning baggy pants, hats of any kind except those with the school name on them, and tops or dresses that look more like underwear than outerwear. Students could be required to put more clothes on or be sent home to change when found in violation of the dress code.

These policies had become part of the way in which educators and parents defined the charter school when talking to prospective and currently enrolled students. They were used to threaten students who were not living up to expectations. One administrator said that when she meets with parents who are interested in sending their children to Montera, she asks them whether they are ready to abide by the dress code. She also said that when a student has several violations of the dress code, she'll say, "You don't want to go to this school. You need to go to a school where they don't have a dress code, and I have shipped them out."

The Self-Fulfilling Prophecy of Niche Marketing

At the same time that Montera educators worked to create a school that was more homogeneous in terms of highly motivated and committed students, educators and parents alike used ethnic diversity as a selling point when marketing the school to prospective parents and students. Diversity was a draw for the white and wealthy parents who were choosing to pull their children out of private schools and enroll them in Montera. These parents told us how and why they valued having their children in a school that better reflected the diversity of their city than the expensive and exclusive private schools.

One of these parents explained what she and her daughter liked about Montera when they came for a tour: "She came to visit and she looked around and she liked the bigness of it and she liked a lot of different kids and she wanted to make a change, and I also liked a lot of different families and parents. I felt I had more in common with public-school families than with private-school families, who tend to be, I don't know, a little more prissy."

Parents we spoke to valued Montera's image as a "diverse public school." They spoke of other parents who still send their children to private schools, which are not preparing their children for the "real world." At the same time, they noted that one benefit of Montera's charter status was that the school could selectively recruit and that it could get rid of students who did not behave appropriately. Thus, the high motivation levels of the students and the almost private school application and expulsion processes made this diverse public school very appealing to parents who wanted to take their children out of private schools to go to Montera.

Although there was less of a need to market Montera once its enrollment had swelled and it had a waiting list, educators and parents still paid close attention to the image of the school and how it was perceived in the community. According to one of Montera's counselors, charter schools like Montera need to market themselves "basically, because we're charter, everybody is coming by choice, so we have to be in a way like a private school and get out and sell ourselves a little bit, and that's actually good, because it makes us keep on top of what we're doing and think about what we're doing. You know we don't just take it for granted, because we don't just have students automatically coming to us. They have to make a conscious choice to come to us."

A teacher noted that "we are selling product here. And we have to get that message across to parents, that this is a product and you know this is what you will get if you come here . . . Nobody is forcing you to come to Montera, but this is what you're going to get. We're selling it."

Access to Knowledge and Curricular Reform

In addition to engineering student diversity through selective recruitment, discipline policies, and image marketing, Montera Charter transformed its academic offerings with an abundance of new programs. While it was not clear how many of these programs were implemented because Montera was a charter school, their development subsequent to the school's becoming a charter school meant that charter status and the programs were often linked in the minds of educators and parents. At the same time, these programs were often designed to narrow the achievement gaps between the community students and the transfer students. Therefore they tackled issues such as tracking and access to knowledge. For instance, many of these programs shifted the school away from an isolated "basic-skills" approach to learning toward one that emphasized thematic, interdisciplinary learning and problem solving. For example, the math and science departments replaced most of their single-subject classes, such as algebra and physical science, with sequential, integrated courses, such as integrated math and science. The English department implemented a "Humanitas" program in which students integrated English with either drama, art, or world cultures in a two-period block. Montera also launched a media academy where academic subjects were integrated with the specific skills and technology used in the film and recording industries.

Montera's curriculum reforms were complemented by an increased commitment to providing students with multiple forms of academic assistance. A campus tutoring center, largely staffed by parent, community, and student volunteers, was open throughout the day and after school. Montera also opened a satellite tutoring center in a more convenient location for many of its transfer students. In addition, transfer students benefited from the Success program, which provided study skills training, mentoring, and support for students who felt that they were not working up to their academic potential. Although any student could participate in Success, the program typically attracted transfer students preparing for, or enrolled in, the school's high-status Advanced Placement (AP) and honors courses—courses in which transfers often were underrepresented.

Each of these academic reforms (and numerous others throughout the school) reflected the interests and aspirations of many of Montera's educators who hoped to breathe life into traditional subjects and increase the academic success of all of Montera's students. Although these widely shared goals may appear uncontroversial, some parents and teachers criticized the school's reforms as having an adverse impact on high-achieving students, who were generally, though not always, the white and wealthy students from the local community. Across disciplines, the tension between serving the needs of the high-achieving students and those of the school's general population was a recurring theme.

Because this tension was shaded by issues of race and class, it raised thorny questions about the role that power and privilege play in securing access to knowledge. We explore these questions, first, by considering how the pressure for honors and AP courses shaped the debate over reform across disciplines. Next, we show how reforms aimed at integrating the curriculum in math, science, and the humanities were influenced by beliefs about which students were best served by specific educational approaches. Finally, we examine the relationship between Montera's academic support programs and its commitment to providing equitable educational opportunities.

The Press for Honors and Advanced Placement

The tension surrounding Montera's academic reforms reflected the school's unique demographic composition and social location within the district. While Montera had a long tradition of educating many of the district's most affluent and academically successful students, its charter resolved to better prepare greater numbers of students—particularly transfer students—for admissions into highly competitive college campuses. Still, given its history and location, Montera's academic reforms were often analyzed and interpreted in terms of how well they served the needs of the school's highest achievers, not the general student body. This split resulted in ongoing negotiations and compromises between those who sought to preserve traditional, hierarchical academic distinctions exemplified by honors and AP courses, and those who wished to reduce curricular differentiation and expand academic opportunities by offering similarly challenging courses to all students.

Conversations about which students were best served by competing academic reforms must be understood in the context of the school's demographic makeup as it relates to achievement and course placement. Overall, the mostly minority transfer students—who made up 65 percent of the student population—had lower test scores and grade-point averages than the mostly white local students. These differences produced disparities in the ethnic makeup of honors and AP courses. As one teacher commented, "If you were to come into my classes, in my regular classes, I have two white kids, maybe three, in every class. If you were to go into the honors classes you would see a completely different thing . . . mostly white probably."

In turn, these enrollment disparities frustrated efforts to reduce achievement differences between community and transfer students and subtly polarized discussions about what kinds of courses should be offered and how enrollment decisions should be made at the school. For years Principal McCann had been tackling the difficult issues surrounding race, class, and academic achievement, negotiating deft compromises between groups that held opposing views about curriculum and instruction.

McCann, whose skillful leadership won him lofty (and nearly universal) praise from parents and teachers, said he felt that economic and social differences contributed to the "achievement gap" between community and transfer students. Pointing to a detailed computer printout showing student performance broken down into various demographic categories, he noted that "the biggest dilemma of this school is . . . if we're accountable for narrowing the gap between the community students, primarily whites and Asian, and the underrepresented kids, how do you stop the achievement of kids who have access to the world through family resources—where they travel, libraries, museum[s]?"

But McCann also recognized that social as well as economic resources played an important role in securing access to high-status courses for students. Because the prestigious University of California system favors applicants with honors and AP courses, savvy parents are quick to get their children identified as gifted to improve their chances of enrolling in such classes. He was forthright about his disappointment with a system that punishes parents who are less familiar with its operations: "Excuse me, but damn the

UC system for their honors credit, because what that has done, in a multi-ethnic school, . . . [while the parents of white] kids . . . are there getting them identified at kindergarten . . . the [transfer] kids don't have anybody pushing them."

Access to honors courses was perceived by many to be the most important factor for community residents deciding between Montera and private schools. According to English teacher Randy Leonard, "The local kids, the parents bring them here, they want them in honors. And we're told that if we kill the honors program, what we will do is we will lose the population. We will have kids that will go to other schools."

Attempts to Reduce Student Tracking

With the strong community attachment to honors and AP, Montera attempted to equalize access to these courses in two important ways. First, after much discussion, the school eliminated "honors" courses in the ninth grade and decided to use teacher recommendations as the central factor in selecting students for the honors and AP classes in grades ten through twelve. While this move did not entirely eliminate ninth-grade course distinctions (the Humanitas program, for example, was considered by some to be a de facto honors program for ninth graders), it facilitated more shared experiences and learning during the first year of high school. This decision also allowed teachers to help promising ninth graders gain access to high-status courses, even if their K–8 transcripts were less than stellar.

While most of the teachers we talked to supported the school's more liberal honors and AP policy, some felt that it diluted the quality of those classes. For example, one teacher lamented the relative ease with which students could be assigned to honors and AP courses: "What we now have is far less honors than it was [in the past]. For example, before, we took in only the cream of the crop for AP, now we take in all comers. [Before] we took in twenty-five kids, now we'll fill the class with forty. We've opened our doors a lot . . . and we take them in. Before, we used to be far more elite. Why do we do that now? So the parents won't bitch. I want my kid in AP? Let him in."

The second major strategy at Montera for widening access to honors and AP courses involved providing strong tutoring and academic support. McCann said this assistance could help modify the differences in academic preparation between the local and transfer students. Speaking softly but firmly, McCann reiterated his belief that Montera—with the assistance of the tutoring and Success programs—could prepare larger number of under-represented students for honors and AP courses. He said, "We're constantly providing the resources, the study skills, the tutoring centers, the motivation, the goal setting." Later, he went on: "Someone cynically said, 'What do we do, lock them [the affluent high achievers] up for three years while we try to push these other kids up?' So [intervention] with the transfer kids . . . that's the overriding dynamic of what we're trying to do here. Because without constant intervention everything will sift out again."

Even with the enthusiasm of the majority of the faculty for expanding access to AP and honors courses, Montera needed the support of the school's parent community. In addition to the practical importance of garnering parental approval before making broad changes in curriculum or instruction, the school's charter explicitly mandated shared decision-making authority with parents through a site-governance council. Via parent involvement at the school and parent representation on the council, the white and wealthy parents from the local community were vastly overrepresented. And although these involved parents ceded the ninth-grade honors program, they were less enthusiastic about other changes that they felt might jeopardize the integrity of high-status courses.

For example, a proposal to reorganize the school day to accommodate a ninety-minute "block schedule" in which students would rotate to different classes on different days drew broad teacher support but was ultimately voted down at a parent meeting. According to English teacher Wendell Daly, parents of AP students led the fight against block scheduling, fearing that it would detract from their children's preparations for the AP exams. Many of those parents also fought to shape the implementation of the integrated curriculum to allow reform to take place while maintaining honors and AP course options, particularly at the upper grade levels.

Integrated Math and Science

The decision to adopt integrated math and science curricula engendered considerable controversy. Some parents felt that the integrated approach, particularly in mathematics, was confusing and inferior to the traditional, sequential course offerings. Others felt that integrated courses were acceptable so long as school provided an "honors" integrated mathematics option for top students—a compromise that was ultimately agreed upon.

The science department's move to an integrated curriculum generated less parental resistance. Unlike the math department, the science department was able to eliminate the honors distinction altogether. However, the science department retained its AP courses, a move that may have helped defuse any anxiety over the loss of honors courses. Still, a white parent from the local Montera community voiced her frustration with the reforms being implemented in the science department to help lower-achieving students (often the transfer students): "There's another big issue and that is that the science department has dropped the all-honors-level class. They just offer AP and regular classes. And their rationale for that is the heterogeneous groupings will pull up the lower-end kids. OK, fine. But how about the honors-level kids? They say that if they're really honors level, then they should be able to take AP."

A substantial number of parents criticized curriculum integration with respect to its impact on AP and honors courses. Particularly in math, many parents were confused by the integrated approach, and they felt powerless to help their children master the new problem-solving strategies used by the textbook. McCann noted:

> The math debate is still going on—you know, Is the integrated reform curriculum better than the old traditional? . . . We do parent meetings where we bring in the teachers, we put them through the simulated exercises, and we go through all the rationale that, if all you learn is a formula and then apply it to the fifteen problems and memorize it for the test Friday and then go on to the next thing, if you don't see how it's applied, you don't internalize it, you're not learning in the same way as if you see the application and really understand conceptually.

For McCann, and especially for many of Montera's math teachers, the ultimate goal for mathematics teaching was understanding, not memorizing. To bolster their case for the merits of integrated math and science, Montera's faculty drew from at least two highly respected institutions—a local university and the National Science Foundation (NSF). Nearly every new hire in the mathematics department between 1992 and 1998 was trained in the university's teacher education program. They brought with them an institutional perspective that challenged traditional course offerings and promoted the type of conceptual approach to learning that was the foundation of the integrated math program. These teachers ushered in integrated mathematics and were among its most staunch defenders. Support for hands-on math and science training—key features of the integrated curriculum—also came from the National Science Foundation. In fact, the NSF has funded an initiative to reform mathematics and science teaching nationwide. Still, even with the support of the university and the NSF, many of Montera's vocal community parents remained skeptical of the merits of integrated math and science.

Thus, despite impressive efforts by faculty in both departments and some evidence of student success in the program, McCann noted continued parental resistance: "The test scores go up and the performance levels go up, [but] all it takes is a couple of parents whose kids are struggling, and we go right back to square one. [Parents ask] 'Why aren't [you] teaching algebra and geometry the way we learned it?'"

Humanitas

The English department also adopted an integrated curriculum through its Humanitas program. Humanitas, a popular program in California, uses team teaching and thematic units to integrate English with social studies. Although the Humanitas program was originally developed for the ninth grade only, its popularity facilitated its expansion into grades ten through twelve. Unlike math and science integration, Humanitas created very little controversy, in part because it was an elective rather than a mandatory program. Another reason for its acceptance was that the parents of high-achieving students viewed Humanitas as a quasi-honors program.

The coordinator of the program, history teacher Carl Ringoir, acknowledged the appeal of Humanitas among honors-oriented students but argued that, overall, the program was quite diverse. Ringoir told us, "Parents in this community feel a constant need of making sure their students are taking those courses that will not only challenge them . . . but that colleges will look at with more favor." He then added: "Humanitas, in the ninth grade particularly, . . . has . . . the perception—and although often times it's not true, the perception—that it is a . . . quasi-honors program. Simply because most of the students would be in the honors program if indeed they weren't in the ninth-grade Humanitas. Having said that, it is not an honors program . . . It's a huge mix, huge mix."

Even without an official honors designation, Humanitas indeed appeared to be a favorite among students who might otherwise have been enrolled in honors classes. Furthermore, we learned from another counselor that students who enrolled in Humanitas as ninth graders had to take a mandatory health class during summer school instead of during the school year like most students. This could present a particular difficulty for transfer students who did not have transportation to attend summer school.

The Humanitas program revealed the curious relationship between status and coursework at Montera Charter High School. Although it was not officially an honors course, it enjoyed honors status among parents. Given this elevated status, the program encountered much less controversy than integrated math, which was conceptually and philosophically similar but was perceived by many parents as a threat to the honors system. Even programs simply being considered for adoption by the school faced considerable scrutiny as to which students they were intended to serve—children at the top of the academic ladder or those who occupied the rungs below.

Outreach and Tutoring

At the same time that tension over these curricular reforms was swirling around the school, Montera made a strong commitment to tutoring and support programs for transfer students. Principal McCann said he hoped that the Success program could help prepare students for demanding high school courses, describing it as a "program where we identify early on the under-represented kids, give them goal-setting intervention, expectations, and work with the parents, so that by the time they get here they're able to—they're ready to—move on to honors, AP-level classes."

As we noted, the Success program provided study skills, mentoring, and support for low-performing students. The founder of Success shared Mc-Cann's goal of using the program to boost transfer-student participation in honors and AP courses. Math teacher Bianca Lester, who was herself once a transfer student at Montera, reflected back on her own experience at the school when she decided to launch the Success program. She recalled: "I have lots of friends who went to college, but they weren't in the honors programs . . . Most of them went to Cal States [the second-tier universities in the state system]. A couple of them might have got into [University of California] because they got straight A's in their regular classes. Even though I was a flake in my classes, just the fact that I took honors everything throughout school, I got into every place that I applied. It makes a big difference." After supporting the Success program at Montera, McCann helped start related programs in nearby elementary and middle schools.

Even with the Success program, Montera was still a school divided by the disparate achievement levels of its community students and transfer students. Although these divisions were linked to the different economic, educational, and social backgrounds of the students, they were also related to the organization of the curriculum in the school. Access to high-level AP and honors courses favored community students whose parents could exercise greater control over the tracking process. Similarly, efforts to diminish hierarchical course distinctions were opposed by these parents whose children had an important stake in the current system. In light of these forces, however, Montera had done an admirable job of raising key questions about the relationships between race, class, and achievement—and maintaining a sustained dialogue between parents, teachers, and administrators geared toward narrowing the achievement differences between community and transfer students.

The Uneven Voices of Montera Parents

At Montera Charter High School tensions ran high over whom the school best served. As evidenced by the debate over academic reforms, teachers and administrators continually struggled to meet the demands of the powerful local parents while simultaneously providing meaningful academic opportunities for the larger group of transfer students. Administrators, in particular, continually worked to resolve the many competing demands of these two groups of charter "clients." In many ways, the school's survival hinged on satisfying the demands of both.

Who had voice, therefore, was a contentious issue at Montera. While the charter and the concurrent site-based management reforms brought a more inclusive governance structure to the school, larger social issues of power and wealth often dictated who—when all is said and done—had the most voice.

Montera's community parents had long served as leaders of reform efforts at the school, and after the school won its charter, they became intimately involved with virtually every aspect of the school's operations and programs. Powerfully positioned to win concessions from the school board downtown for Montera's reforms, and able to attract the resources required to make those reforms a reality, these community parents found the school's administration generally very responsive to their needs and demands.

Montera's transfer parents, on the other hand, whose children made up the bulk of the school's student population, were less powerful in terms of being heard at the school. Because of the geographic distance separating them from the school and from each other, these transfer parents were far less organized and informed than the community parents and had sacrificed much to provide their children with a better educational opportunity in a distant community. In the end, transfer parents reported that they felt like guests on the Montera campus. While the principal was welcoming, the community parents were less willing to include them in the school's decision-making process.

Community Parents: Power Brokers and Reformers

Although most white parents took their children out of Montera when busing for desegregation began in the district, a core group of community parents stayed, and they remained committed to revitalizing Montera High and its feeder schools when enrollment dropped. One of the central tasks of this core group of parents was to establish and maintain a legacy of community parent involvement at Montera. As Carmen Mitchell, a highly involved local parent, observed: "I think what we've been lucky with here is that there's been a hard-core committed group that [has] sort of passed the baton, and everybody tries to initiate the people two or three years behind them, or a year or two behind them, pull them in, and identify who is able to give that kind of commitment. And we've been lucky we've had that sort of legacy."

This core group of parents mobilized to save Montera when it was threatened with closure, and thus they took much of the credit for turning the school around. Mitchell noted: "Years ago they were talking about closing the schools because there wasn't enough student body. So those of us that have been here over a couple of decades have seen an incredible transformation. We were part of the transformation, I think we drove the transformation, if you want the truth."

The parents at Montera who had originally instigated the charter idea as a means to revitalize the school found themselves trying to garner involvement and "buy-in" from teachers and administrators. As another highly involved local parent, Billie Kennedy, explained:

> I think the parents' role became proportionately less important, which was our goal. The point was that we really felt that we were never going to get reform if it was all parent driven, and we understood from the beginning

that we needed the participation. You had to be, you had to have buy-in from all the groups so they [would] participate. The teachers are obviously very powerful in that regard, and should be. So our goal was really to make everyone feel invested in this process, and to bridge that resistance gap and that barrier that often exists between parents and faculty and where the faculty feels the parents are meddling. We always try to take the approach of "What can we do to help?" rather than "Here's what you should be doing."

These local parents then drew on their political and financial resources to enable the passage—and ensure the success—of the charter. In a district with an embattled and politically unpopular school board, Montera's community parents were able to use their political power to push the charter idea through in spite of some objections raised by several civil rights groups that the charter was an effort by Montera to become elitist. As Billie Kennedy explained: "I think . . . from a PR point of view it would look terrible if they had denied our charter. And I think we had also begun to show them that we were really determined to maintain a diverse student body, and that we had already established some of the programs to meet the needs of the kids from all the different backgrounds. We certainly had something to stand on. But, again, it's always political. We still feel that they don't really care what we're doing, they still want to paint us as being elitist."

The parents were able to amass a tremendous amount of financial and in-kind support for the charter—resources that were continually renewed to make the charter and other related reforms successful. As Principal McCann noted, the resources these parents brought in terms of money and expertise were invaluable, especially given the lack of financial and technical support available for the conversion to charter status. Yet these donations required, from a political point of view, that he pay extra heed to these parents' concerns. According to McCann: "I have tens if not hundreds of thousands of resources just in the expertise of the people who are in the parent or local community, which is not to say that they don't constantly have to be reinforced and stroked and responded to. I'm here till eight or nine at night returning phone messages because I won't leave until every phone message is returned. Because each one of those parents is somebody who potentially or already has contributed to the school."

While McCann made an effort to keep every parent involved and informed, this involvement in turn invited scrutiny: "We're overwhelmed with the parents' scrutinizing . . . but I think that keeps everybody on their toes. We have to justify everything we do, including every grade that's issued." McCann recognized that it was the parents, particularly the well-connected ones, who were central to the charter's success: "You can't create a charter or use the charter unless you have leadership in the school community, a set of support systems that include involved parents who are willing to commit energy, time, and have a passion for what they're doing, and then connect it to other resource systems."

For their part, the local parents were extremely involved, even though many of them—mothers and fathers—worked full-time. In fact, some of the mothers who did not work outside of the home volunteered at Montera full-time. Carmen Mitchell, local parent and the volunteer coordinator, described the amount of time she had given to Montera:

I was really putting in about fifty hours a week, and that wasn't here, that was at [the nearby] middle school. Now I put in, it's hard to calculate, anywhere between probably fifteen to—it depends on if we're talking about broad issues or writing to congresspeople—then sometimes I probably am up to, depending on the project, thirty, forty, like a couple of times they had a big fund-raiser and for a couple of weeks, it was probably about forty hours a week. As you can see I'm not working [at my job] anymore at the moment. I'm doing this.

The involved local parents are extremely proud of their role in turning Montera around from a school on the brink of closure to one with a waiting list. Yet while they drew many local parents back from private schools and brought a "more committed" group of transfer students to Montera, there were still tensions around issues of race and voice. The white community parents, in particular, were often defensive when it came to issues of race. While they regarded themselves as making every effort at inclusion, they said they were often "written off" by the district and other Montera observers, characterized as racist or "elitist" because of who they were and where they lived. Despite the fact that these parents and their community as a whole carried a lot of political weight in the city and the school district, sometimes their race and wealth worked against them in their efforts to garner resources. One parent recalled the efforts the local parents made to increase transportation to the school for transfer students: The problem of course is that when a white parent from Montera goes, [school board members] don't want to hear from us, and part of what, I think one of the biggest inroads we've made this year is the fact that we gotten a lot of, more of the [transfer] parents to join the parent involvement. So we have some real key leaders, especially in the African American community now."

At the same time, however, there was a sense of ambivalence among community parents toward the transfer parents who, despite efforts to involve them, remained underrepresented. On the one hand, the local parents recognized that transfer parents faced obstacles to getting involved, yet on the other hand they felt that the lack of involvement by the transfer parents somehow indicated a lack of commitment to the school and their children. As one local parent stated: "There are some parents that are what you call the [transfer parents], there are some . . . who do make an effort to get involved in activities and to come to certain things, you know nighttime things, stuff like meetings that are, you know, if they can make them then we usually hold them at night. They are easier for them, I think, than the daytime meetings. But on the whole we see, in terms of the more involved parents, I think you mostly see the neighborhood kids [and parents], but there is a handful of the other.

Billie Kennedy described the difficulty in creating an inclusive governance system with such a diverse and far-flung student population:

> It's a challenge always to get the parents, because how do you determine what constitutes a fair parent vote? We have to make sure they're all notified. How do you deal with the fact that if they have to come to the school site to vote, some of them can't be there at a certain time. It's really, really tricky to get parent votes on these things when you're dealing with a school the size of Montera High and a student body that comes from hundreds of zip codes all around the city. That's one of our biggest challenges.

Yet, despite their reported efforts to get the transfer parents involved, the local parents also found themselves at odds with the transfer parents—as well as with Montera's teachers and administrators—over some of the equity reforms aimed at providing opportunities for the transfer students, as discussed earlier. For instance, many of the local community parents said that they felt frustrated with the efforts to "de-track" the school, and that when it came to curriculum and instruction, their concerns were not addressed. With regard to the integrated math program, Kennedy noted, "Well, we have been actively involved in trying to influence [the math program], and this is a frustration. We've set up committees, we do all these things, we try to have a dialogue, try not to be confrontational; bottom line is, I really do have to question what has been the effectiveness of our role at this point. We don't really see a change. Nobody has said, 'Well you're right, we have to get rid of this program.' And it's always hard to know, is it really the program, is it the teachers?"

Teachers, on the other hand, said they felt bombarded by the demands of the local parents. As Sandra Marx, a Montera teacher, noted, "Parents have an input. That is what it is all about, and I guess that is nice in some ways, but in others it is not. It is too much parent involvement." Overall, however, the teachers and administrators knew that they had cater to the demands of the powerful local parents for their school's survival. As teacher Carl Ringoir observed, "The parents [are] going to get very vocal and active. I'm not saying that's bad; I'm not saying it's good. And frankly, oftentimes the parents don't have the right perspective they need to have on certain matters . . . [But] you can't have parent participation and say, 'But you can't participate.'"

Transfer Parents: Seeking Membership and Voice

Many of the transfer students' parents had applied to Montera hoping that the charter high school would provide their children with a safer and more rigorous academic environment than the one at their neighborhood high school. Most of the parents with whom we spoke said that Montera lived up to their expectations, but many had also come to realize that finding such an environment for their child came at a high personal cost, as transfer parents on the whole were less involved, less informed, and less powerful within the school community.

Most of the transfer parents sent their children long distances to Montera—some by bus, some by car—because they were fearful of the gang problems at their local high school and worried about the safety of their children. One transfer parent described her fear of sending her son to the local high school:

I was in a panic, you know, what am I going to do? I couldn't afford to put him in a private school, and I didn't want to send him to the high school. I mean, he's a good kid, and I just felt like he would not survive [the neighborhood high school]. So I started looking around . . . [and] there was an opening [at the] charter, so [they] accepted him, and he's been there ever since. Otherwise he would have been stuck going to [the neighborhood high school]. I thought I was going to lose my mind, because I was afraid . . . they would eat him alive, he wouldn't survive. Not that Montera is the best, but I felt better about it.

The safe environment for their children, however, came at a price. For instance, as we mentioned earlier, transfer parents said they found it difficult to let their children become involved in after-school activities, due to the lack of adequate after-hours transportation. Even more significant, transfer parents found that the distance between their home and Montera caused them to be less informed and less able to have input at the school. One transfer parent described the dilemma in which many transfer parents found themselves:

I don't make the [parent] meetings, not that I [don't] want to, not that, because, like I told you, when it comes to school I am very vocal. But . . . I have to work. So it's not that easy. And it's hard because you want to do what's best for your child's education, you want it safe . . . it's not safe to send your child to a school in your neighborhood. I mean, that's a fact. So you want to send him somewhere where it's safe, where they'll be exposed to a little bit, but you know, you have to pay the price. And sometimes the price, which really makes you angry—you do get left out, and things go over your head, and you have no control.

The sole transfer parent on the Montera governance council, Fanny Luttrell, said that she was afraid to speak up at meetings because she felt far less informed about the issues up for discussion than the community parents, who had been involved in the Montera community much longer. She explained, "It's kind of intimidating . . . sometimes it's difficult to formulate a question when I don't understand, when I don't understand what's been going on. Yet I'm reluctant to ask what's going on, because I'm the only one that doesn't know what's going on, or maybe I feel I'm the only one that doesn't know what's going on. Everyone just seems so informed because they've been involved, as you've observed, for years."

Many transfer parents said that Principal McCann, in particular, was committed to keeping the transfer community well informed. While they said there were also some teachers and other administrators committed to meeting their needs, there was a general sense among the transfer parents that many in the Montera community did not express a need or desire to include them or their children. As a parent of an African American transfer student noted, "Even though we are accepted by the principal, we still don't feel accepted by the community, by some of the teachers, by some of the administrators, by some of the community members. We still feel like outsiders. So for the [transfer] parents that do take the time to get involved, we're always concerned whether or not our needs are being met. They're sure to meet their needs, but sometimes they overlook ours."

Luttrell, as a governance council member, had several firsthand experiences with what she considered the community parents' resentment toward the transfer students and parents, particularly when teachers and administrators expressed concern for the way certain programs such as tracking—affected the transfer students. Luttrell discussed one instance:

> I went [to] a department meeting and . . . I was the only African American there, and I could tell, I think it was a matter of adding some honors classes, yet some teachers opposed it because it would cause tracking; they saw advantages to having the children together at all achievement levels. . . . And this parent was an advocate, naturally, for her child, and looking at her face, just watching her face, I felt—I could be wrong—but I felt she was thinking something like, "Well, to hell with those niggers."

Other transfer parents said that the school had been less than eager to secure their full participation. Luttrell described one episode that she said was blatantly discriminatory—when a group of local community parents wanted to have a meeting to identify future parent leaders who could best continue the programs they had started. Luttrell said that when they mentioned the meeting to her, it was more for her information as opposed to an invitation to participate. When Luttrell asked whether there were any traveling parents attending the meeting, she was told someone was "working on it." Several days later Luttrell was invited to the meeting, and she informed two other African American parents, who also attended. "If it had not been for me asking that question, we never would have known. [They] didn't consider giving us the training to kind of keep things going, even though we're . . . 70 percent of the school population."

Luttrell also observed that, despite the lack of involvement on the part of black parents, the African American community is much more organized than Latinos or Asians, who make up a significant proportion of the student body.

Montera's satellite tutoring center located in an African American neighborhood had helped to inform and involve more transfer parents. As transfer parent Gerry Kenter observed: "Sometimes the parents don't have any connection with school, and . . . I feel this center is helping to get some parents involved, or to [give them] some way of touching, of getting information from the school that they would never get [otherwise]." Despite this connection, however, transfer parents still remained generally isolated from the core decision-making processes at Montera Charter High School. While many had hoped that the center would provide a meaningful bridge between the transfer community and the local community, that bridge seemed to be more of a one-way street. Even though some community parents had supported establishing the satellite center, many transfer parents resented the fact that the local parents had not expressed much of an enduring interest in the center. As Fanny Luttrell noted, "We can't *make* them accept us, we can't *make* them come here [to the satellite center], but sometimes it's not very comfortable when it's so obvious—when parents immediately attend a meeting [at Montera] but don't even know what the center looks like. When a meeting is called in our territory, they have no interest."

While this reported neglect of traveling parents certainly could occur whether or not the school was a charter school, Montera's charter status and its more decentralized decision-making processes made the stakes a little higher. If charter schools promise greater parent involvement and more democratic decision making, it appeared as though Montera was making that promise come true for only a certain set of parents.

The Dilemma of Decentralized Inequalities

The story of Montera Charter High provides a good example of why the impact of charter school reform is not straightforward or simple. Policy questions about whether or not charter schools are "working," whether or not they are "better" than the traditional public schools, cannot be answered without taking into account both the promises and threats of this reform as it interacts with a highly unequal society.

Montera Charter High School was "working" for most of the students and parents who got in and stayed in. Even the transfer parents who would have liked more voice and support found Montera a much better alternative to the schools in their neighborhoods. Even the community parents who were frustrated with some of the equity-based reforms that educators were trying to implement preferred the image of a diverse public school to an elite private school. For these families, Montera was the best choice.

Yet from a broader public policy perspective, we must question where the "unmotivated" students who would have been sent to Montera before it went charter—or those who have since been asked to leave Montera—currently attend school. How is charter school reform working for those public schools now faced with an even greater concentration of disenfranchised students? How much of Montera's success is attributable to the fact that these students were sent elsewhere, and how much is attributable to the curricular reforms and new governance structure at the school? To what extent does Montera serve a broader public interest, and to what extent is it serving a more narrow set of interests?

We believe that so long as difficult questions such as these remain unanswered, the success and failure, the promise and threat of schools such as Montera cannot be fully assessed. Although researchers and policymakers are quick to draw simple comparisons between charter schools and "matching" public schools by examining student outcomes after a year or two, the story of Montera Charter High should help to illustrate the inability of this approach to measure the full impact of charter schools on public education and on the lives of all students.

CHAPTER 6

Losing Public Accountability:
A Home Schooling Charter

LUIS A. HUERTA

Nestled in the center of California's fruit basket, adjacent to the Sierra Nevada foothills, the settlement that I call Valley Town is situated in a square-mile plot of land surrounded by neat rows of fruit trees. With the exception of two small general stores, there are no businesses in this rural spot that is home to fewer than a thousand people. There are no main thoroughfares either, only six or seven narrow streets lined with houses and large yards. Many of these fenced lots resemble machine storage lots, with pieces of rusting tractors and old cars scattered about. The largest yard, in the middle of town, surrounds the six buildings that house the Valley Unified School District office, the Valley Elementary School (a traditional K–8 school), and the main annex of the Valley Charter School.

Valley Charter School (VCS), which opened its doors in 1994, is perhaps unlike any other charter school in the country in that the majority of its students come from conservative Christian home-school families; others come from antigovernment libertarian families in the San Francisco Bay Area, more than one hundred miles away. Even more unusual is the fact that VCS's students remain home schoolers, rarely setting foot in the public school office or resource centers with which they now are conjoined. One parent explains: "I want them to have the attitude that 'God has given me all these blessings in my life, what can I give back?' That is the foundation that I want for them. And one of the ways to get that is not to have them brainwashed by a group of educators. I don't want to leave my children off somewhere like in a classroom and have them influenced and taught by someone that I am not familiar with."

It may seem strange that Christian home schoolers such as this parent would want to join forces with a public school district; after all, many told me that they had become home schoolers in the first place to remove themselves from the hegemony of a secular and even godless world. But that's exactly what they did—in droves.

Public school officials expected only the eighty families already enrolled in the district's independent study program (ISP) to join the new charter school. But in less than five months, student enrollment surged to more than 400 students as home schooling families learned of the program and joined VCS. Amy Stevens, the school's director and a passionate advocate for the home school families she serves, recalls the frenzy of those first months: "I became the director of the home school and the only full-time employee at the charter school because we only had eighty kids. By April first, I said, 'No more. No matter who calls, I'll not take another student. I cannot survive.' I was working probably, at minimum, eighteen hours a day, and with no clerical staff, and bringing part-time teachers in. And the enrollment at that time . . . was more than four hundred."

The news of a public school dedicated to serving the individual needs of home school families spread quickly around the Central Valley. Stevens recounts the swirl of publicity:

> The local newspaper . . . heard there was a charter school. We were the first one anywhere in the area, so she wanted to do an article, and I kept putting her off until finally she came out, visited with the parents . . . And she wrote quite a good article about an alternate way of educating your children. And it made the front page . . . But then it went on the wire service, and the next day it was on the front page of the *Oakland Tribune.* So we got hundreds and hundreds and hundreds of calls. We had so many calls [from] people interested in knowing more, people who were already home schooling and wanted to hook up with us. But it was like a whirlwind. I would never [have believed] it in a million years, because I would never have advertised like that. I just thought that this alternative was growing by word of mouth. And I didn't have the sense that we needed to grow.

A year later the student population reached its current capacity of nearly 750 students.

If it's unusual that Christian home schoolers would want to join a public school, it's perhaps equally surprising that a school district would want to sponsor a charter largely for evangelical Christians. After all, some districts are wary of sponsoring any kind of charter, much less one that seems so at odds with the legacy of public education. But the Valley school district was in fact eager to grant this charter.

In essence, this chapter details how two apparently incompatible entities, traditionally at loggerheads, created an anomalous public, Christian, home schooling network with enough clout even to establish an annex for mostly libertarian families in the distant Bay Area. While charters sometimes represent a movement in the direction of radical decentralization, the creation of VCS in some ways appears to represent almost the opposite: the creeping centralization of a home schooling constituency that has, until now, insisted on absolute autonomy. But as this story will reveal, VCS, through its loose accountability mechanisms, does not expect families to adapt their home schooling practices to stringent demands from the public authority. Rather, the state reinforces their already decentralized existence and autonomy, allowing families to retain their private identity at public expense.

This chapter explores the motivations among the actors in this unlikely alliance, and the reactions of a subset of home schoolers who define it as an unholy union. I ask questions about both the possibilities and the dangers of such an alliance: Does VCS suggest that the government is beginning to take control of a once fiercely independent movement? Or do we see independent, home schooling Christians learning to take advantage of centralized resources for their private benefit?

I begin by discussing the founding of VCS. I then look at how teachers and the school's four learning annexes serve families in a purely supportive role, leaving core teaching responsibilities to the parents. I explore the developing tensions between VCS families and the "purists," home schooling families who refuse to be "co-opted" by Valley Charter School. These families fear that the home school movement will be poisoned by government, and that VCS families have sold out for the sake of resources supplied by the state. Finally, I discuss whether or not the state has a legitimate role in supporting home schooling charters—charters that operate with little accountability, outside of the public domain.

The Creation of Valley Charter School

Prior to the establishment of the charter school, Valley Unified was one school district, serving just 200 K–8 students and 80 home school students through an independent study program. The ISP had operated since 1990 and had grown steadily as more families learned that it was tailored to meet the specific needs of home schoolers. As the ISP student population increased, so did the burden on the district to meet the needs of ISP students. However, the district staff was limited in serving ISP students due to the demands of students in the regular school program. In an attempt to better serve ISP families that chose home-based instruction, and to provide them with the staff and learning tools needed to successfully educate their children, the Superintendent, Frank Gomez, gathered support for a charter school among the district's teachers and staff and then submitted a petition to the district. The charter was quickly ratified, and the charter school began operating from a small trailer placed on the school district grounds.

In no time at all, a tightly knit community of home schooling parents who for years had been teaching their children themselves was opened up by the opportunity to use public funding for a choice that they previously had financed privately. For many home school families, joining VCS meant no longer worrying if the legal affidavit they filed yearly was sufficient to meet the compulsory education requirements of the state.[1] For these new VCS families, their once private choice to home school was now publicly validated, legitimized, and fully funded.

Like most communities that decide to create charter schools, Valley encountered some financial obstacles in the start-up phase. However, the challenge of founding a new school from scratch was eased by an advance of $250,000 from the district. With this generous sum, which was to be paid back by VCS, the charter school quickly blossomed and was brought to fruition. The rich dividends are best exemplified by the growth of VCS's student population. During the school's first two years of operation, the student population grew from 80 to nearly 750—almost three times the size of the original Valley school district's student population.

Along with the many new students came a surge of state revenue to the small district, increasing the district's budget by more than 300 percent. VCS garnered home school families by providing them with a wealth of materials and instructional support. In exchange for resources, families would mail monthly student learning records to the school. Learning records are the lifeline of the school and serve a dual purpose—outlining the monthly academic content completed by students and serving also as an attendance roster from which VCS staff can calculate average daily attendance (ADA).[2] Thus, parents' self-reported enrollment data permit VCS to receive full capitation grants from the state. Over time the new revenues provided enough money for VCS to pay back the original start-up loan as well as the necessary funds to begin an ambitious expansion that would cross district lines all the way to the San Francisco Bay Area.

VCS students come from an expansive geographical area covering fourteen counties and stretching across 450 miles of the Central Valley—from as far north as Shasta and as far south as Bakersfield. VCS is able to serve such a large and dispersed student population because instruction is home-based and parents provide the primary instruction. In other words, there are no formal classrooms and there is no site that resembles what might be readily recognized as a school. Rather, VCS operates from a main annex, situated in Valley, where only four VCS families reside, and an additional four separate annexes spread throughout the Central Valley and as far west as Oakland.

Considering the large and diverse geographic region from which VCS draws students, the ethnic makeup is very homogeneous. The student population in 1998 was 89 percent Anglo, 7 percent Latino, and 3 percent African American. The superintendent explained that the Oakland annex had helped provide a bit more diversity to the student population, although the low turnover rate of VCS families, combined with the fact that enrollment is capped at 750, lowers any near-term prospect of a more diverse population.

Stevens, a twenty-year veteran teacher and the former curriculum coordinator for the small district, was asked by Superintendent Gomez to become the director of the new charter school. She is respected among her colleagues, one of whom said: "We are very fortunate because Amy has a long history with the small district and is well respected by the community and staff and the school board."

Stevens, a strong supporter of home schooling, is always eager to talk about her school. A conversation with her is never complete without the description of at least one trial the school has faced and the hard-fought triumph that followed. Modest by nature, she likes to give others credit for the school's accomplishments. She describes how she endured the chaos that ensued as news of the opening of VCS spread among home school parents:

> We had been in a trailer that we moved into in January. And we had a small computer lab at one end and a supply room at one end, and my office at the other, and a conference table and our curriculum . . . the logistics were mind-boggling. It's like, all the books we'd order . . . I'd decide what I needed to order late at night before I went home. And then I had a clerical gal that came in the morning and processed those. And then when the or-

ders arrived, they all got delivered to the front office. That meant that they had to be first taken physically over to our facility and then they had to be unpacked and all. But until November that year, I had taught the whole first trimester [at the traditional school], I taught upper grades. So I had upper-grade students that, everyday after morning recess, they'd stop in the office and they'd come over, they'd spend their lunch hours . . . helping me unpack and process the book orders. It became a whole team of people. And the parents within our program, they'd just help.

As self-effacing as Stevens is, she is obviously very proud of what she has created. Her nonstop personality and dedication to her work are reflected in her naturally amplified, high-pitched voice, which always sounds hoarse with fatigue.

The Role of the VCS Teacher

The founding premise of a home schooling charter school such as VCS is that parents are responsible for the education of their children and thus are the primary instructors. The job of VCS teachers, referred to as "education coordinators," is to help provide parents with the tools they need to become more effective teachers of their children. The VCS mission statement explicitly says that teachers will "provide a supportive and encouraging environment in which parents can receive high quality training opportunities, teaching resources, counseling, and a structure to support their educational objectives."[3] Classes are offered but optional, and families may follow a VCS curriculum or any other curriculum of their choice. But in no sense do VCS teachers require attendance or determine curriculum.

While VCS teachers play only a supportive role, they are important nevertheless, as Stevens discovered when she found herself swamped with requests for materials and instructional support during the charter school's first months of operation. Soon she was able to recruit a kindergarten teacher from the traditional school, hiring her as an education coordinator. The new teacher's job entailed meeting with new VCS families, aiding them in outlining their specific curriculum needs, and then ordering the necessary materials. As more families joined VCS, more educational coordinators were hired. Over time, the teachers' role evolved, as Stevens elaborates:

We started out by having grade-level teachers here. And we found that wasn't very fair, because lots of home schoolers have multiple children. So now we're about families. So each family is assigned to a teacher.

We vary [assignments] from over fifty families to down to fifteen families. It's like the person [teacher] that was there the longest, that knows people the best, can accommodate a larger number [of families] because they've already done all the background. The goal is that it's going to be fairly even. I would say . . . the teacher would have 100 or more students. And those students could represent thirty, fifty families, depending on how many students per family. So then they sit down. They've gone to the orientation, most of them come visit while they're on the waiting list, and then they just sit there and they really talk about their children. What kinds of things they can get, hook into, that will work. At that time too, they also make curriculum choices, because we have a catalog. We have a variety of choices for each.

Hiring new education coordinators to monitor the needs of VCS families was a well thought out process and involved carefully selecting teachers who would buy into the mission of VCS: supporting parents and providing them with the tools to be better teachers of their children. Stevens's ability to select the right teachers would soon prove to be perhaps the most important factor in the successful development of the school.

After the kindergarten teacher started to work for VCS, Stevens recruited two more teachers from the community, Ms. Fischer and Ms. Kirby. These two women, both former public school teachers, were also home schooling parents, and they were members of two different local home schooling collectives. Kirby had also been the director of a local "cover school" serving private home schooling families.[4]

These two teachers would prove instrumental in the continued growth of the school. Their firsthand experience and their knowledge of the specific needs of home schooling families, as well as their personal relationships and contacts, helped them persuade families from the private home school collectives to join VCS. Thus, with minimal but carefully selected staff, VCS quickly became a powerful force within the home schooling community and a competitive threat to the church-based cover schools.

While the teachers were careful never to usurp the role of parents, they did offer an optional classroom experience for home schooling students— a concept foreign to most home schoolers. This was developed by Amy Stevens, who did not believe that books and materials were enough to meet the educational needs of VCS families. She was determined to offer them new opportunities: "That spring, I felt like if these people are going to sign up for a school, they needed more than a book and a lady at the other end of the phone and an occasional meeting with a teacher . . . So, I thought the best thing I can do right now is get some classes going and get the word out to them so they can get their child participating in some good classes. Thinking, that'll get us through until the summer and then we'll regroup and see where we're going."

To increase the services provided to VCS families, Stevens hired fifty part-time instructors and five more full-time educational coordinators who began providing instruction in science, history, physical education, art, computer education, and many other areas. An educational coordinator explains:

> We want the parents to come together and learn. We have a computer lab and have eight-week sessions. They come and we have curriculum we work on there. We have hands-on science class. Some of them are focused on single topics. We have projects. We have a choral music program. We have about one hundred students involved in that. They break it into grade-level sectors. The older group is going to be doing the musical *Davy Crockett.* Last year we did a Christmas production in the state theater and filled it up with parents. It was all choral music. We have an instrumental band that comes to our facilities. We have creative writing classes in Modesto. That is done according to grade-level group. They work on writing process, whether expository writing or poetry. We have art instruction. We have a limit of how many art units they can take, so parents have to pick and choose. But they do sculptures and basic drawings. We have physical education in the gymnastics studio. Those are just some of the things. We have field trips that we do. We had a fine arts fair. We had artists come in.

Still, teachers are peripheral to the home schooling mission of VCS. They work, by design, in only a limited capacity, facilitating lessons for students and parents. A teacher describes her role:

> Amy [Stevens] is really good about reminding us all . . . that our classes are enrichment only. Our classes are to support what the parents are already doing. So they [the parents] are really doing all the hard work at home. So when they come here it's more just to give the children an opportunity for a group experience, and also just to enrich what they are doing at home. But they are having to do the hard work at home.
> . . . A California history class that I do, it's mainly an activity class and then I give all kinds of ideas and books and they take them home and they do all the instruction. I am just enriching the unit.

In essence, the responsibilities of the school staff seem to make them consultants to the parents rather than teachers to the students. But among staff, there is some confusion as to just what responsibilities should fit what title. As one VCS teacher says:

> Our new title is education counselor. The first title was grade-level coordinator . . . and then we were saying, instead of grade-level coordinators, education coordinators. So now we were thinking more, "We are really . . . helping to counsel families rather than coordinating them." We are not saying, "This is what is good for your family"; they are coming in, saying this area needs some work, and we give it to them. The idea is that we are going to move from grade-level coordinator to more education consultant, or coordinator.

The teachers finally settled on education coordinator as their title. As education coordinators, they are always at the disposal of the parents, providing advice or assistance to parents only when called upon. Says one: "What parents like is that they can call one of us and say, 'I'm stuck here. I'm frustrated, can you help me?' And then we have a chance to meet with them . . . We try to be available, accessible, but not act like we're breathing down their neck or requiring production from them."

The Far-Flung Annexes

The fact that parents had a lot of trust in like-minded teachers gave this far-flung school community a kind of coherence. So did the creation of three VCS annexes spread throughout the Central Valley and an additional one in the San Francisco Bay Area. The annexes made members of the VCS community feel that they were part of a real "school," albeit an unusual and somewhat fragmented one. The annexes also gave parents a practical incentive to join VCS: within them are stored an abundance of instructional materials, from books to microscopes to educational software. Three of the annexes organize these services and materials into a "learning center," although the fourth is simply a garage stocked with textbooks.

The annexes are intended to ease parents' access to learning resources. Parents can either go directly to the annexes to borrow materials or they may request that materials be mailed to their home. A visit to the main annex hints at the school's unconventional nature. The main annex is housed in a temporary structure at the back of Valley Elementary's main school yard. It has wide, solid-wood front stairs, a shaded front porch, and double

French doors and windows. All in all, the facade seems to resemble that of an old one-room country schoolhouse. But inside, the modestly decorated annex features modern institutional furniture, shelves filled with brand-new materials, an impressive computer lab, and well-equipped offices for several of the teachers and the school's administrator.

Another annex, located about four miles away in a neighboring town, contains additional offices for teachers as well as the central stockpile of materials. Along the walls, tall shelves tower toward the high ceiling, tightly packed with a plethora of books and other instructional materials. The floor area is also lined with many long rows of well-stocked shelves. In the air is the smell of new books, giving one the sense of browsing through a cozy bookstore.

Parents do indeed browse through the annex, deciding what materials they want to borrow, and they may order additional materials and charge them to their $150-per-child personal curriculum account provided by VCS. The annex also houses the VCS Internet server and mainframe computer. From here VCS provides e-mail accounts at no cost to all families with computers at home. And the teachers are expanding their use of technology, developing a long-distance learning program that will allow students and teachers to interact and take advantage of additional resources over the Internet.

At first glance, the environment inside the annex seems to mimic that of a well-structured business office rather than a school. Teachers work at their desks, answering e-mail or taking phone calls from their client families. Others use the round tables in the middle of the room to review student learning records or browse new materials that are regularly arriving. On different days of the week, however, the annex adopts a more school-like atmosphere. Students, accompanied by parents, fill the computer lab for a math class or an Internet research lesson, or they sit around the tables for a social studies lesson.

The Religious Right at Valley Charter School

Although the teachers seem to be open to helping any family, several emphatically state that "Valley Charter is not for everyone." A similar sentiment is echoed in the VCS annual report, which describes the VCS educational approach—parents educating their children at home—as "not for everyone." If VCS is not for everyone, then just who are the families who are attracted to the school?

The answer is revealed in conversations with VCS staff and parents, as well as in a VCS survey. The survey indicates that the majority of VCS families have had prior home school experience; that less then one-third came to VCS new to home schooling. As described by the district superintendent, the majority of families are "right-wing Christians" and are home schooling on account of religious conviction, though he quickly adds that VCS provides only secular materials to families.

The superintendent's description of VCS families is affirmed by the survey results, which reveal that the most popular reason for home schooling is the "inclusion of family morals and values in the curriculum."[5] Parents overwhelmingly reported that church activities were the most popular non-school extracurricular activities for their children. Parents also mentioned disillusionment with public schools as a popular reason for choosing to home school—a disillusionment that stemmed in part from the structure of traditional classrooms: "Many parents felt that single grade/age classes as found in the regular public or private schools were artificial bureaucratic contrivances that did not adequately prepare children for the real world. These parents preferred the multi-age, familial, community, church, and other intergenerational social and educational experiences made possible through home schooling, over the sort-and-select, lock-step groupings of traditional public or private schools."[6]

Religious families explain their reasons for choosing home schooling in various ways, but a common theme—their desire to keep government influence out of their family life—surfaces as the principal reason for choosing to home school their children. One parent explains:

> I am raising my kids the way I want to raise them, not the way government-run schools think I should. And that's the biggest thing. See, children are individuals, you put them in a classroom, and the teacher spends the first three weeks trying to figure out where everyone is and then you try to find a middle ground. And you try to work a little with the lower kids and you try to give the higher kids a little extra, but you are really working at the middle ground and trying to cover as many kids as you can. Well, my kids are all different. They are not in the middle. All six of them are all so different in the way they take in things. My son who is eleven is an incredible communicator, while my daughter who doesn't yak in my ear all the time, she concerns me because she is not a communicator.
>
> See, people don't get to agree with what I believe is right for my children, because I brought them into this world, I went through the labor pains. No

government entity feeds them. We totally support them. And I believe it's
my right to pass on the values that I believe.

Another parent shares a similar sentiment:

> I would say that my main reason [for joining VCS], was for religious rea-
> sons, plus the other things, together [referring to materials and services] . . .
> I have a very protective view of my children in that I don't want them, es-
> pecially at a younger age, having that constant, day-in-and-day-out, secu-
> lar, humanistic viewpoint. But at the same time I try to educate them in
> what's out there so that they are discerning. So I am not an isolationist,
> where I pull them in and keep them innocent of all the things of the world.
> That is not my personal viewpoint, so . . . different Christians take it from
> different views.

A look at the students' learning records reveals the use of religious materials in daily instruction, illustrating the private freedoms that families are
allowed to preserve as members of a public home schooling program.
Learning record samples, provided to new families in a VCS informational
how-to guide, show how parents can integrate Bible reading and devotions
in their daily curriculum. The reference guide indicates that the models
"were selected to demonstrate the variety of record keeping and reporting at
different grade level groups which we believe satisfy the purpose of the
learning records."[7] Parents freely include such items as "write and read Luke
1:37, memorize Luke 1:37, prayer journal" as lesson plans in learning records. Interestingly, the models are prefaced by an explanation of the importance of learning records:

> Monthly Learning Records are required for all students enrolled in the Val-
> ley Charter School. These records are our official record of work completed
> so that you and your grade level coordinator can track your child's progress
> throughout the year. The Learning Records are also your attendance report.
> Our funding is generated from our attendance count, so without your com-
> pleted records we do not receive funds for your child: thus we will not have
> the money to continue the comprehensive program we now offer.[8]

In essence, parents' private choice to use religious materials in their children's daily lessons is validated by VCS's sample learning records. Thus VCS
parents are encouraged to engage in their private family choices at public
expense.

The Libertarian Minority

VCS also serves a small sector of nonreligious families, mostly from the VCS annex located in the San Francisco Bay Area. Many of these families, steeped in the region's counterculture traditions, describe themselves as "civil libertarians." Like the religious home schooling families in the Central Valley, the libertarian home schoolers also have strong parent networks that have provided peer support for home schooling. While they don't have the religious convictions of the valley's VCS families, these libertarian families are similar in that they resist governmental intrusion in their private lives and their children's education. One parent explains: "I want to keep all government influence out of my children's lives. I don't want them influenced by what the public schools are teaching them. They are individuals and need to be taught by me to be individual thinkers, rather than by state officials."

The libertarian families, like the religious ones, enjoy the benefits of being able to educate their children privately through public means. One parent talked about how he overcame his initial reluctance to join VCS when he realized the freedom the school offered his family: "Well, I guess at the time we still had pretty libertarian—way at the end of the libertarian spectrum—kinds of ideas that we wanted to do this ourselves. So there was a bit of feeling that to enroll in a program [a public program] was going to be somehow limiting. But that idea was offset by the way the program was represented, which was that it was in no way limiting, or only to the extent that you need to document doing work on certain subject areas."

By enabling families to continue privately educating their children while offering them a wealth of materials and services, VCS has managed to enroll en masse the two kinds of families—libertarians and religious conservatives—that most characterize the private home school movement.

At first glance, it seems highly ironic that families with strong sentiments against government institutions and their influence would affiliate with a public charter school such as VCS. The irony, however, may be only superficial. While these families may appear to be moving toward more centralized, state-sponsored schooling, they are not required to relinquish any of their freedoms. In fact, VCS seems to be strengthening their commitment to home schooling by providing them with a powerful community network, in addition to field trips, classes, learning materials, and instructional support. Thus, it seems that private schooling choices and autonomy are actually being reinforced and even expanded through the offerings of a public school system.

Who Is Accountable?

In return for the freedom to operate unencumbered by state regulations, charter schools are obligated to account for their finances and the educational progress of students. California's charter school legislation specifies that schools are to be held "accountable for meeting measurable pupil outcomes" and provides as an intent that schools will "change from rule-based to performance-based accountability systems."[9] However, the California legislation is vague in terms of specifying accountability measures. While charter petitions must clearly state student performance standards and indicate the methods schools will employ to measure student outcomes, the legislation makes no recommendations as to what constitutes an acceptable accountability mechanism.[10]

The vagueness is perhaps understandable in light of the fact that lawmakers wanted to grant as much discretion to charter schools as possible. Nevertheless, the lack of specificity can result in confusion, especially in the case of home charter schools like VCS, where parents are the primary educators and the school provides only supplementary lessons and materials. Who at a school like VCS is ultimately accountable for student learning? What measurements of student achievement should be used? And—perhaps the most important question—is it even possible for a school operating in such a highly autonomous environment to be truly accountable for student outcomes?

The question of who is ultimately accountable for student performance at VCS has resulted in different and sometimes ambiguous answers. District governing board members claim "the parents are accountable to the school" and that the board is "ultimately responsible for the charter school." However, the fact that parents at VCS are clearly intended to be the primary instructors suggests that they—and they alone—are accountable for student performance. This is how the parents appear to see it. When asked who they felt was accountable for student performance, one parent enthusiastically responded, "We are! Oh totally! I see their [the teachers'] role as supporting me in any way that they can, and that's it. That's how I see it. I don't see it as them being responsible for my children as far as what they learn or what they don't. It's my job!" Another said, "Does Valley think they're accountable for my kids learning the scientific method? Does the state think Valley is accountable? I don't want them to—I'm the teacher!"

Teachers agree that primary instruction is the parent's responsibility. As education coordinators, they believe they are limited to consulting and administrative roles. Their job is to aid families, provide teaching advice, evaluate each student's progress by reviewing monthly learning records, and help families only when called upon.

Aware that their unorthodox school can attract scrutiny by outside observers, VCS staff have worked hard to create a system of accountability—for the sake of appearances if nothing else. Stevens explains, "We have to work harder in a charter school to have all of our records correct because we're going to be looked at under a microscope." To address the issue of accountability for student outcomes, and to meet both the legislative requirements and the original school goals described in the charter petition, VCS has developed its own curriculum standards. Progress toward these standards is determined in four primary ways: through standardized tests, learning records, math work samples, and writing work samples.

Standardized Tests

In 1997 California adopted the Stanford 9 as the new state assessment tool.[11] Prior to its implementation, VCS had chosen to use the California Test of Basic Skills (CTBS) to assess student performance. Because many home school families have had no prior experience with standardized tests and are unfamiliar with their structure and purpose, VCS informs parents that the tests are not a requirement.[12] Although most parents choose to participate, some decline. Said one: "Would I test for myself? No, I would not have them take standardized tests for myself. You don't need to. Somebody the other day was talking about tests, and I said, 'Well, a test is when you need to know where they are. Well, they're at my kitchen table. I know where they are.' I don't need the test."

Regardless of some parents' resistance to the test, VCS staff is proud of its student test results and mentions them in every conversation about the school. In 1997, the test was administered to all students in fourth through eighth grade.[13] The test was administered not by parents but by proctors in five test centers. The student results—in spite of the staff's enthusiasm—were not particularly impressive. Grades four, seven, and eight scored at the national average in all subject areas, and grades five and six scored slightly below. But in comparison to their traditional public school counterparts in the Valley Unified School District, the home school students did score slightly higher.

Learning Records

VCS requires that parents submit monthly learning records for each student. A learning record should include an outline of monthly learning goals in each subject, a comprehensive list of assignments that students have completed, and work samples either as chosen by the parent or requested by a teacher. Every month teachers are to evaluate each student's learning records in order to document progress. As described in the VCS *Annual Evaluation Report* for 1997, "A review of work samples and/or lesson plans by an education coordinator forms a foundation for further collaboration with parents. In order to keep this system manageable, one curriculum area is chosen each month for student work submissions."[14] Learning records are also used for attendance purposes, as the number of days of school per year is reflected in the daily lesson plans.

Parents share mixed feelings about the documentation that is required of them, but they also realize that it's a small price to pay for the abundance of materials and services they receive from VCS. As one says, "I hate the records. They drive me crazy. I am not against them. I know Valley is responsible for this. They have taken a lot of responsibility for this. And they need these records for attendance and funding, and to make sure that we are a functioning home schooling program. So I don't have an attitude problem with it, but I just hate doing it."

Work Samples

Math and writing work samples, used as an informal assessment tool, are collected and compiled in a student portfolio. Math samples are classified according to the seven math strands outlined in the California Mathematics Framework; an evaluation of the samples indicates which math areas need further development. Writing samples are graded using a five-point rubric; to track progress, scores from September samples are compared with scores from April samples.

As these evaluation systems suggest, VCS has adopted fairly traditional measures of accountability. Perhaps this isn't surprising, given that most characteristics of the VCS educational program are strikingly similar to traditional schools. The curriculum materials that fill the annexes are similar to the prepackaged materials found at most schools. The learning records and lesson plans submitted by parents, filled with didactic activities and lessons structured according to a textbook, mimic those found on the desks of most teachers. Formal classes are offered to students, and all VCS teachers are credentialed. The school also urges parents to participate in standardized testing of their children. And it sponsors field trips and other extracurricular activities, such as choir, band, and spelling bees.

Why do home schooling parents, who have described much of traditional schooling as "artificial bureaucratic contrivances," import certain qualities and norms from highly structured traditional classrooms into their own home? Perhaps the VCS staff and parents have chosen to adopt rituals common in traditional schools because they are aware that publicly funded home schooling is potentially controversial. Making the school look and operate very much like a traditional school may buy legitimacy from critics who might otherwise frown on such a school. I will return to this subject in the final section of the chapter.

Before we move on from the subject of accountability, it is important to consider the negotiated contractual agreements that VCS originally made with the district. In return for agreeing to sponsor the VCS charter and for reimbursement of the initial $250,000 given to VCS for start-up costs, the district required VCS to surrender 15 percent of its average daily attendance funding to the district's general budget. Today, after five years of operation, VCS continues to surrender 15 percent of student ADA moneys. VCS justifies the payments as fees for a contracted service agreement that buys VCS certain services, such as a psychologist, speech therapist, and resource specialists. These negotiated agreements are potentially troubling because they give the sponsoring board—which is ultimately accountable for VCS—a financial incentive to find the charter school effective.[15]

The Home School Movement Fractures

As news of charters like VCS has spread and attracted more and more recruits from church cover schools, antagonism toward home school charter schools has continued to escalate among traditional home schoolers. This has caused a divide among home school families. As previously described, 70 percent of VCS families are former private home schoolers, and about half teach their children at home for reasons associated with religious conviction. According to Ms. Bancroft, a director of a local private cover school, families that affiliate with a state-sponsored home school charter are in essence allowing government to reenter their life. She states:

> For me it would be hypocritical to go back into a public system. And I have to live by what I feel is right. But I know a lot of families that feel it is OK to do that—but I do not want to be the one to pronounce judgment on them or condemn them for what they're doing in their charter, because ultimately they are the ones who are responsible for their children, for their own conscience. You know it bugs me a little because of my own conviction, but I have to have grace for those who don't [share] our values.

Bancroft's wariness toward the Christian families that have entered home school charters is apparent:

> I feel there is a new breed that is cropping up. You go back ten, twelve, twenty years ago, and those people did [home schooling] because of conviction, religious conviction. They said, "We have reasons, and we are doing it at any cost—we are home schooling, period." In those days there was no charter, you had to go underground and hide out somewhere. It wasn't popular, and they were not sure if it was legal. They did not have attorneys like the Home School Legal Defense Association, they did not have lobbyists like Roy Hanson, they did not have a statewide network like CHEA [Christian Home Educators Association], they did not have all these people to assure them that what they are doing is legal and say, "We are here to back you up if you get in any trouble." So back then it was like, "I am just going to [fade into] the woodwork." Well now it has developed into a movement—it's like, "I am not afraid now, I am going to do it regardless of what anybody says because I know my rights." And now you have the new charter culture that has come out of that, and they are saying, "Well I want my cake and eat it too. I am tired of suffering. I am tired of paying it twice. I am going to do it."

Family networks that have traditionally supported home school families share this wariness. Organizations like Christian Home Educators Association are taking action against families that affiliate with home school charters. Bancroft, a member of CHEA, explains that such families have relinquished any chance of assuming leadership positions in the organization: "If I had a support group and I was in a charter and I wanted to do a home school support group for those charter families, I would not be eligible under the CHEA guidelines because I am affiliated with a charter."

A parent formally affiliated with a private cover school and now a member of VCS describes the stance that CHEA took against her family: "They will not allow Christians of the charter school now to participate in conventions or their workshops . . . [W]e belonged to a [private] home school choir, and we found out after being there for a year that they did not want charter school students in there. That is real sad to me."

Indeed, an exclusionary stance is favored by many private home schoolers. A leader of a local parent home school network based in Sacramento and sanctioned by CHEA says this of the position her organization has taken against home schooling parents affiliated with a public home school:

> We have lost a lot of people that have, in the past, been affiliated with our network but, because of the charter issue, have chosen to move on. And just because they go to a charter does not necessarily mean that they stop subscribing. We have to this point allowed them [to be members]. They're still parent educators. There's no harm in that. But if you're in a charter, you can't be our leaders . . . we changed our bylaws so that leaders could not be affiliated with the public school system in any way. We don't separate out just charter. It's not just charter. You cannot be involved with the public school system and be in leadership.

These concerns are shared by private home schoolers almost everywhere. National home school organizations like the Home School Legal Defense Association take a similar attitude. Its memos published in the newsletters of local home schooling networks explicitly outline how home schoolers affiliated with public institutions will not be eligible for their legal and support services.

Former private home schoolers now affiliated with VCS express anger against the very organizations that once supported them as private home schoolers. A parent formerly affiliated with a private cover school says: "I finally quit taking her newsletter [referring to the director of a local private cover school] because she just had so many articles in there against the charter schools. We were with Valley ISP at the time that they changed into a charter school, and I was going to activities with Apple Valley [the cover school], and all these Apple Valley moms were talking and they were all, 'Can you believe the charter school is going to take everyone away?'"

The same parent explains how the position of private cover schools stems from their fear of government interference: "Some people felt that by more people joining a public institution that's going to cause those that like being free to stand out . . . to be targeted. In other words, when there [are] so many, chances are you are not going to get your file pulled, you know, for someone [government official] to come and check you out. But when there [are] more and more involved in a government institution, there is a fear that those that choose not to do that are going to be flagged."

Libertarian home schoolers in the San Francisco Bay Area have experienced a similar divide in their home school community with the opening of the VCS annex. As VCS gained popularity in the Bay Area among home school families, increasing numbers of families abandoned the traditional support networks and affiliated with the charter. Private network organizers became furious, feeling that VCS was in essence co-opting the grassroots home school movement they had created in their community. A parent in a local private home schooling network put it this way:

> We used to all do things together. See, we had all these classes that volunteers from our community would offer. Then what happened was when VCS came in, VCS said they'd pay for these classes for VCS people. So they took these classes and made them VCS classes that used to be our community classes. Then there weren't enough independents [private home schoolers] left to make more classes for independent people. So a lot of stuff that our community had done for each other got taken. That is the most distressing thing. It hurt our group quite a bit, our support group, you know.

VCS affected the network's membership significantly, explained another parent: "We used to have eighty subscribers. We're down in the fifties now. People aren't renewing. They have their VCS stuff or whatever and, yeah, you get a few new people in but it doesn't make up for what you've lost. I have the list of people who didn't resubscribe and many of them are VCS . . . it's made a large impact on our support community."

Strange Bedfellows against Government

As state-sponsored home school charters grow, traditional home schoolers fear the rise of government involvement in what has historically been a completely unregulated environment. Traditional home school families feel the privacy that they have always enjoyed is threatened by the government. Parents from the Sacramento home educators group passionately voice their concern over the potential threat that public home schools pose to their freedom as private home schoolers. One says:

> Our voice is being diluted by the charter. That's what our fear is, because we have had this freedom and we cherish it. We had to fight for it somewhat in the beginning, at least I did. And I just want my grandchildren to be home schooled as my children were, in total freedom. And our voice is diluted. Now we have people whose curriculum is being funded by the government. And at some point, you know, the government is going to cause more and more restrictions; they're going to tighten the noose; they're going to ask for more accountability; they're going to be in their homes more. And then they're going to say to us, in private home schooling, "They do it. You're going to have to do it too. We need to govern them, so we need to govern you as well." And we renegades will never submit to that.

Bancroft, the cover school operator, echoes the concern:

> If the government schools take off in this magnitude it's going to pose a threat to the private sector. And it certainly has. We have districts that, seven years ago, they wouldn't check our transcripts from high school, they would take them at face value, no problem, they would just take [them]. They would accept our transcripts without any question. And now because their district has a charter they are saying, "Oh no, we are not taking anyone's [private] home school credits anymore."

And this dismay is shared by traditional libertarian home school networks in the Bay Area. An active member of a parent network elaborates:

> We're concerned about our freedoms being whittled away very slowly, and it's very easy to chew chunks until eventually they would have a lot more control than any of us are willing to give up. I'm afraid of the state trying to take control. I know they want to. I know California would be a great state for them to take . . . I am not convinced that they have a master plan, but it wouldn't surprise me.
>
> It's so important to me and to a lot of people I know who have this independence, have this freedom. We have such a free state, we're very lucky. And we can't just give it away . . . I'm convinced that when push comes to shove it's the R-4 affidavit [which registers a home as a private school] you fight for, whether you use it or not, because that's our freedom, period.

Recognizing the potential threat of government regulation of private home schooling, libertarian home school families find themselves in an

ideological alliance with conservative Christians. This is a case of odd bedfellows indeed. As one libertarian explains:

> I'm afraid the state would like to control us; they would love to control us.
> They're against home schooling with the R-4, the higher bureaucrats; they
> think it's illegal. And they are trying to figure out how to close it up. The
> only reason they haven't yet is because we have the Christians on our
> side . . .
>
> Yeah, you know, if they try to change any wording on that [the R-4
> affidavit], I'm telling you, they will get inundated with calls from the Chris-
> tians. This is important to the Christians. This is where the Christians and
> people like me come together. The Christians don't want the state involved
> with their schooling either.
>
> Home schooling is the common thread that holds folks like me and the
> Christians together . . . and there's nothing else that holds us together. And
> there's no way people like me would be able to maintain this freedom with-
> out them. So I'm glad we're on the same side.

As the popularity of home school charters increases, the larger home
school movement—which has long been insulated from mainstream influences—is gaining legitimacy as a schooling alternative. The traditional parent networks and organizations that have played an integral part in the success of home schooling are now faced with challenges in representing home
school parents who have different values and beliefs. Hence a paradox has
emerged. Charter home schoolers, by aligning themselves with public authorities, are bringing a new legitimacy to the movement. New families are
being introduced to what was once a fringe educational alternative and is
now becoming more mainstream. Yet traditional home schoolers, as their
movement gains momentum, feel that their freedom and autonomy are being threatened. Eventually they must decide whether to support the large
and diverse group of families that now embrace home schooling or to confront the government forces that potentially threaten their independence.

Does the State Have a Legitimate Interest in Home Schooling?

In light of the current conflict between the traditional home school movement and the new publicly funded home school charter movement, it is important to discuss the state's interest in sponsoring home schooling. As I
have described, there is fear among traditional home school families that the
influx of home school charters may pose a threat to the autonomy they en-

joy, leading to eventual state regulation of home schooling. However, it is not clear that the state has an interest in placing these families under its jurisdiction, or even that the state has a genuine interest in sponsoring home schooling at all.

The Purists' Political Views

Traditional home schoolers accuse the state of craftily carving a small market niche among the home school movement, thereby laying a foundation for eventually bringing all home school families under the scrutiny of the public authority. One purist put it this way: "I believe that the government is willing to put out a lot of money at the onset for this home schooling thing, but eventually they're going to push people back into the mainstream of regular school. We see it as an investment. They're looking at it as an investment. 'First we get them into the charter school and then start putting in more and more regulation, and pretty soon they're back into the regular schools. Now we got them where we want them.'"

Traditional home schoolers see public school officials as working quietly behind the scenes, building a kind of imperialistic monopoly over all models of education, including home schooling. They fear their numbers will dwindle as fellow home schoolers choose public home school options, jeopardizing the solidarity of a once cohesive grassroots movement. Nevertheless, the traditional home schoolers go on with the business of educating their children, trying to cast aside their fear of state regulation.

The concerns of traditional home school families may not be unfounded, especially in light of recent changes made to California's charter school legislation. In 1998 a state ballot initiative known as the Hastings Initiative (Charter Schools Act of 1998) gained public approval and was slated to appear on the November ballot. Financed by Silicon Valley computer magnate Reed Hastings, the initiative was beset with controversy early on. It strove to place new regulations on charters even as it aimed to expand their numbers. Many charter proponents were concerned that stringent regulation would discourage people from creating more charter schools. Still, the initiative was supported, albeit with mixed feelings, by charter school supporters who welcomed the fact that it allowed for more schools. Within weeks of announcing the proposed initiative, volunteers collected nearly 1.2 million signatures from California citizens, nearly twice the number of signatures required for an initiative to reach the ballot.

The principal objective of the initiative's authors was to lift the original state-imposed cap of 100 charter schools, calling instead for an unlimited number of schools. The authors were concerned as well about the loose accountability mechanisms employed by the state and many charter schools. The initiative required all charter schools to "meet statewide pupil performance standards and conduct the pupil assessments required" of all other noncharter public schools.[16] Also, the initiative required charter school students to exceed the academic achievement of comparable noncharter public school students. Failure to show marked improvement would "result in the revocation of the school's charter."[17] Such new high-stakes requirements were contrary to the intent of the original 1992 charter school legislation, which allowed schools and their charter sponsors wide discretion in determining methods for ensuring pupil progress. The new initiative, moreover, required all charter school teachers to be certified or to show proof of progress toward certification. Lastly, the initiative specifically called for limitations on home schooling, stipulating that charter schools would not receive ADA funding unless primary instruction was provided in person by a certified teacher and employee of the school. This was a direct strike against the home school charter model.

News of the positive public response to the initiative quickly reached the state legislature, and in an unprecedented move, the legislature moved the initiative directly to the floor for debate. Most of the initiative's provisions were approved, including lifting the imposed cap on charter schools from 100 to 250 for the 1998–99 school year and allowing the creation of up to 100 more schools in years thereafter. Provisions requiring charter schools to participate in the state-adopted assessment program also passed, but lawmakers excluded the language stipulating marked achievement gains by charter school students. The legislators also eliminated the provisions that would have required primary instruction be given only in person by certified employees of a charter school. This ensured that the home school charter model could continue.[18]

Views of State Actors

From an economic perspective, a state interest in sponsoring home schooling seems to make little sense. The home school population has always paid taxes that fund public schools, yet their absence from public school enrollment rolls means that the state has not had to pay full ADA funds to districts. Why would the state want to educate home school students when the present situation is profitable?

Certainly by bringing traditional home school families under its jurisdiction, the state can lay claim to promoting the common good. If public schools are indeed founded on principles of democratic citizenship, and are intended to equip all students with the tools needed to be good citizens in our society, then the interest of the common good does weigh heavily against financial considerations—but perhaps not heavily enough, given the substantial investment the state would have to make to bring all home schoolers under its umbrella.

Could it be that the state does have a financial interest in charter home schools, contrary to appearance? The economic benefits the public education sector brings to the state's general economic well-being are an important return on the state's educational investment. Even though public schools are often shielded from the forces of private corporate interests, the public schools provide economic benefits for the entire state by providing such public- and private-sector agencies as teacher and employee labor unions, textbook and materials publishers, and construction and food service companies. Funding more public schools with state money could very well translate into a stronger state economy.

A Hazy Line between Public and Tribal Interests

In the context of Valley Charter School, where state ADA funds are drawn for fewer than 750 students whose educational needs are mostly served in the privacy of their own home, the economic benefits to the state seem insignificant. It hardly seems that the state is promoting the common good in the case of VCS.

Promoting the common good may be difficult, if not impossible, given the vague state legislation that has allowed VCS to operate in such an autonomous environment. It seems that VCS may be less the product of studied intent than of a decentralized state policy that has given communities a free hand to build locally shaped institutions. The result, in the case of VCS, is a strong collective of private home school families who abide by only the most minimal requirements, in the form of learning records. VCS home schooling families obviously are not recentralizing public authority. Instead, the already decentralized status of home school families is being reinforced with public support.

The state finds itself in a political transition, caught between abandoning traditional regulatory efforts to promote a common good and the demands of decentralized school-reform policies calling for local control of public

institutions. In an attempt to recast its authority in an era of fewer bureaucratic controls over schools, the state largely drops its pursuit of the common
good as public authority is devolved to local families.

At the local level, VCS has engaged in symbolic institution building
since its inception. While many charter schools are trying to invent innovative governance structures and curriculum programs, VCS has consciously
sought to look like a traditional school in many respects: adopting "boxed"
curricula as created by textbook publishers, offering structured classes to
home schooled children, and highlighting standardized test results. VCS's
constituents are cognizant of the stigma and lack of public legitimacy that
come with home schooling, and are trying to gain legitimacy by having their
network look somewhat like a traditional school.[19]

The strategy may be working, judging by the growing numbers of families
associated with the school and the growing popularity of the home schooling model. Some home school charters serve as many as 1,500 students,
drawing ADA funds for their entire student enrollment while providing little
accountability for student learning. Charter schools like VCS, it appears, will
continue to challenge state interests with the radically decentralized control
of quasi-public institutions.[20] Whether the private interests of local communities will prevail over the more diverse and democratic interests of the state
remains an open question.

CHAPTER 7

Teachers as Communitarians: A Charter School Cooperative in Minnesota

ERIC ROFES

When I was growing up in the 1960s in the suburbs of New York City, one of the memorable television commercials that frequently flashed before my eyes advertised canned vegetables from the Valley of the Jolly Green Giant. Nostalgically I recall a tall, green woodsman smiling on the screen as he spooned peas and carrots down his gullet.

Green Giant commercials created a homey picture of bucolic life in the Midwest: wholesome families, rural vistas of forests and farmland, and good, healthy food. My Avon lady mother bought Green Giant vegetables when we went food shopping at the A&P. She would tie on an apron and serve them piping hot from the stove during those frigid Northeast winters. I recall can upon can of peas, carrots, and mixed vegetables stacked on our kitchen shelves. When my father told us children, "Eat your vegetables," he was referring to one Green Giant product or another.

I am not sure whether in my boyhood I imagined there was an actual Valley of the Jolly Green Giant. I do know that I was stunned when, three decades later and an hour from Minneapolis, I spotted what appeared to be a green giant towering above the trees on the side of the highway as I entered the town of Le Sueur (population 3,763).

I was in Le Sueur to make my first visit to the Minnesota New Country School. On my drive down from the Twin Cities, I had passed plenty of John Deere tractors, grazing livestock, and red barns rising up from rolling fields—sights that had served to situate this part of southern Minnesota in familiar narratives of small-town life. The farmstands with local produce and the billboards bragging of home-style restaurants affirmed my city dweller's impression of the rural Midwest. I knew I wasn't far from Lake Wobegon and all the Lutherans and Norwegian bachelor farmers in tales spun by Garrison Keillor. Still, I was caught off guard when I suddenly came upon the Green Giant from my childhood, looming high overhead. I almost ran off the side of the road.

The town of Le Sueur is located seventy miles south of the Twin Cities amid the verdant farmland of the Minnesota River Valley. While downtown Le Sueur features several gas stations, a small shopping mall, the offices of the town newspaper, and a few government offices, its distinguishing feature is the abandoned Green Giant plant, consisting of numerous executive office buildings and a three-block-long canning and processing factory. The conspicuous nature of these vacant facilities makes it impossible to forget the town's recent economic decline. Le Sueur was battered not only by the farm crisis of the 1980s that had forced many farm families to the auction block, but also by a decade of corporate buyouts and reorganizations that ultimately resulted in the closure of the Green Giant facility and the loss of hundreds of jobs, many of them well-paying management positions.

When the closure came and Green Giant jobs were shifted out of state, Le Sueur lost a large portion of its middle class and overnight became primarily a blue-collar community. The town attempted to lure new companies into the area but succeeded only in attracting small manufacturing firms offering relatively low-paying jobs. As one local resident told me, "They got several small companies that paid fairly poor wages [to move into Le Sueur]. Nice companies, but you know, they don't pay what Green Giant paid. So you don't have any executives left in town. Even the people who came in here to run the companies don't live here. There's been a lot of houses for sale. At one time there were ninety or more houses for sale, just a few years ago. That is something for people to handle."

A decade after Green Giant's withdrawal from Le Sueur, the public schools in the area began to show evidence of the departure of corporate executives' families. Test scores declined, alarming local residents and educators alike. Public school teachers accustomed to having significant numbers of children from well-educated, upscale families now faced the challenge of teaching large numbers of students from lower-middle-class, blue-collar, and poor families. Local residents no longer felt the same kind of pride in their schools, and some veteran teachers felt burdened by the different student population. It was in this context of economic decline, profound transformation in the rural farming community, and sagging spirits within the school district that the Minnesota New Country School (hereafter referred to as MNCS) and the EdVisions Cooperative were founded.

Communitarian Roots: If Teaching Were Organized Like Farming

Charter schools frequently have been promoted as offering new opportunities for innovation within public education.[1] Yet while charter advocates sometimes refer hopefully to the flourishing of new kinds of pedagogy and curricula, they rarely discuss issues of school governance. If charters are intended to shift power and responsibility from a centralized authority to the local school site, thereby allowing for innovation, it would make sense that they adopt forms of governance congruent with their local community.

For more than a century farm life in the Upper Midwest has been heavily influenced by the cooperative movement, a mode of organization with a long history in America that today is stronger than many realize:

> The history of democratic economic enterprise reaches far back into American history. Formally organized cooperatives, such as mutual fire insurance societies, date back to colonial times. Informal cooperative action pervades our early history in the form of barn raising, threshing bees and the mutually supportive activities of neighborhood, town and village life. But the tradition is much broader than most people realize—well beyond farmers and food consumers, to include people with disabilities and local governments, neighborhood organizations and hardware store wholesalers, all together claiming a membership of 100 million Americans.[2]

Beginning in the mid-nineteenth century, farmers throughout Iowa, Wisconsin, Minnesota, Nebraska, and the Dakotas banded together in producer and consumer cooperatives to protect their interests amid the dramatic economic shifts of the time.[3] They wanted to retain their independence from the new corporate entities that were beginning to dominate the American economy, while still remaining competitive. This meant they had to find new ways of structuring their agricultural enterprises in order to purchase what they needed at the best possible price and sell their products at a profit. Professor Brett Fairbairn of the Centre for the Study of Cooperatives at the University of Saskatchewan links upswings of cooperative activity with the need to respond to economic upheavals: "You could say that all cooperatives have their origins as responses by people to economic restructuring. I've argued elsewhere that the free trade liberalism of the 1860s, which helped spread industrial change, made up a first round of what we now call 'globalization.'"[4]

Examples of the first rural credit co-op can be found in Germany in 1862, the first rural consumers association in Denmark in 1866.[5] Germans and Scandinavians were among the prime groups that emigrated to the Upper Midwest in the late 1800s, bringing with them experience and commitment to cooperative organizing.[6] This immigrant stock was but one of the factors that contributed to making this region a seedbed for cooperatives:

> While the region's people embrace the ideas handed down to all rural Americans by the Jeffersons and the Jacksons, the Northwest has a more narrowly defined culture that was shaped by immigrants, periods of settlement and development, distance from markets, and shared experiences on the frontier. It is a culture that found cooperatives to be a useful tool for development and problem solving in earlier years . . . Northwest residents inherited political approaches to problem solving from immigrant ancestors who settled on the frontier, and from Native Americans who were already there.[7]

A Charter Cooperative Rises

Dan Mott, an attorney who assisted in the founding of the EdVisions teacher cooperative, which designed MNCS's educational program, said that "the co-op concept really is pretty well entrenched in the Midwest. It tends to be focused on agriculture and utility co-ops, and a lot of people in the rural parts of the state are members of a co-op of one sort or another." He explained how co-ops have functioned historically:

> Typically, the co-ops in the Midwest are either supply cooperatives or marketing cooperatives, and what they're doing is taking a grower's product and marketing it on their behalf, or collectively purchasing a service or a product and selling it to the farmers at a reduced cost . . . Historically it was a way for small people—in terms of the scope of their economics—to band together to compete more effectively with larger organizations . . . The people who own it are the ones who use it. And to the extent the co-op makes money, the money is distributed back to the members.

Nadeau and Thompson, in a book on the cooperative revival in America in the late twentieth century, offer a useful explanation of the contemporary function of cooperatives:

A cooperative (or co-op) is a business owned and controlled by the people who use its services. All co-ops share four additional features:

- Service at cost. This means that co-ops are not designed to maximize profits, but rather to provide goods and services to members at a reasonable price.
- Benefits proportional to use. Unlike for-profit businesses, co-ops distribute profits to member-owners on the basis of the amount of business transacted with the co-op during the year rather than the amount of capital invested in the co-op.
- Democratic control. In most cooperatives and credit unions, each member has one vote in the decision-making regardless of the number of shares owned or the amount of business done with the co-op.
- Limited return on equity. People buy equity in co-ops not to make a lot of money on their investments, but rather to enable the co-op to provide the products or services they want. They may get a return on their investment . . . but these dividends are a secondary issue.[8]

Ted Kolderie, a St. Paul–based policy analyst who helped craft Minnesota's innovative charter school law, was visited by MNCS founders during the school's formative phase. Familiar with the cooperative concept from his own midwestern roots, he suggested they consider the co-op model as a way to bring about a shift in the teacher's role from employee-worker to owner. Kolderie explained, "Farmers tend to be owners, and the benefits of productivity always go to the owners, so it's fine when the worker is the owner, owner is the worker. But in the Industrial Era, when the work and ownership [are] separated, the owners who are not the workers take the profits, take the productivity gains, so workers have to organize and strike, trying to fight for their share of the productivity gains to which their labor has contributed."

Kolderie encouraged this small group of educators, farmers, and small business owners to experiment with cooperatives to realize a vision of teacher-owner rather than teacher-worker:

What would happen if teaching were organized like farming? Well you begin to think about what happened to productivity in farming in the nineteenth century, I mean the rate at which the worker-owner took up the machinery that was produced, the crops, the materials, the better methods . . . you look at the whole structure that we put out there through the county agents, and a system to show them how to do better. The worker-owner farmers couldn't just wait to do better. It's what Seymour Sarason calls a self-improving system. You became richer and your labor became easier at the same time. You worked less and you earned more.

Kolderie's suggestion resonated with the MNCS founders and seemed to offer an especially valuable tool in the aftermath of the bankruptcies and decimation suffered by farmers during the preceding decade. After all, the Le Sueur schools had endured a similar crisis in the economic downturn induced by the loss of Green Giant and the subsequent consolidation with a neighboring district. They became determined to draw on the strengths of the cooperative model in establishing their new school. Operating in isolation, and with the example of only one or two other educational ventures in the United States aimed at achieving an authentically cooperative approach to governance, MNCS has broken new ground that merits examination.[9] A close relationship has emerged during the school's first five years between the EdVisions teaching cooperative, which owns the educational program of the school, and the farming cooperative model, with the former repeatedly drawing on the hard-learned lessons of the latter.

At times, it's hard to tease out the differences between the EdVisions teaching cooperative and MNCS—they're a bit like twin brothers engaged in a wrestling match. While the vision for MNCS came before the formation of EdVisions, the teacher cooperative was formed in concert with the formal institutionalization of MNCS. From the start, EdVisions was seen as the creative brain trust out of which MNCS—along with other local educational ventures—would grow. Thus, while the educators in EdVisions shaped much of MNCS's educational program, the school itself was overseen and administered by the MNCS board, which was officially granted the school's charter.

Hence, MNCS has been organized in a unique manner: while the board of directors of the school is vested with oversight responsibility for the school, they have contracted out the total educational program of the school to a cooperative of local educators. MNCS was chartered by the Le Sueur–Henderson school board in November 1993, and it opened in September 1994 as a school of seventy-five students in grades seven through twelve. Since its opening, the unique educational program of the school has been featured in local newspapers and journalistic case studies as an example of an innovative, alternative approach to traditional secondary school.[10] The complex relationship between this charter school and reform activity in the local district schools has been documented in detail.[11] Significant local and national media attention has been directed toward a group of MNCS students whose discovery of large numbers of deformed frogs triggered action on the part of the Minnesota legislature and won them an award for being environmental heroes from the Minnesota Wilderness and Parks Coalition. They even appeared on ABC-TV's *Nightline*.[12]

Yet little attention has been focused on the school's uncommon structure of governance, perhaps its most radical departure from other American schools, whether public, private, or charter. While scholars and educational policymakers have examined the possible blurring of public and private distinctions at some charter schools, and the private management of charter schools has become a point of controversy for journalists, state policymakers, and teachers' unions, few have discussed privatization in the form of a teachers' cooperative owning the educational program of a school.[13] At MNCS, the for-profit cooperative conceptualizes, designs, and implements the entire educational program; hires and evaluates the school staff; plans the budget for the school's educational program, and is responsible for all of the school's day-to-day operations. In short, how does human-scale democracy drive innovative pedagogical practices?

In a bold attempt to rethink teacher identity and teachers' work, the governance structure was designed to afford teachers the opportunity to function as professionals, entrepreneurs, and owners of their work. In the Minnesota River Valley, sugar beet growers have organized themselves cooperatively to sell their beets, and farmers throughout Minnesota, Wisconsin, and other midwestern states have organized themselves cooperatively to own grain elevators, so why shouldn't teachers organize themselves cooperatively to develop, implement, and own the educational program of a school?

This case study of the MNCS suggests that the true potential for innovation emerging from charter schools may lie in the potential to meld local traditions and community-specific forms of organization with public schooling. The Le Sueur–Henderson school district stands as a powerful example of one way in which the charter school initiative may harness the energy and talents of local community members to reenvision how schooling may be organized and delivered. Drawing lessons from ways in which farming has been structured in the Upper Midwest for more than a century, the founders of MNCS and EdVisions not only have initiated a form of school governance that has the potential to complicate, perhaps even shift, debates on privatization, but they've also designed a school where the process of teaching and learning itself resonates with the same agrarian traditions of innovation and self-sufficiency.

Furthermore, the fascinating developments I observed at this school went beyond an innovative form of school governance: as we'll see, teacher identity, student work, and classroom life have all been reconceptualized through the lens of agrarian cooperatives.

A Local Business Provides a New Opportunity

The economic shifts in Le Sueur during the 1980s had a profound impact on the local schools. As noted earlier, the district lost a large number of its higher-paying jobs; a main source of the tax revenue that funded district schools also left with Green Giant. A rural district that had prided itself on its schools and had created a successful college preparatory program serving the children of Green Giant executives fell into decline. As the middle-class students moved elsewhere, and as farm family incomes dwindled, local educators faced a range of new challenges borne out of the shifting economics of the area: increasing numbers of students from unemployed and underemployed families and families on welfare; a fall-off of academically motivated students seeking a college-prep track; increasing numbers of dropouts and incidents of school violence.

Rural districts experiencing dramatic socioeconomic shifts and an out-migration of residents often find themselves facing consolidation. Governmental authorities—ever concerned with the fiscal bottom line and the ability to capture economies of scale—see small rural schools as financially inefficient and often argue that students are best served by transferring to larger schools. It was during such a moment of district consolidation that the seeds of MNCS were sown.

Henderson (population 750) is located a few miles down the Minnesota River from Le Sueur. In the early 1990s, when the state of Minnesota began a process of merging the two districts, resistance emerged. Lost in the shuffle of transferring students, teachers, and programs from one school to another was a unique partnership Henderson High School had forged with a small technology-oriented business. Because Henderson High School had plenty of empty rooms, it had leased vacant office space to the company. In turn, the company provided computer time to the students. Thus the partnership provided students with the chance to gain a great deal of expertise in computers; it also allowed teachers to begin incorporating high-tech activities and working across disciplines. The small program had drawn its share of admirers among students and parents, and when the consolidation resulted in the separation of the high school students from the company, people began thinking of alternatives to giving up the program.

The New Country School Opens Its Doors

Hence out of the consolidation of Henderson and Le Sueur came the impetus to organize a new school. A group of parents and teachers who had learned of Minnesota's recent charter school law began to gather and discuss the possibility of opening a charter in their area. Other interested parties were drawn into the organizing efforts, and by the fall of 1992, an active planning committee had formed. This committee included several local teachers as well as interested parents and community members with strong ties to the land; several key members of the group had been farming in the area for generations.

The founders faced many of the challenges now documented as typical when a community group sets out to gain approval for a charter school. At that time, a hostile superintendent in the area barred the organizers from holding their organizational meetings in his district's schools. They also had to overcome a provision in the state's charter policy that explicitly prevented organizers from forming charter schools in response to consolidation. Those members of the organizing committee employed as teachers at Le Sueur High School sometimes had to face hostility from their peers and the disapprobation of the teachers' union. It took about two years of diligent work, deep disappointments, and school board rejection, but the charter planning group eventually won a charter from the Le Sueur–Henderson School Board, by a vote of six to one, in November of 1993. The state board of education endorsed the charter in January of 1994.

The school opened its doors the following September with seventy-five students and four teachers housed in two storefronts in downtown Le Sueur, one a former drugstore that had been closed for years and the other a bar and café that had shut down a year earlier. When an adjacent carpet store closed after MNCS's first year, the school expanded into that space as well. While such sites may be nontraditional spaces for a school, with their long countertops, sinks in odd places, and built-in cabinetry, oddly, they seemed to fit together nicely with the school's progressive and innovative educational philosophy. It seems appropriate that hanging over the front door was a sign saying, "It might not look like school, but it looks like learning."[14]

Teachers were recruited from the founding committee. Two of them were veterans of the Henderson schools. Another came to the group as a mentor teacher from a nearby university, Mankato State. And the fourth was a noncertified person who was the group's technology expert and who had worked at the small high-tech company that had been housed at Henderson High School. From the start, teachers at MNCS were known as "advisers," which reflected the shift in teacher identity that the charter wanted to highlight.

Strong Demand for a Progressive School

It wasn't hard to find students. The founders held a series of public information meetings in Le Sueur, Henderson, and other local towns that drew anywhere from six to twenty-five participants, often parents seeking alternatives for their children amid the limited options available in rural areas. The initial group of students entering the school included a fair number of "techies"—students eager for the computers and technology-rich curriculum the school promised. A fair number of home schoolers were drawn to MNCS because they welcomed the strong partnership the school aimed to establish between parents, student, and adviser. And an additional group of kids came from what one person called "free-spirit families"—folks seeking open classrooms, free schools, or other alternative models for educating their kids. The school had little trouble finding an adequate number of students, who were then funneled not into rigid age-based slots, but into two simple cohort groups: Level I (generally grades seven through nine) and Level II (grades ten through twelve).

The school's admissions guidelines make it clear that, while the educational program of the school fulfills the Minnesota graduation standards, MNCS "provides a rigorous educational program within a flexible setting and structure," and that it seeks students who are motivated to learn in an informal setting. Yet the school, from its very inception, was straightforward about both its achievements and its shortcomings. After the charter's first year, the founders issued a Foxfire-like compendium of what they'd learned, which included a list entitled "Things That We Found Have Not Worked Well." The two items at the top of this list:

- Students who do not have self-motivation still do not become motivated to do well! Some still refuse to try to fulfill the curriculum, even when they are given every opportunity.

- Students had a very difficult time adjusting to becoming the "worker" rather than the "receiver"! Many still wanted to sit back and let the teacher do the work.

Because of the school's progressive philosophy and flexible educational program, motivation appears key for MNCS students. They need to be self-starters. As one researcher has written, the structuring of time at this year-round school "is a flexible, evolving concept based upon student needs and tasks at hand. It [MNCS] operates more like a workplace than a school."[15] The five cornerstones of the school are technology, parent involvement, teacher-student accountability, community as a place to learn, and the nine "Essential Principles" developed by esteemed school reformer Theodore Sizer. These principles, which have been implemented at several hundred schools, are centered around the notion of "student as worker" and "teacher as coach."

MNCS stresses interdisciplinary learning as opposed to the methodical study of traditional subjects such as English and science. Students are encouraged to tackle topics that capture their imagination, drawing the academic skills and knowledge they need from across several disciplines. Each student at MNCS has a "personal learning plan" that is created, monitored, and evaluated in a partnership between student, teacher, and parents. Students gather daily in advisory groups (twenty students with one teacher) but then, after the meeting, take off in many different directions to pursue their own learning objectives. On any given day this might mean that small, structured groups of students focus on particular areas of inquiry while the majority of students head off to participate in community service work, project-based activities, and individual computer research.

The curriculum of the school does not consist of a neatly tied bundle of skills and knowledge to be mastered, as it does in most schools. It emerges, rather, out of specific learning benchmarks, dubbed "validations." These validations require that students exhibit proficiency in eight key areas: the arts, communications, earth systems, citizenship, mathematics, personal management, technology, and lifelong learning. These areas are cataloged in a volume aptly called "the bible," which students appear to consult frequently. While the Minnesota graduation standards inform the nature of these validations, staff members—as befits the independence and self-sufficiency of co-op members—make use of rubrics they've designed to set standards for each area of competency.

The students' success in meeting these standards is determined largely by portfolio evaluation—including the use of electronic portfolios, which all students are expected to maintain. Drawing on a long tradition in rural schools of exhibition evenings for parents and local community members, the school convenes a monthly Community Presentation Night at which students display and discuss completed projects, perform readings or concerts, and exhibit their research findings to gatherings that might approach one hundred people.

From its very inception the school has been an interesting mix of intensive individualized programming and strong collaborative learning, mirroring the culture of many worker co-ops. The school's emphasis on technology offers students endless opportunities for self-directed exploration on the Internet, where they gather information that they apply to a wide variety of learning areas. At the same time, students participate in community service projects, technology work-study projects in partnership with local businesses, school-to-work apprenticeships, and student-initiated entrepreneurial businesses.

The school's first four years saw a steady growth in students (from seventy-five to ninety-six) and advisers (from four to six, plus an aide). It also expanded its facilities and focused and clarified its educational programs. In addition to tackling the key issue of matching the school's need for highly motivated and self-directed students with its applicant pool, the school also initiated parent and student education on an ongoing basis. Despite the clarity with which the founders articulated their mission and the explicit discussion of the educational philosophy in the school's literature, MNCS has realized that its unorthodox approach to teaching and learning requires that school community members be trained in both the school curriculum and "the meaning of the validation process."[16] An intensive process of reeducation now helps ensure meaningful parent and student participation in developing individualized work plans.

Owners of a Cooperative, Not Employees of a School

As discussed earlier, the founders were determined to draw on the long history of midwestern cooperatives when they received their charter. The founders had three primary motivations for organizing the school's educational program through what became known as the EdVisions Cooperative: to ensure a formal organizational role for themselves so that the school would continue to build on their vision, to provide teachers with a professional identity and an ownership role in the new venture, and to avoid what some experienced as the negative aspects of traditional district-union relations.

Kim Borwege, a founder of the school who became one of MNCS's advisers, has worked at the school almost every day since its doors opened. She cited the desire to maintain the involvement of the entire founding team in the school during its early years. Borwege said, "There are a lot of people who were involved in the starting of the school, and they weren't all teachers. Yet their input into education, their interest is there. We needed their continued involvement and expertise."

Doug Thomas is one of the nonteaching members of the founding team Borwege referred to. A regional coordinator for the Center for School Change at the University of Minnesota and a former member of the Le Sueur–Henderson school board, Thomas had no interest in working at MNCS on a day-to-day basis, though he helped shape the school's philosophy. A co-op member since the inception of EdVisions, Thomas recalled that he thought forming the cooperative was a good idea because, as he said, "I was part of the original planning team, and I wanted to stay involved with the school."

The founders' reasons for their continued involvement seemed to be less about ego or personality or even maintaining collegial connections than about ensuring the continued purity of the school vision. They believed that new charter schools risked departing from their original vision if a way was not found to keep the founders meaningfully involved. Thomas said, "I think one of the downfalls with charter schools—at least from what I've seen—is that the original planners are often left out in the dark. When the school actually starts, they have no role. They don't have any kids in the school, and they don't run for the school board as a parent, and they're not teaching in the school. They're out of the loop. Yet they're the ones who have had the vision from the start."

In addition to wanting to sustain the school's original vision, the founders of EdVision wanted to encourage and enable teachers to reconceptualize their position in the education power structure. Thomas explained that once the founders were awarded a charter by the Le Sueur–Henderson school board, they took the time to consider a range of options for the school's governance and operations—an issue rarely considered at all by the founders of new charter schools who generally assume a narrow range of possibilities: "Once the original group got their sponsorship and we were thinking about ways to organize and ways to keep the group together, and the ways that teachers could be entrepreneurs as a part of this, in a sense, then we decided that one of the ways to organize was that the teachers would be the owners of the instructional program, and would contract with the charter school board."

John Schultz, an MNCS founder and the fiscal liaison and school planner during its first four years, summarized the difference between the organizational structure eventually adopted by MNCS's founders and that of teachers in the district's traditional schools: "We're all owners of a cooperative," he stated, "rather than employees of a school." Schultz insisted that a key part of the founders' decision to organize as a cooperative involved their insistence that teachers develop an identity *distinct* from that of district employee. They wanted teachers, or advisers, in their co-op to bring a new attitude to work: "It [the co-op] requires people to have a professional perspective on their work and on their organizational relationships. This is no different than what doctors, architects, engineers do—there is no difference."

Dan Mott, a St. Paul attorney who was recruited by the founders to create the legal documents that formed EdVisions, remembered that school founders were seeking to create a new kind of professional role for teachers. "Why is it that lawyers and doctors and accountants organize together as professional associations, but teachers simply work as employees for some school?" Mott asked. He pointed out that Minnesota maintains a "professional corporation statute" that allows licensed professionals such as architects, nurses, and lawyers to organize themselves into associations. Yet, amazingly enough, teachers had never been permitted to form such an association. Mott recalled the early conversations about organizing as a cooperative: "I think the people at New Country School liked the concept of it being a co-op. It sounded good. Out in the rural community, everybody knows what co-ops are. It's an accepted way of organizing a venture, and I think they liked that idea. It really fit the model for them to create a professional association using the co-op structure."

Mott practices in the area of co-op law with Doherty, Rumble, and Butler, one of the nation's leading law firms specializing in cooperatives. While in law school, he was legislative analyst to the chair of the K–12 finance division of the Minnesota senate education committee. Thus his expertise includes both co-op law and education policy. Mott supported the founders' interest in organizing as a co-op because, he said, "To me, it's a model for how you . . . professionalize teaching, by treating teachers as professionals. I think it gives them a chance to get out of the traditional mold."

A New Professional Identity for Teachers

Teachers at MNCS departed from the traditional mold in two ways: not only did they reject the circumscribed role of employee-worker but they also became fully fledged members of the EdVisions Cooperative, which allowed them to take on assignments for the cooperative beyond their daily work with MNCS. In a very real sense, they became educational entrepreneurs. As John Schultz said, "Educators don't just limit their vision to this locale, the site they are at. They realize there is a larger reality that they're part of and need to stay plugged in to and be active in . . . they're concerned that we have contracts with more than one place."

Linked to the desire to professionalize the role of teachers in the school was a parallel desire to circumvent unionization. Malcolm Maxwell, a retired farmer who served as chairman of the board of MNCS for three of its initial four years of operation and was the parent of an MNCS student, believed the cooperative offered an appealing alternative to a teacher's union. "Teachers feel they should be regarded as professionals, and I have no problem with a professional association," Maxwell stated emphatically. "But an association is quite different from a labor union."

Maxwell had served a term on the board of a local school district and during that time had become frustrated with the district bureaucracy:

I've somewhat felt that the traditional school system is not as cost-effective as it could be because of the many layers of management: superintendent, assistant superintendent, business manager . . . then there's the activities director, and a dean of students. All people who are drawing a larger salary than the classroom teacher, the person who actually does the work. Somebody's got to be the boss and I've very easily accepted that, but they don't have to have all of that huge stack there before the work gets done down here. And I feel considerable funds are wasted in that administrative stack up there that could be applied down here.

Maxwell said he felt MNCS has avoided what he sees as administrative waste by organizing as a cooperative. "What I have a problem with is the bureaucracy that the [district] engenders. That's my big problem. Here, we don't need the bureaucracy because we're small. The staff and people can sit down over a cup of coffee and hammer things out."

Maxwell's support for the cooperative model at MNCS existed in inverse proportion to his frustration with the traditional school bureaucracy. "Often the bureaucracy protects—and the union protects—incompetence and mediocrity. And that I don't like," he insisted. "Because in my industry—farming—the marketplace weeds us out of there in a hurry. If you don't measure up—pssssst!—you're gone." Indeed, Maxwell cited the marketplace model as key to the cooperative's success:

> The members of the cooperative are professionals—they are real teachers, and they know that they have to perform or there won't be anybody in their school. It's simple as that. It's a business, in a very real way. They realize that individually. At least some of the people even had businesses of their own. Dean was a farmer, he tried farming. The eighties came along, the farm depression of the eighties, and he was knocked out. He thought he'd try teaching again. That's fine. He understands that. Doug Thomas was in construction. He understands how to run a business.

Doug Thomas also spoke of the ways in which the cooperative offers a better alternative to a teachers' union, citing both the professional role teachers assume when they are owners rather than employees and the ability to avoid cumbersome district-union collective bargaining: "I think there is a genuine excitement about not having to go through the traditional patterns and negotiations and all of that crap. That is destructive to the whole educational process . . . In that old mode you're not really thinking about yourself as a professional, you're gonna wind up in a fight because you're just not on the same plane as the other side."

Attorney Mott argued that one of the unique features of the MNCS-EdVisions partnership is the impact it has on labor relations. "This is not the traditional employer-employee model," he mused. "What we're doing is not something that really is consistent at all with the labor movement or labor union concept." Mott went on to say: "Theoretically the members of a teacher association, teacher cooperative, could be members of a union, but I'm not sure why they would be. I mean they can't bargain with anybody, because they are it. They're setting their own direction in compensation, in dealing with their own policies on how you run your operation. So it changes pretty dramatically the employer-employee relationship. I don't know whether that's good, bad, or indifferent, but it is a very different model from what the traditional policymaker has looked at."

Dean Lind, a former farmer in the area and one of the school's current advisers, suggested that giving teachers more authority was the key to the cooperative model. Under that model teachers have "a lot more ownership" and the opportunity to share power in the day-to-day management of the school.

Likewise, Mott also saw shifts in teacher work, authority, and power as keys to the success of the cooperative structure:

> What you are really talking about is a group of teachers who have formed an association to provide services on a broader scale than one site, and they're doing it sort of in a collective model, where they decide, and they govern themselves, and they decide how they're going to operate, and how they're gonna divide up their compensation, and at the end of the day how they're going to share the profits . . . The exciting piece of this from the teachers' perspective is that it professionalizes what they're doing by saying, "We're not going to just be employees of a school anymore, we're going to try to develop a business that relates to teaching."

Thus the formation of the cooperative frequently was linked in the minds of its members with professionalization, autonomy, empowerment, and personal pride.

Three Political Players

MNCS derives much of its strength from its unique structure of governance, characterized by three key entities that all have a stake in the success of the school. These are the Le Sueur–Henderson School District, which chartered the school; the MNCS board of directors, which oversees the school; and the EdVisions Cooperative, which provides the educational program of the school. An "outcome-based school contract" between Le Sueur–Henderson School District and MNCS's board of directors serves as the school's charter and identifies the basic conditions under which the school operates. An "instructional services agreement" between MNCS's board of directors and EdVisions Cooperative sets out the conditions under which EdVisions will provide the school's curriculum development and educational services. The

Le Sueur–Henderson district contracts with the MNCS board, which, in turn, contracts with EdVisions for the day-to-day operation of the school.

The school district's role is primarily related to its chartering of MNCS and holding it accountable for key outcomes. While a vote of the Le Sueur–Henderson school board chartered MNCS, the Minnesota charter law ensures that the school is legally constituted with a status similar to that of a tiny, independent school district. While the charter's contract sets forth the purpose of the school ("improve pupil learning," "encourage the use of different and innovative teaching methods," "create new professional opportunities for teachers"), MNCS is granted exemptions from specific statutes and rules that apply to most traditional public schools. State laws that continue to apply include certain statutory requirements ("no tuition charges," "non-sectarian," "applicable state and local health and safety requirements"); admissions policies (student selection must be by lottery, and between 25 and 75 percent of the school must include residents of the district, with first-option availability given to parents of currently enrolled students); and financial considerations (the school must be revenue neutral in regard to the district).

Following Minnesota's charter law, the contract requires that the MNCS board of directors comprise a majority of teachers at the school and ensures that the remainder of the board be made up of current parents. The first contract was for a period of three years; in 1997 the school board voted six to one to renew the charter for an additional five years.

The job of the MNCS board is to maintain the legal status of the school by ensuring that the requirements of the contract with Le Sueur–Henderson are fulfilled. The board has generally maintained a membership of seven: three are parents of current students and four are teachers (advisers) at the school (and hence also members of the EdVisions Cooperative). The MNCS board meets monthly to consider broad policy and planning issues within its jurisdiction, while leaving everyday educational decisions to those at the school site. The board has seen its primary responsibility as contracting out the design and management of the educational program of the school and regularly evaluating the success of that contract. Hence the MNCS board has eschewed the traditional school board functions of employer and manager of day-to-day operations, instead becoming a contractor overseeing the school's general operations. This kind of change in board duties and responsibilities has been proposed for other district school boards in several recent scholarly works.[17]

Organizational Foundations

The EdVisions Cooperative is responsible for providing "all curriculum development and educational services" to MNCS students, according to the
services agreement between EdVisions and MNCS. This involves a range of
tasks that are usually assumed by boards of directors at other charter schools
and that are rarely contracted out by traditional school districts. EdVisions
hires, reviews, and retains or terminates the staff of MNCS, struggles with issues surrounding curriculum and student achievement, and crafts the rules,
rituals, and social processes that constitute everyday life at MNCS. In addition, EdVisions is also the seedbed for a range of educational ventures: conferences for educators, marketing of the MNCS curriculum, and the founding of new charter schools. The cooperative owns the instructional program
of the school; it is not the property of the MNCS board of directors.

The articles of incorporation of EdVisions spell out the specific purpose of
the cooperative: "The Association is organized as a cooperative association
by associating a number of education professionals for the purpose of providing employment and income to its members in a manner that will permit
them, individually and in concert with each other, on a cooperative basis, to
employ their skills, talents and resources for the development and implementation of instructional programs."

Educators involved with the cooperative are eligible to apply to become
voting members and hold a share of the association's common stock. Since
its inception, an average of about fifteen members have made up the co-op's
membership, in two distinct categories: full members and nonstockholder
members. Full membership entails the purchase of a share of stock at $100,
which grants voting privileges. Nonstockholder membership requires the
payment of a co-op fee of $25. The majority of members have been stock-
holders (full members); the nonstockholder members tend to be supporters
of the cooperative who live at a distance from Le Sueur. The cooperative
functions primarily through its executive committee, which handles day-to-
day operations and meets with the membership monthly to decide key policy issues.

Because EdVisions was started in part to ensure that the crafters of the
school's original vision would continue to serve as a resource to the school,
the cooperative includes nonteachers, some of whom have little or no day-
to-day involvement with the school. John Schultz, for instance, the president of the cooperative during its early years, is not a teacher and yet has

been a school administrator and a key visionary for the school's educational program. Another important feature of the cooperative is that it allows teachers to leave their day-to-day work in the school and still maintain a connection to the school's operation by remaining members of the cooperative.

While the co-op membership has remained stable at about fifteen members, with a few original members departing and new ones joining in, EdVisions was expecting to expand in the school's fifth year for the simple reason that it had to hire additional educators as it enlarged its student population. As it seeks out new members, MNCS must ensure that it recruits individuals who share the school's overarching commitment to teacher professionalization. As John Schultz noted, "If you're not interested in taking on a professional role, then don't do the co-op model, because it won't do you any good. This is a lot of hard work."

When asked about how they see their primary relationship to the EdVisions-MNCS partnership—are they members of the cooperative or teachers at the school?—EdVisions members' responses fell into two distinct categories. The first is exemplified by founder Doug Thomas, who was never a teacher at the school or formally involved in its day-to-day operations. Thomas responded to the question without a moment's consideration: "I'm definitely, definitely part of EdVisions. That is my only role here. I'm an interested adviser in the sense that I'm a member of the co-op. That's my only connection to the school, other than that I am on the sponsoring board [the Le Sueur–Henderson School Committee]. But as a sponsoring board member, I wouldn't be stopping down here once a week and talking to the teachers and the students or anything like that. That is a different role. I do that as a co-op member."

Thomas's identification as a co-op member was shared by the other nonteachers in the cooperative who were interviewed, including John Schultz, who worked half-time as the school's fiscal administrator and has been central in developing the educational vision for the school and cooperative.

Differing Models of Membership

Those cooperative members who actually work in the school identified with the charter enterprise in a much different way. For instance, teacher Kim

Borwege, who has been with school since it opened, identifies primarily with MNCS, not EdVisions.

> My first love is MNCS. That's where my heart is. When people say, "Where do you work?" I don't say I work for EdVisions. I always say I work at MNCS or that I work for the school. I don't think of it as "I work for EdVisions." To me, I work at the school, and this is my job . . . I will do whatever it takes to be where I am now, and to keep the school up and going. And EdVisions is second to me. Maybe that's not right, I don't know. But this is how I feel, because MNCS is my business. The co-op may or may not be there, but to me, if MNCS goes down, that's when I go down. I don't think, "If the co-op dies, then I'm done." Know what I mean?

At the close of my interview with Borwege, I asked, "Is there anything I haven't asked you today that you'd like to talk about, specifically about the co-op? Anything we haven't covered?" She promptly answered, "Not really. I don't think about the co-op much, you know? It's funny you should ask that."

It is understandable that MNCS teachers such as Borwege would identify with the school rather than with the coop. The cooperative, after all, was organized as an entrepreneurial association that would take on a variety of projects in addition to MNCS. MNCS was EdVisions' first project and was seen as becoming but one of several projects—perhaps several schools—that would capture the cooperative's time, energy, and creativity. Yet throughout the first four years, MNCS has been pretty much EdVisions' only project. The cooperative has organized a conference; sold its curriculum to eight schools in Pennsylvania, Michigan, and Minnesota; and applied (without success) to Minnesota's charter school network to provide professional development services. But the overwhelming thrust of the cooperative's work has been toward getting MNCS up and running.

This was expected to change dramatically in the school's fifth year. At the end of the period under study, members of the EdVisions Cooperative were laying the groundwork for substantial growth at MNCS, including a move into the school's own site in Henderson, an increase in student enrollment, and the opening of a satellite site in a unique partnership with a Hutterite community—a small, faith-based community located thirty miles west of Henderson. At the same time, members also anticipated moving the co-op's work beyond MNCS by signing contracts that would facilitate the development of additional charter schools in Minnesota. They have, in fact, a goal of developing two new rural charters each year.

Sustaining the Cooperative Spirit

This growth might bring about a change in another key area of interest to cooperative members: the fiscal bottom line. At the end of each year, the co-operative, as a for-profit association, is expected to divide up its surplus. In the school's first four years, the co-op avoided the potentially contentious process of division by not turning a profit. John Schultz explained:

> The fact that we haven't had to divide up the profit has been on purpose. We haven't sought to make any profit, but that is the direction we're start-ing to go into now, with the consulting we've been doing. Any extra mon-eys we've generated from selling curriculum or whatever, was used up for staff development, postage, travel, whatever. But I think if we get the con-tract with the Mankato group, and right now there's also a group from Mil-waukee that is considering giving us some kind of contract, there's serious dollars flowing through EdVisions over the next year. In that case, it's possi-ble there's going to be some profit.

A few individuals have remained members of the co-op because they ex-pect to turn a profit on the venture over the next few years. Doug Thomas doesn't see it this way: "It's really interesting that there are a few people around who have stayed members of the co-op, including the insurance man, who believe that there's some money going to come from all this [EdVisions] down the road. I look at them like, what?"

Regardless of whether people remain cooperative members because they expect to make money, alter the professional stature of teachers, or simply create educational programs that are innovative and appealing to students, one thing is clear: the cooperative model, while cumbersome and time con-suming at times, has created and bound together a group of educational pio-neers who maintain a steady and steadfast commitment to MNCS.

Teaching and Learning at MNCS

A visitor dropping in at the Minnesota New Country School in Le Sueur might easily become disoriented. On first entering one of its downtown storefronts, one would find a room filled with activity, but not the sorts of activity one expects to observe in a typical classroom. Teenagers pal around informally with one another, as if they were in a clubhouse, the family rec room, or a summer camp meeting hall. Some sit in front of one of the dozens of computer terminals—working alone or with friends—surfing the Internet, pointing out discoveries to neighbors at adjacent terminals, deliberating over mathematics challenges, playing computer games. Other students come and go freely from the building, dashing off to a local store or restaurant, a class at a local community college, or an internship with a nearby community organization. One small group of determined-looking teens huddle around a large table and debate plans for an upcoming holiday fund-raiser. A few earnest adults move about the room, casually checking in with the adolescents, pulling books off of shelves, pointing out a page on which song lyrics are scrawled.

The room is filled with noise, but not the sort of noise typically heard in a classroom. A telephone rings and a young woman runs and grabs it. One teenager puts a tape into a boom box and blasts some music he'd told a friend about. A pair of girls at a computer terminal laugh loudly, point at the screen, and then call out to a friend on the other side of the room to come join them. Doors slam, backpacks rustle, a boy in a baseball cap sits in a corner strumming a guitar. A few students consult charts of academic goals that they keep in individual three-ring binders and loudly haggle with the adults over expectations and standards. The group discussing the holiday fund-raiser gets into a boisterous discussion, disagreeing, arguing, shouting. An adult comes over and tells them gently, "Keep it down, folks," then moves on.

The walls of the room are covered with materials pulled from popular culture—Far Side cartoons, posters of Garfield, a small plastic statue of Bart Simpson on his skateboard. A blackboard lists the names of those in the class and their current independent work projects, including "aviation," "practical writing," "subwoofer," "frogs," and "math." Coats and backpacks are scattered throughout the room; books are strewn willy-nilly; a fraying poster from Wall Drug in South Dakota looms over a computer terminal. The room has a feeling of informality—busy but not chaotic, ragtag but not purposeless.

Somehow the look of the room captures the spirit behind the educational philosophy of the school founders. While they articulate their mission as technology-driven, project-based, and intended to cultivate the intrinsic motivation of each student, they seem wholly unaware of the ways in which the same cooperative tradition driving teachers' work at this school also infuses life at MNCS for the students. If the school's staff is opting for identities as owners and professionals rather than employees and workers, student identity at MNCS has also been reconceptualized in a powerful way, resonating with key parts of the cooperative model. The students, like the teachers, seem to feel a powerful sense of ownership in the school.

I spent a day shadowing a seventeen-year-old boy, a farmer's son, who'd come to MNCS as a refugee from a local high school where he'd felt socially isolated. Certainly not a model student—neither in the traditional school from which he'd come nor in this progressive charter school—Michael aptly summarized the altered sense of relations he observed among students and between students and teachers at MNCS: "People are just a lot nicer here, you know. There are really no social classes, and you can really work on what you like." Michael here highlights three features that are critical components to rural cooperative organizing: comfortable face-to-face relationships with other members, a flattened hierarchy, and a significant measure of autonomy.

Notes taken from a student focus group that convened after the school's first year reflected how students as well as teachers had reshaped education according to more cooperative models.[18] Students appeared keenly aware that learning takes place in many ways and that students have a responsibility to become active, self-starting learners. When asked, "How do you learn at MNCS?" students had answered:

Accomplish.
Work in the community.
Learn by doing.
Pursue personal interests.
"Involve me and I learn."
By experience.
Optional classes.
Research projects.
Individual or group.
Student lead.
High school classes.
Learn from others.

When asked to describe the way they learn the most, students had answered:

Learning by seeing.

Research projects tailored to what interested in doing.

Getting involved.

Can see what people are talking about. Internalize it.

By doing it.

Work on own.

Read, experience, variety of ways of learning.

Follow own interest.

Identify what it is you want to learn and then go ahead and learn it.

Former farmer and current adviser Dean Lind's insistence that the EdVisions Cooperative offers teachers "a lot more ownership" and the chance to "share power" in the management of the school could just as easily be applied to the students. The radical shift MNCS students are expected to make—from passive receivers of information to the designers and directors of their own learning programs—is essentially about assuming responsibility and ownership of their own schooling. While such a shift has been traditionally linked in educational circles to the work of Paulo Freire and other champions of critical pedagogy and to feminist theorists, in this rural Midwest context, its roots may be more appropriately seen as emerging out of a century of cooperative organizing.[19]

MNCS Frog Group serves as a wonderful illustration of how the school offers its students the freedom of discovery and the chance to transform themselves as learners. A group of students studying the local environment during August 1995 discovered a large number of deformed frogs in a small pond not far from the school. Some of the frogs had three back legs rather than two, or were missing a leg; several had deformities of the eye. Adviser Cindy Reinitz worked with the students to observe and catalog the deformities and also participated in efforts by state and federal scientists to explore the causes of the deformities.

In a short period of time, the project mushroomed into a national media sensation. Dozens of local and national newspapers and television stations picked up the story, and the ABC-TV news show *Nightline* highlighted the case of the deformed frogs, including the investigative work MNCS students had done. *National Geographic* called. The cable-television *Discovery* channel broadcast a reenactment of how the students had discovered the deformed frogs. Reinitz and a student were flown to San Diego, where Sea World presented them with an award of $12,500 for environmental education.

While Reinitz and the students organized their work into an ongoing research project, offering the eleven- to fourteen-year-old frog scientists the chance to acquire a range of skills related to scientific inquiry, students were at the same time learning about testifying before government regulatory bodies, the funding of scientific research, and the joys and headaches of working with the media. Students were empowered to see themselves not as people too young and inexperienced to have an impact on public discourse or to participate in the arena of public policy, but as activists, spokespeople, environmentalists, and scientists. While the Frog Group, as it became known, serves as a powerful example of experiential education, one cannot help but see ways in which aspects of the cooperative model—democratic participation, individual empowerment rather than hierarchical sources of authority, and the collaboration-rooted impetus to confront problems head on rather than ceding that onerous responsibility to others—suffuse teaching and learning at MNCS. Doug Thomas and Kim Borwege summed up the school's pedagogy in a manner rife with the values of midwestern cooperatives:

> The design of the Minnesota New Country School reflects a very different approach to schooling. The school is founded on the beliefs that young people have a strong desire to learn, that faith in that desire needs to be restored, and that it can be restored through a sensible, involved, and caring program. Furthermore, schools can no longer do "to" and "for" students and communities, but must work "with" others to help future generations be productive and responsible.[20]

This emphasis on productivity and responsibility, caring and involvement, working with rather than doing to or for, is parallel to the values that have driven midwestern rural co-ops for the past hundred years.

When Organizational Innovation Runs Deep

What's especially impressive about MNCS is that, unlike many charter schools, it has lived up to the mission of ambitious innovation promised by charter school reform.[21] The school's philosophical commitment to cooperative organizing not only structures the organization of the school and its educational program, but also shapes daily classroom life. Innovation, woven almost seamlessly into the fabric of school life, runs deep at MNCS.

As MNCS ends its founding period and enters a phase of formalization and institutionalization, it will be interesting to observe whether key stakeholders are able to keep alive the commitment to cooperation. The 1998–99 school year at MNCS included a move from Le Sueur to Henderson, where a new building was constructed to suit the school's pedagogy; the opening of a satellite site thirty miles away primarily for children from an isolated religious sect culturally distinct from the current MNCS community; and an expansion in the size of the student body. At the same time, the EdVisions Cooperative was also to undergo a major transition: the co-op's original aim of providing educational services to several schools has been realized, and contracts have been signed for the co-op to assist in the development of three additional schools in rural Minnesota.

Historians of education have suggested that the reforms that take hold in public schools in America are often hybrids, emerging out of an intensive, politicized process of negotiation among interest groups (teachers, administrators, parents, students, public officials, unions, academics) within schools.[22] This certainly appears to be true of district-based reforms, as the power of bureaucratic organizations sets formidable restraints on change. Stable but often unproductive institutional forms and processes emerge from such systems.[23] While we rely on the bureaucratic organization of public schooling to withstand the vicissitudes of ideological shifts, pedagogical trends, and frequent cultural quirks that impose themselves on classroom life, such a system of organization significantly reduces the potential for innovations that are radical departures from contemporary norms.

While MNCS's cooperative model clearly springs from the rich soil of the Upper Midwest, where it has helped farmers withstand the hardship of natural disasters, demographic change, and profound economic transitions, policymakers seeking alternative forms for public schooling would do well to consider seriously the organization of MNCS. During an era in which the political right tenaciously pursues voucher programs as the messiah of public education, this charter school offers a compelling school-choice alternative to the individualism and cultural fragmentation that characterize vouchers.[24] And during a period in which the left campaigns against the privatization of public schooling on account of its potential to disempower teachers while extracting corporate profits, this humble site in the Minnesota River Valley introduces a new form of privatization in which educators are not only professionals but also owners able to profit from the fruits of their own labor.[25]

CHAPTER 8

Breaking Away or Pulling Together?
Making Decentralization Work

BRUCE FULLER

Dreams consist largely of imaginary conversations . . . to be imagined is to become real, in a social sense. The imaginations which
people have of one another are the solid facts of society. The social
person is a group of sentiments attached to some symbol which
keeps them together and from which the whole idea is named.

Charles Horton Cooley, *Human Nature and the Social Order* (1902)

Whether cruising on bikes along suburban sidewalks or atop
skateboards on city streets, children humanize our neighborhoods. In turn,
the social worlds of grown-ups spring to life around our kids. Serving in the
co-op preschool, arranging play dates and birthday parties, attending the
high school basketball game on Friday night—these are basic rituals that
create public spaces and enrich our constructed communities.

Charter schools, at one level, offer an inspiring story about activist parents
and teachers eager to create more fulfilling communities for themselves and
their children. The grandmother who helped to found El-Shabazz Academy
sticks in my head: her grandson had been killed by a youth gang, and she
blamed the public schools. Or the Latina grandmother I met at Amigos
Charter, who watered the garden. She simply wanted to lend a hand.

These individuals have joined like-minded families to organize an option,
to imagine a safer, more nurturing community. Indeed, a broad spectrum of
families from across the country are making a clean break from neighborhood schools by exercising their new-found market right. We have seen
how small charter organizations are pulling together committed parents and
teachers in new and invigorating ways. Great promises, along with less vivid
perils, accompany this human-scale search for community.

As revealed in our school cases, the skyrocketing hopes people hold for charter schools—as with earlier utopian movements—often are pulled back to earth by the nitty-gritty problems associated with building a sustainable and effective organization. Our reporting on the Amigos and Montera charter schools demonstrate that an emboldened spirit alone is not enough.

Charter advocates have yet to recognize the two paradoxes that beset the movement, as put forward in Chapter 1. Will charter schools, by eroding central government authority, end up undermining broad public interests that go beyond the tribal commitments that mark many charter communities? And might the rise of market forms of choice—increasingly designed to give blue-collar and disadvantaged children new opportunities—end up exacerbating inequities that already plague public education?

Crafting Just and Effective Forms of Decentralization

This final chapter aims to corral these and other major lessons learned from the six case studies. I cannot advance sweeping generalizations from just a handful of schools, no matter how many months or years our contributors spent exploring life inside them. Indeed the rapid spread of these small-scale institutions creates new challenges for policymakers and scholars who are eager to paint clear portraits of universal realities. Instead we must do a better job of representing on more than one canvas the diverse colors and forms of these bright new organizations.

Our case studies do serve to complement empirical findings to date on the common attributes and uneven effects of charter schooling, as reviewed in the first chapter. Evaluations from a growing number of states are beginning to confirm some claims and challenge others made by the radical decentralists. On the one hand, many charter schools are sparking democratic participation by parents and teachers in shaping innovative school communities. On the other hand, charters have yet to demonstrate a broad ability to boost children's learning through more effective classroom practices, to nurture more accountable schools, or to create competitive pressures on still moribund urban systems. Charter reformers thus far are scoring high on process and low on hardcore results. One could applaud charter founders for their advances in democratic decision making. But the growth of "virtual charters" over the Web, private school management firms, and exclusionary admissions practices are threatening the participatory spirit of the movement.

I have argued that the growth of charter schools is motivated in part by Americans' commitment to communitarian ideals, a rendition of nineteenth-century village republicanism, but with a newfound focus on one's own village rather than on unifying villages across the republic. Parents and educators may be reacting to larger forces in society, not only to the depersonalizing and insular attributes of big school bureaucracies. For example, if economic forces are hollowing out central cities and sharpening America's class hierarchy, then the charter movement and its organizations may be a phenomenon over which the state will have little long-term influence. Under these dynamics, government can only ride out the storm of economic change that erodes communities, as charter activists attempt to dam the floodwaters.[1]

Uncovering What's Working

Scholars in many policy arenas mobilize evidence to advance claims about the overall effectiveness of a social institution or program, and so it has been with assessments of the public schools and earlier renditions of school reform. Rich empirical discoveries also can be used to illuminate what's working or pinpoint weaknesses to guide future improvements. The latter analytic approach is compelling, especially given that charter schools are so young and diverse.

The question then becomes: How can we build from empirical lessons to make charter schools and radical decentralization work better and yield more equitable results? This framing urges consideration of how we can prevent the ills engendered by radical decentralization, especially in terms of the inequities and plain ineffectiveness that are cropping up as hundreds of charter schools bloom in the dark, in a largely unaccountable manner.

Why take this formative tack? Hard and fast opponents of school choice—as well as policymakers pursuing the counterstrategy of state-led reform—would eschew this pragmatic framing. So would true believers in charters, who typically abstain from asking tough questions about their movement.

Yet this pivotal moment in America's political history demands that we be rigorous and vigilant in assessing the effect of decentralized public programs, from charter schools to welfare reform. This tough-minded tack is desirable for several reasons. The political and cultural forces underlying the recurring romance with radically decentralized governance are not going to wane. If anything, rising respect for ethnicity and the widening political bases it provides for Latino, African American, and, most recently, Asian American groups will intensify support for allocating more government resources to local agencies and human-scale organizations, from child-care centers and health clinics to charter schools.

The strange bedfellows backing radical decentralization—including evangelical Christians and this new generation of local black and Latino activists—will likely grow stronger and more dynamic, relative to the old bureaucracies that formerly dominated public programs and institutions. And this situation comes on top of an American political culture that, from Tocqueville's day forward, has expressed a distrust of concentrated political authority, be it lodged inside the Washington beltway or an insular city school board.

The seeming inability of school administrators and teachers' unions to reform the system from within represents another reality that will continue to erode the credibility of professional educators and energize support for debureaucratization. While the counterstrategy to school choice—state-led accountability measures—will play out in large urban states, the unions and administrators' associations will lobby to water down attempts from above to exact school-level change. California governor Gray Davis, for example, has settled for a somewhat decentralized, district-by-district accountability structure, in part because his political future rests on support from the education establishment.[2]

Contributing to the allure of choice is a tenet of our contemporary political culture that requires reformers to pay homage to market remedies for public problems. After the sudden collapse of centralized socialism in 1989, followed by a decade of sustained economic expansion in the West, faith in market dynamics and direct accountability between consumers and producers has climbed steadily. Public policies linked to parental choice, economic incentives, or tax credits—despite their uneven ability to actually alter behavior or advance public interests at the grassroots—now enjoy strong credibility.

Emile Durkheim, back in the nineteenth century, pointed out that primitive religions invented the idea that a universal force could energize the moral and economic life of a society.[3] In our time, this omnipotent force is embodied by the amoral marketplace. Never mind that how we raise our children involves the most fundamental social mores and, one hopes, a core set of democratic ideas that help to hold our centrifugal society together. Instead market dynamics and the pursuit of individualistic interests are, many assert, the forces that will improve our public schools and provide more effective alternatives to them. America's old symbol of idealism and unity, the common school, is being replaced by a new totem: McDonald's golden arches.

Most recently we have heard moderate Republicans, like George W. Bush and Representative J. C. Watts of Oklahoma, talk of "compassionate conservatism," a curious fusion of a fresh adjective and an old noun. They acknowledge that markets don't always help working-class families or those surviving within impoverished inner cities. They argue that a combination of targeted incentives and human-scale aid from local institutions—churches, self-help groups, and community action agencies—can complement impersonal market forces.[4]

Ironically this compassionate conservatism flows in part from the left's post-1960s investment in local nonprofit organizations to run child-care centers, health clinics, and housing programs. This line of attack on big government by the right is consistent with the very same empowerment metaphor that energizes charter school advocates. Unfortunately, the attack on the centralized state undermines its very ability to demand accountability from the local schools and community organizations that deliver publicly funded services. We have returned to a contemporary rendition of Madison's eighteenth-century split from Jefferson.[5]

In short, "there's no putting the school choice genie back in the bottle," as Michigan professor Gary Sykes recently commented. Choice will continue to alter the array of schools available to families and local educators.

Thus the pressing question facing activists—those in and around government and those in charter schools—is how to raise the efficacy of charters without eroding government's capacity to address wider public interests. Only central public agencies, like state governments and school boards, can push hard for gains in accountability and equity. And as we have seen so vividly in the case studies, charter activists within neighborhoods can choose to either complement or undercut these basic public priorities.

Forces that Determine Charter Schools' Efficacy

Making charter schools work better is a slippery task, given that different schools are pursuing quite different goals. Nevertheless, policymakers and charter advocates generally ask two fundamental questions when assessing the success of charters: Are charter schools expanding the number of parents and teachers involved in school governance, and enriching the core teaching and learning processes? And are charter schools advancing the so-

cial, cognitive, and moral development of children in different or more effective ways?

Of course, not all charters accept the assumptions on which these questions are based. Some school directors do not, in fact, hope to see stronger
parental participation. Their schools were founded by teachers eager to
shake free of district regulation, and they are not necessarily dedicated in
any clear way to new forms of democratic participation. Many charter educators are more interested in broad socialization agendas—advancing religious convictions, ethnic identity, or simply personal discipline—than in
demonstrating improved student achievement per se. We also saw how the
creation of small, safe environments is a preeminent goal. Yet I would argue
that a charter school—and the movement at large—is failing to deliver on its
promises if it does not recast teacher and parental involvement or raise children's learning curves.[6]

Within this conception of effectiveness our case studies revealed that
charter leaders must successfully address four key factors if their schools are
to work better:

- Charter schools must *take advantage of resource interdependencies*—links
  with economic sponsors and organizations that provide political legitimacy and funding. The rhetoric of "autonomy" is invigorating, but
  charter schools that show sustained strength have built tight relationships with their host district or state education department, as well as
  with private benefactors. Building interdependencies also involves the
  crafting of a crisp identity, and communal links to local parents and
  funders, whether by affirming the value of religious home schooling, by
  offering no-nonsense direct instruction, or by hiring a Spanish-speaking teaching staff.
- Charter schools must develop an internal organization to *differentiate
  school management from issues of pedagogical renewal and innovation*. Too often these tandem challenges become blurred, with organizational crises
  eclipsing serious pursuit of pedagogical gains. The dilemma is that a
  philosophy of full-fledged democratic participation encourages teachers
  to become involved in many areas of school policy, often reducing the
  time and attention that they can devote to the development of more effective classroom practices.
- Charter schools must *forge a shared understanding of how parents should be
  involved* in both the school organization and at home with their chil-

dren's schoolwork. This does not happen easily. Our case studies suggest that social-class differences, and at times teachers' aura of authority, continue to separate educators from families, resulting in peripheral or ceremonial roles for parents. Few charter founders have attempted to alter how parents aid their children's learning at home. Only at the Valley Home School Charter are (willing) parents directly coached on how they could play a more effective role at home.

- Charters must *balance tribal cohesion with democratic discourse.* Despite the particularistic agendas of many charter schools, two of our case studies reveal an occasional commitment to inviting a diverse set of children, then devising innovative programs to serve them under one roof. Leaders of Montera Charter High School and Minnesota New Country School have defined community not as an insular tribe but as a public space that is enriched by diverse voices, a rainbow of ideas and arguments. This is a version of pluralistic community, first incorporated into the modern urban state, and then brought into progressive classrooms by John Dewey. It also bridges to the liberal arts, a pedagogical approach that gets little hearing in many charter schools.

Market Niches, Institutional Conditions

These internal tensions play out in many charter schools. But to sustain their organizational lives, charters must pay attention to the outside political economy as well. Charter leaders, for instance, must create schools that maximize demand among families who are disaffected by neighborhood schools. And they must tap into resources flowing from the state, businesses, and foundations. Charter leaders, then, must be adept readers of both market dynamics and institutional symbols that can bring greater legitimacy to their fledgling organization.

One lesson we learned about the local political economy in which charter schools operate is that the chartering agency—be it a local school board or a state education department—can make or break an individual school. Montera High, for example, originally negotiated with its district office for an entirely new conception of student diversity: it could retain transportation support by recruiting more middle-class students of color. Even after charters are established, they must continually negotiate, as we have seen, for categorical funding and inclusion in staff development and health insurance programs, and liability insurance pools. Tussles with school districts or state agencies occur in a swirling mix of political and economic interests, advanced by competing local education lobbies, and can have telling consequences for a charter school's long-term vitality.

During an earlier debate over how to decentralize school management in the early 1980s, Stanford University's Milbrey McLaughlin argued that autonomy alone may not bring real results, other than slightly broadening the range of parents involved in decision making. In addition, she said, the state must set clear performance standards *and* provide teachers with an effective form of support.[7] The escape to freedom, so eagerly sought by charter pioneers, often leaves behind the necessary resources and support, including professional development and in-service programs, that inventive states and local education offices can still provide. We have to think more about how mindful public agencies might help to sustain the decentralized experiments embodied in charter schools. Radical decentralization may become effective only if central agencies lend a steady hand.

Indeed, charter founders and teachers express many worries about the lack of resources and social supports in their environment. Abby Weiss recently published a study of Massachusetts's charter schools, revealingly titled *Going It Alone,* in which she found that "autonomy creates isolation . . . [staff] often feel isolated from their community, and many are not accessing the valuable resources in the community. Educational issues are not being given the attention that they need because the schools are weighted down by the more urgent organizational issues [resulting] in a system in which these schools are functioning with little support and assistance."[8]

We also discovered that beneath this very political surface, the institutional and cultural topography of a community determines the organizational forms that win legitimacy for charter founders. That is, charter schools must advance images and themes that converge with preferences of local parents and public benefactors. Chelmsford Charter makes use of a symbol of democratic participation with its morning "town hall" meetings, a model to which affluent New England parents are naturally attracted. Meanwhile, in Lansing, El-Shabazz features strong discipline and authoritative forms of pedagogy to attract its families. The guiding philosophies and key symbols fit their respective market niches.

A final fact, linked to the surrouding environment, often remains unspoken in charter schools: life inside may be more orderly or more supportive of its members relative to that in large neighborhood schools, but student achievement rises modestly, if at all. Student performance remained low to mediocre in the Amigos, El-Shabazz, and Valley Charter schools, and it continued to be highly stratified along ethnic and class lines at Montera Charter High School. Students at Chelmsford did just fine both before and after entering their charter school. And as noted in Chapter 1, evaluators working on a recent study of charter schools in Los Angeles had to struggle long and hard to eke out hazy indications that their learning curves may be rising more steeply compared with those in neighborhood schools.

These patterns suggest that charter schools, like many education reforms, have done little to change the surrounding economic and institutional inequalities that stratify which kids do well in school. Terry Moe, coauthor of *Politics, Markets, and America's Schools,* argued at a 1999 seminar in Sacramento that we shouldn't worry about achievement gains if parents are happy, saying, "Tens of thousands of parents can't be wrong." I agree in one sense: in gauging my own children's development, I don't simply don my green eyeshades and study only their test scores. However, if proponents promise higher learning curves, then parents need to know whether evidence backs these claims. I will return to this basic issue and its implications for the state and would-be reformers. But first let me detail, drawing from our case studies, how the four key factors outlined on pages 235–236 appear to be influencing the efficacy of particular charter schools.

Interdependencies and Legitimating Symbols

> While the region's people embrace the ideas handed down . . . by the Jeffersons and the Jacksons, the Northwest has a more narrowly defined culture that was shaped by immigrants . . . by shared experiences on the frontier.
>
> Lee Egerstrom, on cooperative organization

Advocates for charter schools speak endlessly of autonomy, the organizational magic that will ensue when parents and teachers break free of local school districts or state education departments. Other reformers take other approaches, insisting that tighter accountability to the state is essential, or that networks of schools must be formed to follow a commonly held vision, such as the Coalition for Essential Schools or E. D. Hirsh's Core Knowledge Schools. It may be that "going it alone" is a necessary yet insufficient condition for becoming a sustainable and effective charter school, as *New York Times* writer James Traub recently documented.[9]

One key finding from our case studies is that even if charter founders act out during their organizational adolescence—adamantly insisting on their independence—they eventually (re)build linkages with their host school district or other public institution to gain resources and legitimacy. Conversion charters, those schools crafted by educators inside districts, benefit from preexisting bonds with the administrators who hold the dollars and the parents who may be ready to sign up. Original charters, begun by parents or dissident teachers who choose to leave the comfort of an established system, must work harder to build interdependencies. While both types of schools flaunt their rhetorical autonomy, they eventually move to rely on well-established public institutions for support, or the consolidated capital offered by foundations and wealthy individuals.

Charter founders must establish trust and reliable resource flows at two levels. First, they must attract families, establishing sustainable levels of parental demand. This has not been much of a problem for the typical small organizations that rarely serve more than 200 children. Importantly, the "founding mothers" of many charters have a long history in their community; trust in these charismatic educators has already been established. Dr. Ruby Helton of the El-Shabazz Academy in Lansing had worked in leadership roles in the public school system for more than two decades. Before founding Amigos Charter Academy, Magarita Ortíz was the highly respected principal of the Lakeville feeder school to the (undesirable) public middle school. Valley Charter School was begun by Superintendent Gomez, a trusted small-town entrepreneur. In short, market relationships do not appear out of thin air. They are built on precontractual forms of trust and commonly held sentiment, as Adam Smith emphasized two centuries ago.[10]

Second, key charter activists, situated in their own neighborhood, often are linked to institutions beyond their public school system. They must forge alliances with local churches, foundations, corporate donors, and local political networks. These linkages—along with the material resources they bring—are essential if a school is to compete within the local political economy, especially in a large urban area where costs are high for charters, facilities are scarce, and competition is stiff for public and quasi-public funding. Charter advocates have been slow to recognize the classic inequities in the wealth and poverty of local societies.

Community associations also allow charter founders to make use of symbols and models that yield broader-based legitimacy. Valley Charter School, for instance, incorporated the home schooling concept, tacking on learning centers and loosely coupled "education coordinators," to justify receiving millions of dollars in state education aid. In a more inspiring instance, activists at the Minnesota New Country School mobilized the agricultural cooperative metaphor to create a teacher cooperative. Dr. Freya Rivers, the influential board member at El-Shabazz, had long been linked to the independent black schools movement, and Principal Helton consistently hired teachers and support staff who were black and from the local community—often adults who already knew the families served by the charter.

In each case, the symbols appropriated from the social environment boosted the new charter school's credibility, bringing in parents and benefactors who shared the school's core ideals. Sometimes these collective commitments related to a certain pedagogical approach, such as direct instruction, high-tech instruction, or a progressive learning-in-the-community strategy. At other times the symbolism was linked to culturally bounded values implicit in such things as ethnocentric curricula, the moral emphasis of *educación,* or the Christian right's belief that parents must educate their own children.

But sometimes there's trouble in paradise. The creation of tightly knit, homogenous communities—and the draw on public resources that charters demand—often leads to conflict inside local settings.[11] We saw in southern California, for example, how families and kids remained highly segmented at Montera Charter High, with affluent parents reinforcing the school's agenda much more than ethnic minority parents, who tended to live miles from the school. Valley Charter School has driven church-based "cover schools" out of business, creating deep conflicts with local churches. And the Valley school board's consideration of a new home-schooling secondary curriculum has undercut efforts to build a second high school in this rural California county.

The character of these links between charters and community agencies can evolve dramatically over time. When Ortíz and her *compadres* at Amigos initially submitted their charter petition, it was voted down by the Oakland school board. They appealed to the county office of education and won. The defeated district then became obstinate, arguing that Amigos had to go it alone. Amigos had to buy its own liability insurance; it wasn't able to draw all the categorical aid for low-achieving students for which it was eligible. Amigos students were literally dropped from the district's student information system during their middle school years. But over the three-year period that we worked inside Amigos, relations with the district thawed considerably. When the tireless politician Jerry Brown successfully campaigned for mayor of Oakland in 1998, he was the headliner at a rally to support the rechartering of Amigos. Mayor Brown is now lobbying for several new charter schools, including a military-academy charter to be run by the National Guard.

The development of interdependencies between charter organizers and local public or private organizations is a two-way street. The resource providers—school boards, state education departments, churches, and private donors—receive legitimacy and political popularity by aiding start-up charter schools. Local politicians have come to realize that the symbols of choice and innovation resonate loudly in the minds of voters who are perennially worried about the quality of public schools. Their symbolic acts get downright amusing at times: witness Michigan governor John Engler's push to require local high schools to include charter and home-schooled athletes on their sports teams.[12] The virtues of choice and accountability—and apparently liberal eligibility for athletes attending "autonomous" schools—are refrains that parents like to hear.

In addition, the rechartering processes that we have observed—where school directors present self-study documents to local boards—are remarkable in their lack of tough-minded assessments. This system is driven by local political actors' dependence on charters and the ray of hope that they represent. Local board members win political points by recognizing parental demand and get a symbolic bang by supporting charters, not by asking tough questions.[13] Ironically this resembles the very same political process that explains why public school funding and categorical programs have grown rapidly over the past four decades, despite sometimes disappointing results. Charter schools were to become the pristine model for accountability and stronger school effectiveness. But as in all public organizations, once a threshold level of legitimacy is reached with the agencies that allocate crucial resources, demonstrating effectiveness becomes a muddy exercise.

Cohesive Organization, Effective Pedagogy

> For there to be real change, the whole school has to change. The entire school has to come together and say, "What's our vision?" That's what the public schools can learn from what we've done here. That's what's unique to charter schools.
>
> Chelmsford Charter principal Sue Jamback

Our contributors saw firsthand how charter schools can offer small and personal settings for teachers and children. But just because a school operates on a more human scale does not necessarily mean that it will better serve the needs of teachers and students. Even into the school's fifth year of operation, Amigos Charter was still losing up to two-thirds of its small staff annually. Well into its third year, the director of Valley Charter School was trying to answer the fundamental question of who was really responsible for children's learning, parent home schoolers or paid education coordinators. By way of contrast, the staffs at El-Shabazz and the Minnesota New Country School worked together as finely tuned teams, committed to their school's spirit and basic pedagogical tenets.

Leadership, without question, is important. Strong and respected leaders, like Peter McCann at Montera and Dr. Helton at El-Shabazz, played crucial roles in guiding the creation of coherent and sustainable charter organizations. Sometimes these more effective leaders limited democratic participation in order to get things done. They understood the difficulties faced by a school like Amigos Charter, where an exceptionally strong commitment to shared decision making cut deeply into teachers' time to work seriously on curricular and pedagogical improvement.

Looking across our six schools, one can see two mechanisms that repeatedly affected the schools' stability and attention to classroom practices. First, the charters appeared to be more cohesive and effective when a clear division of labor operated between the principal and the teaching staff, especially in terms of teachers understanding what kinds of schoolwide policies they can influence. Second, the degree of freedom teachers had to craft their own classroom practices varied enormously across our school cases. This was driven by the extent to which principals, teachers, and parents wanted to support a particular kind of instructional approach.

Dr. Helton at El-Shabazz represents one end of this spectrum. She had accumulated authority over a long career, so she could essentially dictate a hierarchical, direct-instruction form of pedagogy. If a teacher candidate was not comfortable with this form of instruction, they were not likely to be hired. The classrooms observed by Patty Yancey exhibited this highly disciplined, didactic method of instruction. Pedagogical alternatives were not really considered; one unitary approach was enforced by the school's determined founders. This approach was linked to the school's organizational identity and market niche: serving black youths who were not doing well in public schools.[14]

Montera Charter High represents a far less uniform model in which instructional experimentation was encouraged. Peter McCann injected moral or "cultural" guidance into discussions of how best to serve the high school's varied student population. New program models were then developed by committed teachers, at times aimed at integrating adolescents from affluent and working-class backgrounds, at other times aimed at serving only college-prep students. No single set of pedagogical principles unified the teaching staff, nor was this even a legitimate topic of discussion, given that student stratification had created a differentiated set of curricular programs and tracks. Similar to El-Shabazz, the stratified curricular structure at Montera matches the market niche crafted by its founders.

Amigos Charter is an extreme case of what can happen when politicized teachers want to be involved in the full range of school policies, from deciding student suspension procedures to determining how parents should be involved in the school's daily work and maintenance. When the founding mother, Margarita Ortíz, ran the school, she exercised significant authority in advancing her rendition of schoolwide policy. But once she left, the new principal ceded substantial authority to the small teaching staff in order to build her own credibility. Eventually the weekly teacher meetings broke down into debates over fund-raising, facilities, and all sorts of problems unrelated to pedagogy and classroom practices. By the school's fifth birthday, several teachers were complaining to our research team that the school still lacked a recognizable curricular framework. Unfocused democratic participation was undercutting teacher morale and organizational effectiveness.

Coherent schools can be built only when the staff is stable and comes to share the basic moral and instructional tenets of the institution. In charter schools, the hiring and retention of efficacious teachers is key. But effectiveness becomes a locally situated concept when charters are advancing a sharp identity and a particular projection of what they stand for. Dr. Helton, for example, was determined to hire real people from the (African American) community in Lansing. The Le Sueur teacher cooperative selected new colleagues who were normatively committed to the spirit of the community-based teaching that undergirds the organization's philosophy. In both cases, these schools remain popular because they are able to recruit and retain teachers who know how to be effective within the moral and instructional tenets of the institution. This requires that teachers' roles and commitment be clear. If they are not, the charter's fragile foundations can quickly crumble.

Another pair of issues arose less frequently in our case-study schools: the need for sound student assessment and the importance of involving parents in core learning activities. Only Dr. Helton had seriously gauged student achievement over multiple years, leading her to discover significant gains in children's math achievement and more modest progress in reading. In other schools, attention to tracking kids' learning was spotty or simply absent. When Amigos was readying its case for rechartering, the principal asked our institute to analyze student test scores over time, comparing Amigos graduates' scores against those of the nearby public middle school. Our research team discovered, however, that not all Amigos students took standardized tests over their three years in attendance, and that the district had simply purged the students' records from their information system because district administrators did not see the charter as part of their district. Despite all the rhetoric around effectiveness and accountability, only at El-Shabazz did we find an eagerness and a basic capacity to assess how well children were performing over time.

Finally, we rarely heard discussion inside these schools about how parents could aid the learning process by watching after homework, checking up on their children's performance, or contributing time inside classrooms. The institutionalized borders of what constitutes legitimate parent participation—imported from typical public schools—confined the discourse around how parents should be involved, even among charter educators who are otherwise quite innovative. This is a troubling example of how charter educators fail to look beyond school walls to affect the more lasting contexts in which children are raised.

Constructing Democratic Participation

> It [school] can be fun when you don't have people mad at you. You get to play in Kiswahili, and we do geographic games. I like recess, too.
>
> A child attending El-Shabazz

Warm and personal communities feel like nurturing families, especially for kids, as Patty Yancey reported from El-Shabazz school. Parents are always invoked by charter activists as being key to both the educational and the participatory values of their schools. The family metaphor was discussed explicitly by Dr. Helton in Lansing and by various school staffers at Amigos

Charter in the Bay Area. This metaphor manifests a small-scale cultural model that powerfully defines core behaviors and beliefs. In Helton's words, "Parents need to know we're them and they are us." The founding principal at Amigos drew on a maternal model in one of our interviews, talking about "protecting" children from the dangers of urban schools and maintaining family values and mores within her small school. And without a doubt, the parents in Valley Charter School remain in control of their youngsters' upbringing and academic learning.

This book's contributors discovered two distinct forms of parental empowerment. The first rests with the simple ability to choose. Whether it be among working-class parents in rural Minnesota or affluent parents in southern California, the ability to opt out of a mediocre neighborhood school or to avoid homogenous private schools is certainly a form of empowerment. In communities with multiple charters or magnet schools, as in Lansing, with its two African American schools displaying contrasting educational philosophies, parents enjoy even more options. Like moving into a better community or choosing one's own physician, actively selecting another school for one's child represents an important opportunity.

The second form of parental empowerment, highly variable across charters, relates to participation in the core work of schools. Many charters require that parents contribute a certain number of hours to the school each month, or they invite parents to lend a hand in various ways. In the end, only a select few serve on a school's board, while a wider circle contributes to peripheral maintenance tasks. Many parents don't feel comfortable working inside classrooms, especially some less educated parents who believe that their status and knowledge is far below that of professional teachers. This emerged several times in our parent interviews at Amigos.

Dr. Helton at El-Shabazz said that many parents still see school as a place of failure, given their own upbringing and disappointing level of achievement when they were students. No more than ten parents would show up for the periodic board meetings. At Montera Charter High School, we saw how parental participation and political influence remained quite stratified along racial and class lines. And at Valley Charter, fewer than one-third of the home schooling parents used the resource centers or enrolled their child in organized classes at the learning centers. No strong normative frame nudged this last group of parents to participate in any "schoolwide" activities once they had eagerly picked up their free curricular materials.

If charters are to truly foster democratic school communities, parents must be deeply engaged partners. How can this be better achieved? First of all, parents must clearly understand what they are buying into from a market perspective. At both Amigos and El-Shabazz, parents are certainly investing in a small school that seems more orderly, disciplined, and supportive of their particular child, relative to garden-variety public schools. At Montera Charter High, parents are buying into the promise of high-quality teachers at a high-status and highly integrated school.

But the next and more essential step—encouraging parents to participate in the core mission of the school or to aid their youngsters at home with schoolwork—has yielded mixed results. It seems that the former, working inside the school, is much easier to achieve than the latter, improving home practices. Only the breadth of Dr. Helton's vision included this deeper facet of parental involvement. One problem is that patterns of participation are clearly linked to parents' social position and their prior history with public institutions.

One parent at El-Shabazz, enthusiastic about the school, said she worked until 11:00 P.M. on week nights and simply could not attend school meetings. Several low-income parents interviewed by Amy Wells and colleagues were appreciative of the opportunity to send their child to a high-quality suburban school but didn't feel welcome at school events, which were largely organized by their affluent counterparts. And Valley's lower-middle-class home schoolers essentially trade signing up with the district for the free materials and occasional courses provided by the resource centers. In a very real way, their identity is signaled by their *not* participating in a common educational community.

Where comfortable roles can be carved out for parents, our contributors do report some success. At Amigos, researchers Eddie Wexler and Luis Huerta often chatted with Spanish-speaking parents who helped tend the small courtyard garden, assisted with weekend cleanups, and came to celebrations and political rallies to help sustain the school. At Montera, affluent parents were involved in helping to create programs that would serve their children, sometimes developing innovative initiatives linked to the higher curricular tracks.

Yet overall, many charter founders seem disinterested in advancing a small-scale civil society. They have a clear agenda for the kind of curriculum and social relations to which teachers and students should conform. Winning "autonomy" from the school bureaucracy does not equate with respect for democratic discourse, whether it's among parents or teachers. No parent in California's rural Central Valley joins Valley Charter if she questions the efficacy of home schooling. And if you disagree with Dr. Helton's commitment to strict discipline and didacticism, you are more likely to pull your child from El-Shabazz than to exercise your voice to urge moderation. When reformers in the 1970s began to emphasize the importance of building a clear mission within a school, they didn't anticipate that this meant stamping out dissonant voices or denying a Deweyan conception of inclusive democratic relations. But this is precisely what we often saw in our modest sample of charter schools.

Community and Diversity

> I want them [children] to have the attitude, God has given me all these blessings . . . what can I give back? One of the ways to get that is not have them brainwashed by a group of educators that I'm not familiar with. I don't want to leave my children off . . . and have them influenced and taught by someone I'm not familiar with.
>
> A mother at Valley Charter School

Reinforcing one's own community often involves circling the wagons and ensuring social homogeneity, as highlighted by this mother's words at Valley Charter. This is both a strength and a severe limitation of charter schools. Charter schools face a troubling dilemma: they must breed sameness and familiarity internally, clearly signaling their identity and market appeal—at the very same time that advocates celebrate charters as havens for organizational liberation and democratic participation. This leads to troubling worries over whether tribal organizations truly advance broader public interests. Few would argue that hog-tied and unresponsive school bureaucracies are advancing the public's interest. But it remains murky whether a rendition of radical decentralization that offers taxpayer support for highly Balkanized communities is the best pathway to school reform.

As the school desegregation movement began to collapse in the 1980s, it became clear that many urban families did not want their children bused out to suburban schools or to magnet schools. They preferred to improve their own neighborhood schools. The empowerment metaphor gained currency again, as it had in the nineteenth century when ethnic and religious groups sought to wrest control over their schools from downtown bureaucrats and professional educators. Many charter schools start with this thrust, representing what might be called "enabling tribalism." That is, families conclude that strengthening the borders of their own community—whether it is situated in a gray inner city or a leafy suburb—will sharpen core cultural and moral precepts, fostering stronger ways of raising their children. This conflicts directly with the earlier integrationist conception of institution building: inviting a variety of diverse families and children into a public place to create an engaging democratic ethic.

Some charter founders have boldly confronted the question of whether they are furthering social homogeneity or diversity. The principal at Montera, for instance, has consistently attempted to attract a wide range of kids from diverse areas of the city. Fostering diversity is central to the school's interest. Attracting a range of children not only increases enrollment but also ensures the flow of categorical-aid dollars from the school district, for magnet and bilingual programs and for busing services. By changing its past image as an affluent enclave in an increasingly diverse city, Montera advances its legitimacy within the metropolitan political economy. And from a more altruistic view, in the minds of Peter McCann, his teachers, and the progressively minded parents, Montera truly is a beacon of diversity, having achieved the integration of many kinds of families into a richer whole.

This same spirit permeates the guiding ethic of Minnesota's New Country School. Situated in small-town Le Sueur, drawing from a virtually all white population, the school is understandably more homogenous in ethnic terms than Montera. Yet the Minnesota teacher cooperative is committed to serving children from a variety of social-class backgrounds. Additionally, the philosophy of getting students out into the community and having them work with adults in a range of workplaces demonstrates the school's integrative philosophy. Its guiding mission does not involve circling the wagons around a homogenous group of families and teachers. Instead, learning and human development are linked to diverse experiences involving a pluralistic range of students and adults.

Mindful States, Deepening Inequality

We have seen how the local players in this story—those who artfully sculpt real schools from the lumpy rhetorical clay of radical decentralization—exhibit grand hopes and boundless enthusiasm. For anyone who has wandered the catacombs of a downtown city schools office, then peeked into the classrooms of an invigorating charter school, the contrast couldn't be more vivid and enlightening. The energy and ideals of many charter leaders and families at the grassroots can be plainly seductive.

But if the high hopes held by charter enthusiasts are to be achieved, we must back away from discussing specific schools and the movement's own romantic polemics. We shouldn't lose touch with the palpable commitment and social electricity felt in many charters, yet we must get on the outside and place this gaggle of fledgling organizations within two tandem contexts. The centuries-old world of school reform in America is already filled with stories of high hopes and dashed expectations. Let's get real.

The Rough Seas of Family Poverty

If you believe that school reform alone—be it led by inventive governors or carried out via radical decentralization—will substantially raise and equalize children's achievement levels, consider the following facts. As early as the second grade, black children nationwide are on average already one year behind white youngsters in their reading skills. Similarly, one recent analysis found that almost half of all the variability in California students' test scores could be explained by knowing just a few social-class characteristics of their parents, independent of the school's qualities.[15]

Students' own voices can also help us grasp the engulfing context of family poverty. In one study, sociologist Roslyn Mickelson interviewed a large sample of black working-class adolescents in Los Angeles. Most clearly understood America's faith in hard work and getting ahead. But when they reflected on their own lives, they visualized quite limited futures. They understood that for *other* high school students, out in the suburbs, doing well in school would be rewarded with a good job and broad opportunities. But kids like themselves couldn't expect that kind of payoff.[16]

The structural inequalities that mark American society and erode the hopes of so many children often are ignored by school reformers. This is the first context surrounding the charter isle of high hopes that must be navigated. Middle-class parents invest heavily in education, reading to their toddlers, moving to communities with good schools, watching after their kids' homework. For these parents, education has delivered economic returns and social openings. They pass on this faith in formal schooling to their children through specific practices inside the home. But for parents who work swing shifts, who face violence and intimidation in their urban neighborhood, who can't afford to move to quiet suburbs and better schools, tinkering with the local governance of schooling may have only a marginal effect on their children's achievement.

Charter schools, like other forms of school choice, do allow eager parents in blue-collar and poor communities to escape what they see as lousy schools. It is difficult to argue that government should discourage these families from searching out safer, higher-quality schools. The state must always offer incentives and opportunities for parents who go up against long odds to improve their children's lives.

The problem is that advocates of choice want us to believe that by simply altering the governance of local schools—debureaucratizing education and shifting to market dynamics—the contextual constraints and structural inequalities marking local communities will dissolve. It's the policymaker's rendition of the magician's sleight of hand. We become so distracted by all the politics around school control and governance that we lose sight of the real hand in which true remedies are held. I truly hope that charter schools become one effective part of the solution, rather than simply distracting both the state and champions of the market from a more serious discussion about inequality in America.

Shaking the Foundations of Civil Society

The second context for charter schools is related to the first. This broad political quandary relates to where we situate public authority and resources to address shared public interests. Civil society must find a way of holding public educators more accountable. This broad public concern is not motivated only by a desire to have our children learn more, or to become more productive workers. Most parents are not so narrowly utilitarian. The recurring search for "more effective" schools involves a deeper yearning to have our children grow up in more thoroughly moral ways. As parents, we are eager to socialize our children to value certain forms of cooperation, to respect each other, to think and act in ways that reinforce our very local conception of community. Our basic values and cultural tenets vary widely across American's pluralistic social fabric. But together we hunger for schools that will somehow contribute more strongly to how we hope our children will turn out.

The political question then comes back into focus: in what level of public governance do we vest the power to push schools to become more effective and more morally engaged places for our children? Urban school boards have shown uneven rigor in demanding stronger school organizations. They often are influenced, in large cities at least, by educational interest groups that weigh members' interests over the futures facing our kids. Washington can target resources to specific public concerns, but that level of government is too distant from schools to make a substantial difference. This suggests that state governments are right in taking a stronger role in finding ways of holding schools accountable, while providing flexibility for local educators in how they organize to become more effective.

If more accountable schools represent a shared public interest, then how do we come together to encourage state or local governments to pursue this agenda? And do market remedies—focusing on the pursuit of private interests—buy us much in this arena? Apropos of these questions, let's listen to the words of conservative student of government George Will, writing in *Statecraft as Soulcraft:*

> Once politics is defined negatively, as an enterprise for drawing a protective circle around the individual's sphere of self-interested action, then public concerns are by definition distinct from, and secondary to, private concerns. When people are taught by philosophy (and the social climate) that they need not govern their actions by calculations of public good, they will come to blame all social shortcomings on the agency of collective considerations, the government, and will absolve themselves.[17]

In terms of the charter school debate, we must ask whether this movement, at its core, is really about using public resources to allow Balkanized private groups to pursue their particularistic agendas, or whether this form of experimentation can complement state-led attempts at crafting more effective, more accountable schools for a wider public. In some cases the combination of *state-led* accountability and parents' *direct* demands for accountability (voting with their feet) will represent powerful, tandem forces. But the convergent pressures of state-led reform (simplifying the curriculum, for example) will undoubtedly come into conflict with the inventive visions of teaching and learning being operationalized by charter school activists. No radical decentralist believes that a single gardener can cultivate a thousand blooming wildflowers.

Will the State Become an Effective, Mindful Force?

The last century taught us much about the down side of urban political economies. Teachers' unions and professional education groups can come to dominate local agencies, undercutting efforts to hold them to account for their school-level failures—and meanwhile school quality becomes lopsided in favor of affluent parents, who can best manipulate local political elites. Left with mediocre schools and no clear recourse are working-class and many middle-income families. As Madison predicted, when higher levels of government surrender authority, local elites will come to dominate the micropolitics of city-states.

The earlier ideal of common schooling squarely addressed the risk of letting local political economies take over. Advocates of this unifying form of schooling retained a good deal of local governance while ensuring that state governments would advance shared moral and curricular structures, address wide gaps in school quality, and progressively redistribute public resources to help poor families. The American political system has yet to deliver on Horace Mann's ideals, especially when it comes to making sure that children from poor and blue-collar families attend schools that are safe and staffed by motivating teachers—or even schools where the toilets work and the roof doesn't leak. The state government's authority is crucial to ensure that local villages, and their schools, account for their effectiveness and explain inequities.

Backing up into a broader context, it may be that the communitarian instincts of charter school activists are fueled by larger economic forces that are eroding the early foundations of the public good. Rising faith in market relations, the hollowing out of inner cities as jobs flock overseas, and the sharpening class divisions that mark America's income structure represent powerful exogenous forces that Washington and state capitals often simply ignore.[18]

This holds a pair of distressing implications. First, public school performance will continue to look bad, since the underlying cause of low student achievement in poor and blue-collar communities has as much to do with parents' economic insecurity and lack of time for quality child rearing as it does with school quality. As voters wring their hands over low school performance, they will continue to support experimentation, even if it means radically decentralized attempts at reform. The central state becomes weaker as global, not domestic, forces further stratify the structure of labor and thus family wealth. And centrist politicians must now genuflect in deference to the virtues of market-oriented "public" policies. Poverty and inequality—and our unwillingness to confront them—thus feed hopeful trysts with radical decentralization.

Second, the legitimacy and technical efficacy of public agencies—be they situated locally or in state capitals—in smoothing the serrated edges of school choice reforms may diminish over time. Even though many charter schools are struggling, at times grasping for lifelines, they were designed to prove themselves in the rough seas of market competition. Even though the sustainability of charter schools in poor communities remains an open question, states are slow to provide more equitable support, since this violates the spirit of market rules. And even though private firms are cashing in on taxpayer dollars by enrolling "students" over the Web, increased regulation is opposed by many, since such rip-offs are allegedly part of the wondrous magic of the sacred market.

In sum, after considering all the arguments and early evidence, I am left with one unsettling fear: that charter advocates, along with their less balanced allies in the school choice movement, will unearth the moral bedrock that supports the ideals of public schooling. The traditional discourse of common schooling is giving way to a conversation that exudes faith in private choice, tribal agendas, and competitive pressures. As George Will argued fifteen years ago, we are drawing "a protective circle around the individual's sphere of self-interested action." The constitutive rules of America's political structure are coming to require that we respect an individual's desire to circle the wagons around his or her own tribe. Then, we are to use public resources to further deepen the fissures that already split American society.

The rub is that bureaucratized schools and the education interest groups that dominate urban education often circle their wagons around their insular agendas, as well. The charter movement offers an important counterforce. But in experimenting with radical decentralization, we must avoid eroding the basic tenets of civil society in ways that weaken the state's ability to attack the underlying causes of low achievement and mediocre public schools. If charter schools prove not to be an effective piece in the school reform puzzle but only a colorful distraction, we will have squandered the energy of many engaged parents and teachers, and the democratic state's unifying spirit will have been diminished.

We must find a balance between Jefferson's faith in political energy sparked at the grassroots and Madison's realistic understanding that localized struggles for community do not always strengthen our commonwealth or build more accountable public institutions. Our political leaders must do better on both levels. And all school reformers must be mindful that while their target for change is the school, they often seek to rearrange the basic building blocks of public authority. When we no longer trust government to address the corrosive effects of family poverty or to find stronger teachers who can help raise our children in more fulfilling ways, the unleashed pursuit of private and tribal interests will only grow more intense.

Yet the equally troubling question is whether calcified urban schools—and their increasingly reluctant benefactor, the state—can devise more inviting, human-scale organizations. If they can, we will witness the blooming of new institutions, like charter schools, from which, in philosopher Alan Wolfe's words, "people will feel less need to escape."[19]

NOTES

CONTRIBUTORS

INDEX

Notes

Acknowledgments

1. Thanks to Paul Elie for this wonderful historical fact, from his article on the late Manhattan progressive Dorothy Day, "The Patron Saint of Paradox," *New York Times Magazine* November 8, 1998, pp. 44–47.
2. Bruce Fuller et al., *School Choice: Abundant Hopes, Scarce Evidence of Results* (Berkeley: Policy Analysis for California Education, University of California, 1999).

Introduction

1. Margarita Ortíz and Amigos Academy are pseudonyms.
2. Discussions of the forms of democracy that are to be pursued by government and other institutions appear in: John Dewey, *Democracy and Education* (New York: Norton, 1932); Mary Ann Glendon, *Rights Talk: The Impoverishment of Political Discourse* (New York: Free Press, 1991); Richard Tarnas, *The Passion of the Western Mind: Understanding the Ideas That Have Shaped Our World View* (New York: Ballantine Books, 1991); Alain Touraine, *What Is Democracy?* trans. David Macey (Boulder: Westview Press, 1997).
3. David Johnston, "Gap between Rich and Poor Found Substantially Wider," *New York Times*, September 9, 1999 p. A14. Deborah Reed, *California's Rising Income Inequality: Causes and Concerns* (San Francisco: Public Policy Institute of California, 1999). In 1996 the average income in the top fifth of families with children equaled $117,000. Mean income for the bottom fifth was $9,254. In urban states, like California and New York, these gaps have grown worse over the past generation. Since the early 1980s, the number of children living in poverty climbed from 4.4 million to more than 6 million. Much of this rise is due to worsening family poverty and inequality in California, New York, and Texas. In Los Angeles County, for instance, the number of children in households living below the poverty line has doubled since 1992, now equaling one in every three children.

4. Daryl Kelley, "As Suburbs Change, They Still Satisfy," *Los Angeles Times*, October 19, 1999, pp. A1, A13.

5. Christopher Jencks and Meredith Phillips, *The Black-White Test-Score Gap* (Washington, D.C.: Brookings Institution Press, 1998).

1. The Public Square, Big or Small?

1. Michael J. Sandel, *Democracy's Discontent: American in search of a Public Philosophy.* (Cambridge, Mass.: Harvard University Press, Belknap Press, 1996).

2. Social theorists, since the modern state's nineteenth-century birth, have long struggled with the issue of large public spheres versus government that essentially reinforces local villages and city-states. Should the notions of civil rights, norms governing social tolerance of minority groups, and dominant ways of raising children be attached to nationwide public institutions or be allowed to vary across local communities? Emile Durkheim framed this as an almost religious issue: should guiding symbols and social rituals be reinforced on the large national canvas, or within town or tribe-specific portraits? Raymond Williams took a different tack, emphasizing that surface-level contention and ideological debates in the society rarely reshape the institutionalized role of the school and collateral agencies of the state. This is why it's useful to frame the charter-school debate as being between self-interested actors battling for political advantage, or as a deeper issue involving which level of society or community should hold public authority. The latter issue is much more fundamental to how we organize the nation-state over time. See: Emile Durkheim, *The Elementary Forms of Religious Life*, trans. Karen E. Fields (New York: Free Press, 1995). Raymond Williams, *The Sociology of Culture* (Chicago: University of Chicago Press, 1995).

3. David Tyack, *The One Best System: A History of American Urban Education* (Cambridge, Mass.: Harvard University Press, 1974).

4. Published by the Brookings Institution (Washington, D.C.) under the tutelage of Paul Peterson, a Harvard political scientist who would become an advocate of vouchers by the mid-1990s.

5. Quoted by Edward Wyatt, "Investors See Room for Profit in the Demand for Education," *New York Times*, November 4, 1999, p. A21.

6. Carl F. Kaestle, *Pillars of the Republic: Common Schools and American Society, 1780–1860* (New York: Hill and Wang, 1983), p. x.

7. Julian Guthrie, "How Brits Shaped Wilson's School Reform," *San Francisco Examiner*, October 18, 1998, p. 1.

8. Quoted in Duke Helfand, "Some Professors Resist State's Reform Formula," *Los Angeles Times*, October 25, 1998, pp. A1, A15.

9. Young quoted in Martha Groves, "3,750 Receive Grants for Private Schools," *Los Angeles Times*, April 22, 1999, p. A12.

10. Anemona Hartocollis, "Test-tube Babies: Private Public Schools," *New York Times*, January 3, 1999, p. WK3. Lynn Schnaiberg, "Buildings in Hand, Church Leaders Float Charter Ideas," *Education Week*, February 10, 1999, p. 1.

11. Quoted in Jeff Archer's coverage, "Catholics Gather to Discuss 'Moral Issue' of Choice," *Education Week,* February 17, 1999, p. 6.
12. From a September 1997 speech at the San Carlos (California) Charter Learning Center. Excerpts of the speech appear on the Thomas Fordham Foundation Web site: edexcellence.net/issuespl.
13. Lawrence M. Mead, "Telling the Poor What To Do," *The Public Interest* 132 (Summer 1998): 97–112. For this simultaneous pursuit of authoritative and promarket policies by centrists and conservatives, see Peter Skerry, "Immigrants, Bureaucrats, and Life Choices," in *The Debate in the United States over Immigration,* ed. P. Duignan and L. Gann (Stanford, Calif.: Hoover Institution Press, 1997), pp. 227–233.
14. See Steve Fenton, *Durkheim and Modern Sociology* (Cambridge: Cambridge University Press, 1984).
15. Chubb and Moe, *Politics, Markets, and America's Schools.* The argument is that local and central interest groups push for a variety of fragmented programs which then harden the programmatic "arteries" of the education bureaucracy, eroding the school-level authority of the principal and leading to insularity vis-à-vis parents' own preferences.
16. Martin E. Marty, *The One and the Many: America's Struggle for the Common Good* (Cambridge, Mass.: Harvard University Press, 1997).
17. Here again, while one may disagree with their derived policy remedies, Chubb and Moe's (1990) analysis regarding the political-economic forces that surround and stultify many urban school boards is quite convincing.
18. Bruce Fuller, Gerald Hayward, and Michael Kirst, with Mark DiCamillo, *Californians Speak on Education and Reform Options* (Berkeley: Policy Analysis for California Education, University of California, 1998).
19. Joseph Ellis, *American Sphinx: The Character of Thomas Jefferson* (New York: Random House, 1996).
20. Jack Rakove, *Original Meanings: Politics and Ideas in the Making of the Constitution* (New York: Random House, 1996).
21. State-level or local school boards that are granted authority by state legislatures to charter new schools can set certain standards or rules that all groups petitioning for a charter school must follow. For instance, it is virtually impossible to get a charter school approved by the San Francisco school board without stipulating that union-level wages will be paid to teachers.
22. *The Random House Dictionary of the English Language* ed. Laurence Urdang (New York: Random House, 1969), p. 227.
23. These origins of the charter movement are detailed in Joe Nathan, *Charter Schools: Creating Hope and Opportunity for American Education* (San Francisco: Jossey-Bass, 1996).
24. Albert Shanker, "Convention Plots New Course: A Charter for Change," *New York Times,* July 10, 1988, p. E7. Historical antecedents to the charter movement are reviewed, albeit with a romantic spin, in Chester Finn, Jr., Bruno Manno, and Gregg Vanourek, *Charter Schools in Action* (Princeton: Princeton University Press, 2000).

25. Robin J. Lake and Marc Dean Millot, "Accountability for Charter Schools: A Comparative Assessment of Charter School Laws," manuscript, University of Washington, 1998. For a discussion of how states' authorizing legislation varies, see Bryan Hassel, "Charter Schools: Politics and Practice in Four States," in Paul Peterson and Bryan Hassel, eds., *Learning from School Choice* (Washington, D.C.: Brookings Institution Press, 1998), pp. 249–274.

26. SRI International, *Evaluation of Charter School Effectiveness*, (Menlo Park, Calif.: SRI, 1997).Teacher views of autonomy are reported in Julie Koppich, *New Rules, New Roles? The Professional Work Lives of Charter School Teachers* (Washington, D.C.: National Education Association, 1998).

27. Lake and Millot, "Accountability for Charter Schools."

28. Thomas Toch, "The New Education Bazaar: Charter Schools Represent the Free Market in Action, with All Its Problems," *U.S. News and World Report,* April 27, 1998, pp. 35–46.

29. Associated Press, "Principal Is Convicted of Assaulting Reporter," *New York Times,* August 11, 1997, p. A12.

30. UCLA Charter School Study, *Beyond the Rhetoric of Charter School Reform: A Study of Ten California School Districts* (Los Angeles: UCLA Graduate School of Education and Information Studies, 1998).

31. Vicki Haddock and Katherine Seligman, "In the Virtual Classroom," *San Francisco Examiner,* October 17, 1999, pp. A1, A14.

32. For a review of Durkheim's focus on how institutions create and make tacit fundamental "social facts" and "collective representations," see Randall Collins, *Four Sociological Traditions* (New York: Oxford University Press, 1994), chap. 3.

33. The brief yet celebrated life of Ivan Huerta, contributor Luis Huerta's late son, still lends for me an immediacy to the life-affirming power of close community and its collectively held symbols.

34. Haddock and Seligman, "Virtual Classroom." In the summer of 1999 the California legislature did pass a bill requiring that districts operating home-school or computer-based classes can enroll only students who live in the host county or an adjacent county. But the basic funding mechanism remains in place.

35. Paul Berman et al., *A National Study of Charter Schools: Second-Year Report* (Washington, D.C.: U.S. Department of Education, 1998).

36. Gene V. Glass, Education Policy Analysis Archives (1999), vol 7, no. 1 (http://epaa.asu/epaa/v7n1/).

37. Berman et al., *National Study,* p. 63.

38. Center for Applied Research and Educational Improvement (CAREI), *Minnesota Charter Schools Evaluation* (Minneapolis: CAREI, University of Minnesota, 1997). For a review of additional evidence on parental participation, see Bruce Fuller et al., *School Choice: Abundant Hopes, Scarce Evidence of Results* (Berkeley: Policy Analysis for California Education, University of California, 1999).

39. SRI, *Evaluation of Charter School Effectiveness.*

40. Ibid.

41. These findings are reported in Eric Hirsch, "Education Program: Charter

Schools Brief," presented at the National Conference of State Legislatures, Denver, 1998; see the March 1998 Web site posting, www.ncsl.org.

42. Joanne Izu et al., *Cross-Site Report: An Evaluation of Charter Schools in Los Angeles Unified School District* (San Francisco: WestEd, 1998).

43. Ibid.

44. Quoted in Gail Russell Chaddock, "Lofty Claims by Charters? States Say, 'Prove It,'" *Christian Science Monitor,* January 12, 1999, Web site, p. 3.

45. Another weak spot is that evaluators have yet to track children over more than a year to assess whether achievement differences are truly sustained. Recent assessments of voucher experiments are attempting to do this. Foundations and government could do a tremendous service by seriously supporting longitudinal evaluations of how well children fare over a three- to five-year period as they move through charter schools.

46. Priscilla Wohlstetter, "Promoting School-Based Management: Are Dollars Decentralized Too?" in *Rethinking School Finance,* ed. A. Odden (San Francisco: Jossey-Bass, 1992).

47. In 1997 *U.S. News and World Report* conducted a national survey, in part asking what issues in education should receive the most attention. The top concerns: teaching children "values and discipline" (26 percent), keeping drugs away from schools (25 percent), and ensuring that schools are safe (12 percent). *Education Week,* "Hot Issues in Education," October 15, 1997, p. 4.

48. National Center for Educational Statistics (NCES), "School Choice in Public and Private Schools," Bulletin 97–287 (Washington, D.C.: U.S. Department of Education, 1997). Fall 1996 data were provided by NCES via a special tabulation.

49. These statistics and trends are detailed in Fuller et al., *School Choice.*

50. This review was informed by Amy Stuart Wells's early history, *Time to Choose: America at the Crossroads of School Choice Policy* (New York: Hill and Wang, 1993).

51. David Tyack and Larry Cuban, *Tinkering toward Utopia: A Century of Public School Reform* (Cambridge, Mass.: Harvard University Press, 1995).

52. Cited in ibid., pp. 100–101.

53. A. S. Neill, *Summerhill: A Radical Approach to Child Rearing* (New York: Hart Publishing, 1960), p. 4.

54. Wells, *Time to Choose,* p. 35.

55. Quoted in ibid., p. 40.

56. Fuller et al., *School Choice.*

57. Rolf E. Blank, Roger E. Levine, and Lauri Steel, "After 15 Years: Magnet Schools in Urban Education," in *Who Chooses? Who Loses? Culture, Institutions, and the Unequal Effects of School Choice,* ed. Bruce Fuller and Richard F. Elmore (New York: Teachers College Press, 1996), pp. 154–172.

58. These local studies are critically reviewed in Fuller et al., *School Choice.*

59. Laurie Steel and Roger E. Levine, *Educational Innovation in Multiracial Contexts: The Growth of Magnet Schools in American Education* (Washington, D.C.: U.S. Department of Education, 1994).

60. Adam Gamoran, "Student Achievement in Public Magnet, Public Comprehensive, and Private City High Schools," *Educational Evaluation and Policy Analysis* 18 (1996): 1–18.

61. Robert Crain, Amy Heebner, and Yiu-Pong Si, *The Effectiveness of New York City's Career Magnet Schools: An Evaluation of Ninth-Grade Performance Using an Experimental Design* (Berkeley: National Center for Research in Vocational Education, 1992).

62. Claire Smrekar and Ellen Goldring, *School Choice in Urban America: Magnet Schools and the Pursuit of Equity* (New York: Teachers College Press, 1999).

63. Education Commission of the States, *Choice: Open Enrollment, Vouchers, Tax Deductions and Credits* (Denver: Education Commission of the States, 1997).

64. Amy Pyle, "Drawn to Magnet Schools," *Los Angeles Times*, January 16, 1998, p. A1.

65. Details of the Massachusetts and Minnesota programs are discussed in Fuller et al., *School Choice*.

66. Jeffrey Henig, *Rethinking School Choice: Limits of the Market Metaphor* (Princeton: Princeton University Press, 1994).

67. For the most detailed history of the Milwaukee voucher program, see John Witte, *The Market Approach to Education: An Analysis of America's First Voucher Program* (Princeton: Princeton University Press, 1999).

68. John F. Witte, "Who Benefits from the Milwaukee Choice Program?" in *Who Chooses? Who Loses? Culture, Institutions, and the Unequal Effects of School Choice*, ed. Bruce Fuller and Richard Elmore (New York: Teachers College Press, 1996), pp. 118–137.

69. Jay Greene, Paul Peterson, and J. Du, "Effectiveness of School Choice: The Milwaukee Experiment," Department of Government, Harvard University, 1997.

70. Cecilia Rouse, "Private School Vouchers and Student Achievement: An Evaluation of the Milwaukee Parental Choice Program, *Quarterly Journal of Economics* 113, no. 2 (May 1998): 553–603.

71. Peterson and a team of researchers also found that the parents who applied for vouchers, while generally of a low-income or working-class background, were better educated, more often Anglo, and more frequently members of two-parent households, compared with New York City families overall. Paul Peterson et al., "Initial Findings from the Evaluation of the New York School Choice Scholarship Program" (Washington, D.C.: Mathematica Policy Research Inc., 1997).

72. Technical findings are reviewed by Paul E. Peterson, "Vouchers and Test Scores: What the Numbers Show," *Policy Review* 93 (January–February 1999): 10–15.

73. This issue has been the subject of considerable empirical inquiry. One of the most thorough analyses appears in Anthony S. Bryk, Valerie E. Lee, and Peter B. Holland, *Catholic Schools and the Common Good* (Cambridge, Mass.: Harvard University Press, 1993).

74. Stanley Elam, Lowell Rose, and Alec Gallup, "The 23rd Annual Gallup Poll of

the Public's Attitudes toward the Public Schools," *Phi Delta Kappan* 73 (1991): 41–56.

75. Lowell C. Rose and Alec M. Gallup, "The 30th Annual Gallup Poll of the Public's Attitudes toward the Public Schools," *Phi Delta Kappan* 80 (1998): 41–56.

76. Bruce Fuller, Gerald Hayward, and Michael Kirst, with Mark DiCamillo, *Californians Speak on Education and Reform Options* (Berkeley: Policy Analysis for California Education, University of California, 1998).

77. These trends in poll findings are reviewed in Adrienne D. Coles, "Poll Finds Americans Split over Public Financing of Private Education," *Education Week,* September 9, 1998, 6.

78. National Public Radio, "Henry J. Kaiser Family Foundation–Harvard University Kennedy School of Government Education Survey," National Public Radio, Washington, D.C., September 1999. On the Web at http://www.npr.org/programs/specials/poll/education/education.front.html

79. Fuller, Hayward, and Kirst, with DiCamillo, "Californians Speak on Education and Reform Options."

80. Richard Cooper, "House Approves Toughest School Standards Ever," *Los Angeles Times,* October 22, 1999, A1, A8.

81. National Commission on Excellence in Education, *A Nation at Risk: The Imperative of Educational Reform* (Washington, D.C.: U.S. Department of Education, 1983), p. 1.

82. David C. Berliner and Bruce J. Biddle, *The Manufactured Crisis: Myths, Fraud, and the Attack on America's Public Schools* (Reading, Mass.: Addison-Wesley, 1995), p. 139.

83. Terrel Bell, *The Thirteenth Man: A Reagan Cabinet Member* (New York: Free Press, 1988). Craig Fuller, Reagan's cabinet secretary, also has reported on how White House staff decided to give force and spin to Secretary Bell's report in early 1983. I review this intriguing episode in terms of the state-led agency and the symbolism it represents, in Bruce Fuller, *Growing Up Modern* (New York: Routledge, 1992).

84. In their thorough analysis Berliner and Biddle *(The Manufactured Crisis)* could find only one gauge—SAT scores—that showed some decline. They argue that this decline is due to the widening mix of high school seniors who are taking the test. For example, in California in 1998, 57 percent of all who took the SAT were non-Anglo, and English was not the native language of fully one-fifth of all test takers. See Gerald Hayward, "How Well Are California's Students Doing? Briefing Paper for the Assembly Education Committee" (Berkeley: Policy Analysis for California Education, University of California, 1998). Berliner and Biddle also report how average scores on basic "intelligence tests" have risen about 15 percent over the past half decade. They ask whether children's intelligence is really rising, or whether schools are getting better and boosting average scores. Richard Rothstein also details how sinking SAT scores, observed until the early 1990s, were likely the result of an increasingly diverse set of high school students sitting for this college entrance exam. In 1941, the

first year the SAT was offered, just 1 percent of all graduating seniors took the exam. By 1997 this proportion had risen to 30 percent. See Rothstein's *The Way We Were? The Myth and Realities of America's Student Achievement* (New York: Century Foundation Press, 1998).

85. David Grissmer, Ann Flanagan, and Stephanie Williamson, "Why Did the Black-White Score Gap Narrow in the 1970s and 1980s?" in *The Black-White Test-Score Gap,* ed. Christopher Jencks and Meredith Phillips (Washington, D.C.: Brookings Institution Press, 1998), pp. 182–228.

86. Eric A. Hanushek and Steven G. Rivkin, "Understanding the Twentieth-Century Growth in U.S. School Spending," *Journal of Human Resources* 22 (1996): 35–67.

87. Michael Cohen, "Key Issues Confronting State Policymakers," in *Restructuring Schools: The Next Generation of Educational Reform,* ed. R. Elmore (San Francisco: Jossey-Bass, 1990), pp. 251–288.

88. "The Text of the President's State of the Union Address to Congress," *New York Times,* January 20, 1999, pp. A22–A23. For empirical substantiation, see David Grissmer and Ann Flanagan, *Exploring Rapid Achievement Gains in North Carolina and Texas* (Washington, D.C.: U.S. Department of Education, National Education Goals Panel, 1998). The key pillars of "systemic reform" are laid bare by historian Maris Vinovskis in *History and Educational Policy Making* (New Haven: Yale University Press, 1999).

89. These findings were reviewed by Richard Lee Colvin, "Recalculating the Standards of Math Instruction," *Los Angeles Times,* November 11, 1998, p. B2.

90. Peter Applebome, "Students' Test Scores Show Slow but Steady Gains at Nation's Schools," *New York Times,* September 3, 1997, p. A12.

91. David J. Hoff and Kathleen Kennedy Manzo, "U.S. Students Bounce Back in Reading: But NAEP Results Still Short of Goals," *Education Week,* February 17, 1999, p. 1. For technical details on reading scores, see Patricia Donahue et al., *The NAEP 1998 Reading Report Card for the Nation* (Washington, D.C.: U.S. Department of Education, 1999).

92. Kerry White, "High-Poverty Schools Score Big on Kentucky Assessment," *Education Week,* May 5, 1999, pp. 18–20.

93. David J. Hoff and Kathleen Kennedy Manzo, "States Committed to Standards Reforms Reap NAEP Gains," *Education Week,* March 10, 1999, p. 1.

94. Achievement gains are detailed in Grissmer, Flanagan, and Williamson, "Black-White Score Gap." Grissmer, a researcher at the RAND Corporation, has conducted much of the statistical analysis aimed at understanding which children are benefiting from the Texas reforms. Also see Texas Association of School Boards, "Reasons You Should Stand Up and Cheer for Texas Public Schools," in a special edition of the *Texas Lone Star* (Austin, 1998). I want to thank Professor Uri Treisman, University of Texas, for helping to provide this evidence.

95. Herbert J. Walberg, "Incentivized School Standards Work," *Education Week,* November 4, 1998, p. 4.

96. Valerie Lee has documented, studying a national school sample, the positive achievement effect stemming from moving students into more demanding academic courses in math and science. See Valerie E. Lee, Julia B. Smith, and Robert G. Croninger, "How High School Organization Influences Equitable Distribution of Learning in Mathematics and Science," *Sociology of Education* 70, no. 2 (April 1997): 128–150.

97. Peter Beinart, "Republican Heartthrobs," *New Republic* December 28, 1998, p. 28.

98. Alexis de Tocqueville, *Democracy in America, Volume 1* (New York: Vintage Books, 1990), pp. 69–71.

99. Michael B. Katz, *Class, Bureaucracy, and Schools: The Illusion of Educational Change in America.* (New York: Praeger, 1971).

100. This historical nexus between who governs the schools (which citizens and at what level of public authority) and the organizational models that have gained status and popular legitimacy has been explored in George S. Counts, *Dare the School Build a New Social Order?* (New York: John Day Company, 1932), pp. 3–5. Diane Ravitch, *The Troubled Crusade: American Education, 1945–1980.* (New York: Basic Books, 1983), chap. 8. David B. Tyack, *The One Best System: A History of Urban Education* (Cambridge, Mass.: Harvard University Press, 1974).

101. Institutional theorists have spent the past generation documenting the ways in which actors inside schools buffer external pressures for change. See, for example, John W. Meyer and Brian Rowan, "Institutionalized Organizations: Formal Structure as Myth and Ceremony," *American Journal of Sociology* 83 (1977): 340–363. For a review, see W. Richard Scott, *Institutions and Organizations* (Thousand Oaks, Calif.: Sage Publications, 1995).

102. Tyack and Cuban, *Tinkering toward Utopia.*

103. The field of cultural models and script theory informs this conception of how behavior in highly institutionalized settings is so hard to alter in a sustained way. See, for example, Naomi Quinn and Dorothy Holland, "Culture and Cognition," in *Cultural Models in Language and Thought,* ed. D. Holland and N. Quinn (Cambridge: Cambridge University Press, 1987), pp. 3–40. For a thorough review of the cultural models construct, see Bradd Shore, *Culture in Mind: Cognition, Culture, and the Problem of Meaning* (New York: Oxford University Press, 1996).

104. Joseph Kahne, "Democratic Communities, Equity, and Excellence: A Deweyan Reframing of Educational Policy Analysis," *Educational Evaluation and Policy Analysis* 16, no. 3 (Fall 1994): 233–248.

105. Diane Ravitch, *The Troubled Crusade: American Education, 1945–1980* (New York: Basic Books, 1983).

2. We Hold on to Our Kids, We Hold on Tight

1. Drew Lindsay, "Michigan Judge Strikes Down Charter Law," *Education Week,* November 9, 1994, pp. 1, 14.

2. Christine L. Emmons, James P. Comer, and Norris M. Haynes, "Translating Theory into Practice: Comer's Theory of School Reform," in *Rallying the Whole Village: The Comer Process for Reforming Education*, ed. James P. Comer et al. (New York: Teachers College Press, 1996), p. 29.

3. James P. Comer, Norris M. Haynes, and Edward T. Joyner, "The School Development Program," in *Rallying the Whole Village*, ed. Comer et al. (New York: Teachers College Press, 1996).

4. Lynn Schnaiberg, "Michigan Tests Show Charter Schools Lagging," *Education Week on the Web*, September 24, 1997.

5. RPP International and the University of Minnesota, *A Study of Charter Schools: Second-Year Report*, Contract no. RC 95 196001 (Washington, D.C.: U.S. Department of Education, Office of Educational Research and Improvement, 1998).

6. M. Mayes, "Resegregation in Lansing Schools," *Lansing State Journal*, April 5, 1998, pp. 1A, 4A.

7. Robert Hollingsworth, "Charter Schools Cater to Our Clients' Needs," *Lansing State Journal*, April 21, 1998, p. 5A.

8. J. D. Ratteray, "Independent Neighborhood Schools: A Framework for the Education of African Americans," *Journal of Negro Education* 61, no. 2 (1992): 139–151.

9. Ibid. Mwalimu J. Shujaa, "Afrocentric Transformation and Parental Choice in African American Independent Schools," *Journal of Negro Education* 61, no. 2 (1992): 148–154.

10. Ratteray, "Independent Neighborhood Schools."

11. S. T. Johnson and D. K. Anderson, "Legacies and Lessons from Independent Schools," *Journal of Negro Education* 61 no. 2 (1992): 121–124.

12. Aisha Shule/W. E. B. Dubois Preparatory Academy, *Aisha Shule Annual Education Report*, Detroit, 1996–97.

13. Kofi Lomotey, "Independent Black Institutions: African-Centered Education Models," *Journal of Negro Education* 61, no. 4 (1992): 455–462.

14. Carol D. Lee, "Profile of an Independent Black Institution: African-Centered Education at Work," *Journal of Negro Education* 61, no. 2 (1992): 160–177.

15. Ibid., p. 168.

16. Maulana Karenga, 1989, quoted in ibid.

17. Lomotey, "Independent Black Institutions. Shujaa, "Afrocentric Transformation and Parental Choice."

18. J. D. Ratteray and Mwalimu J. Shujaa, 1987, in Shujaa, "Afrocentric Transformation and Parental Choice."

19. Eric Rofes, *How Are School Districts Responding to Charter Laws and the Advent of Charter Schools?* (Berkeley: Policy Analysis for California Education, University of California, 1998).

3. An Empowering Spirit Is Not Enough

Susan Puryear contributed greatly to this chapter through parent interviews and her thinking about cultural models of parent participation.

Pseudonyms are used for the individuals and institutions named in this chapter.

1. See Claude Goldenberg and Ronald Gallimore, "Immigrant Latino Parents' Values and Beliefs about Their Children's Education: Continuities and Discontinuities across Cultures and Generations," in *Advances in Motivation and Achievement* 9 (1995): 183–228; Guadalupe Valdes, *Con Respeto: Bridging the Distances between Culturally Diverse Families and Schools* (New York: Teachers College Press, 1996).
2. California Basic Educational Data System, 1998 (Sacramento: California Department of Education).
3. Ibid.

4. Selling Air

1. Peter Senge et al., *The Fifth Discipline Fieldbook: Strategies and Tools for Building a Learning Organization* (New York: Doubleday, 1994), p. 484.

5. Diversity and Inequality

The second and third authors contributed equally to this chapter and are listed alphabetically.
Pseudonyms are used for the individuals and institutions named in this chapter.

1. UCLA Charter School Study, *Beyond the Rhetoric of Charter School Reform: A Study of Ten California School Districts* (Los Angeles: UCLA Graduate School of Education and Information Studies, 1998).

6. Losing Public Accountability

Pseudonyms are used for the individuals and institutions named in this chapter.

1. In California there are several legal ways to school children at home. The most popular option is filing an R-4 affidavit with a local school district. The affidavit establishes a home as a private school. Private schools are not regulated in California, and private school teachers are not required to hold a state teaching credential. Thus, the affidavit essentially permits any home to register as a private school (see California Education Code, Sections 33190, 48222). Another option is to enroll in one of the independent study programs offered by most districts. The ISP option is usually an extension of existing school-based programs and, through teacher involvement, it permits students to learn at home with parent supervision (see California Education Code, Section 51745). A third option is private tutoring: parents who hold a valid California teaching credential may file for an exemption from state compulsory public school attendance law and teach their children at home (see California Education Code, Sections 48200, 48224). A fourth option is enrollment in a charter school that offers support services for home study. This option will be described in detail throughout the chapter. It is important to note that the California Department

of Education does not recognize "home schooling" as a legal option but does recognize the options described above as choices for parents who want to provide their children with a schooling alternative outside the traditional public school setting.

2. Schools in California receive most of their state funding based on student average daily attendance. The ADA is equivalent to days of actual student attendance divided by the number of instructional days in a school year. A school district's basic per-pupil revenue limit (basic state aid excluding funds from categorical programs) is calculated according to student ADA.

3. From the school district's annual evaluation of Valley Charter School, 1996–1997. To protect the school's anonymity, no citation included.

4. Cover schools are private schools that provide support to families who home school their children. A cover school's primary service is to file an affidavit with the state that verifies minors are being educated per state compulsory public school attendance laws. Most cover schools are affiliated with local parishes and are aligned with the religious beliefs and values of the families they serve.

5. See note 3.

6. See note 3.

7. From the district's reference binder for Valley Charter School, 1997–1998. To protect the school's anonymity, no citation included.

8. See note 7.

9. See California Education Code, Section 47601(f), 1992.

10. See California Education Code, Sections 47605(3)(B) and 47605(3)(C).

11. In 1998 the legislature revised the original California Charter Schools Act of 1992. Effective January 1, 1999, all charter schools were required to participate in the new state-adopted pupil assessment program, including the Stanford 9 exam.

12. Declining to participate is an option available to all students in California, where any parent petitions the state for a waiver releasing a student from the requirement to take the test.

13. The CTBS tests were not administered to K–3 students.

14. See note 3.

15. As of January 1, 1999, an amendment to the California Charter Schools Act of 1992 limits a chartering agency's ability to charge for "supervisorial oversight" to no more then 1 percent of a charter school's revenue, or 3 percent if the charter school receives "substantial rent free" facilities from the agency. However, the legislation does not define supervisorial oversight costs nor does it stipulate how these costs should be calculated. See California Education Code, Section 47613.7(a).

16. Charter Public Schools Act of 1998, Section 8, Section 47602.3 of the California Education Code.

17. Charter Public Schools Act of 1998, Section 10, Section 47605(1)(1) of the California Education Code.

18. Officials in the California Department of Education have speculated that the Hastings Initiative as originally written would have forced the legislature to engage in a debate to define home schooling, thus opening up a Pandora's box. Because the term *home schooling* does not appear anywhere in the entire California Education Code, a fierce legal battle might have ensued had the restrictions on home schoolers been debated.

    During the initiative process, the California Network of Educational Charters (CANEC), an influential parent-run organization that acts as both a charter school information clearinghouse and a technical-assistance organization for parents and communities operating charter schools, remained quiet on the sidelines and provided only lukewarm backing for the initiative. The organization was faced with a difficult decision, and it was unclear whether CANEC supported the initiative. It would have allowed an expansion in the number of charter schools but also, through increased regulation, would have ultimately closed nearly one-third of California's charter schools that operated as home school charters, affecting nearly half of the total charter school student population.

19. Borrowing from institutional theory, the outside legitimacy that VCS has garnered has allowed the school to create a protective shell that deflects criticism of what is occurring within the inner core of VCS. During the successful evolution of VCS, the school's outer shell "decoupled" from the inner core; the outer shell continues to buy outside legitimacy for the school, and the inner core continues supporting an unorthodox schooling model. Essentially, the inner core—made up of parents, teachers, and administrators—is allowed to continue about its business of privately educating children at home, while the outer shell, through implementation of symbolic measures and standards of accountability, allows the organization to deflect potential attacks on the schooling model employed at VCS. See, for example, John W. Meyer and Brian Rowan, "The Structure of Educational Organizations," in Meyer and Rowan, *Environment and Organizations* (San Francisco: Jossey-Bass, 1978), pp. 78–109. John W. Meyer and Brian Rowan, "Institutionalized Organizations: Formal Structure as Myth and Ceremony," *American Journal of Sociology* 83, no. 2 (1978): 340–363.

20. In May of 1999 another attempt to close home school charters was launched. This time the attack came from Democratic state senators who learned of the loose attendance and instructional accounting systems used by home school charters. Senators called for the closing of all charter schools employing "home-based" instruction models. Their attack, however, was diffused in legislative debates. After agreeing on concessions that again spared home school charters from elimination, the California legislature passed SB 434 in July, which further amended California's original charter school legislation, implementing more regulation on all charter schools and placing additional restrictions on home school charters.

    Since January 1, 2000, all California charter schools have been subject to stricter attendance accounting regulations, as well as minimum instructional minute requirements. SB 434 also requires all home school charters to operate under current independent study program regulations, which require a teacher-to-student ratio equal to that of other district schools and compliance with attendance zones, which limit enrollment options and prohibit students from enrolling in charter schools that are not in either the county in which they reside or an immediately bordering county. The attendance zone requirement, along with other independent study program regulations, will certainly affect the operation of many home school charters that draw enrollment from counties throughout the state. Whether home school families return to private home schooling or choose to remain within a more regulated public home schooling environment deserves close attention.

7. Teachers as Communitarians

1. Joe Nathan, *Charter Schools: Creating Hope and Opportunity for American Education* (San Francisco: Jossey-Bass, 1999), pp. 76–81; Mary Bixby, "Charter Schools: 'More Than We Ever Expected,'" *Education Week,* February 4, 1998, p. 47; Chester Finn, Bruno Manno, and Louann Bierlein, *Charter Schools in Action: What We Have Learned* (Indianapolis: Hudson Institute, 1996).

2. William Nelson and Judy Ziewacz, "Foreword," in E. G. Nadeau and David J. Thompson, *Cooperation Works! How People Are Using Cooperative Action to Rebuild Communities and Revitalize the Economy* (Rochester, Minn.: Lone Oak Press, 1996), p. 5.

3. Lee Egerstrom, *Make No Small Plans: A Cooperative Revival for Rural America* (Rochester, Minn.: Lone Oak Press, 1994), pp. 23–69.

4. Brett Fairbairn, Centre for the Study of Cooperatives, University of Saskatchewan, Saskatoon, Saskatchewan. Cited in Egerstrom, *Make No Small Plans,* p. 37.

5. Lee Egerstrom, *Make No Small Plans,* p. 37. See also Brett Fairbairn, "Cooperatives and Globalization: Market-Driven Change and the Origins of Cooperatives in the Nineteenth and Twentieth Centuries," in *Globalization and the Relevance of Cooperatives* (Saskatoon: Centre for the Study of Cooperatives, University of Saskatchewan, 1991).

6. Lee Egerstrom, *Make No Small Plans,* pp. 37–38.

7. Ibid., pp. 33–35.

8. Nadeau and Thompson, *Cooperation Works,* p. 8.

9. Ted Kolderie, "Childspace: A Nonprofit + Workers Cooperative," unpublished paper, n.d.; Ted Kolderie, "Could a Teacher Co-op Own a School?" unpublished paper, June 9, 1990.

10. John Wensman, "A Case Study of the Minnesota New Country School," unpublished paper, February 1995.

11. Eric Rofes, *How Are School Districts Responding to Charter Laws and the Advent of Charter Schools?* (Berkeley: Policy Analysis for California Education, University

of California, 1998); Ross Corson, "Le Sueur–Henderson: Minnesota New Country School," *The American Prospect,* July–August 1998, pp. 56–57.

12. Robert Franklin, "Le Sueur's Frog Group Basks in Limelight," *Minneapolis Star Tribune,* October 5, 1997, p. B1.; Anne Brataas, "A Croak of Alarm," *Saint Paul Pioneer Press,* May 9, 1996, p. D1.

13. Amy Wells, Alejandra Lopez, J. Scott, and Jennifer Jellison, "Charter Schools as Postmodern Institutions: Rethinking Social Stratification in an Age of Deregulated School Choice," paper presented at the annual meeting of the Sociology of Education Association, Monterey, Calif., 1997. American Federation of Teachers, *Charter School Laws: Do They Measure Up?* (Washington, D.C.: American Federation of Teachers, 1996); Jerry Ackerman, "Schoolchildren as Commodities? For-Profits Seek to Revive Education," *Boston Globe,* January 25, 1998, p. C1; Lauren Morando Rhim, "Franchising Public Education: An Analysis of the Linkage of Charter Schools and Private Education Management Companies," paper presented at the annual meeting of the American Educational Research Association, San Diego, Calif., April 13–17, 1998.

14. The research on which this chapter is based occurred over a three-year period while MNCS was situated in Le Sueur. In year five of its operation, the school moved to a new site located in Henderson.

15. Wensman, "A Case Study," p. 5.

16. Evaluation Redesign Team of ISD #2397 and ISD #4007, "The Second Year: A Study of the Minnesota New Country School," Le Sueur–Henderson, Minn., December 1, 1996, p. 7.

17. RAND Corporation, Institute on Education and Training, "Contracting: The Case for Privately Operated Public Schools," Santa Monica, Calif., February 1995.

18. Board Study Committee of ISD #2397, *The First Year: A Study of Minnesota New Country School,* Le Sueur–Henderson, Minn., August 21, 1995, pp. 14–20.

19. Paulo Freire, *Pedagogy of the Oppressed* (New York: Continuum, 1973). Michael Apple, *Education and Power* (Boston: Routledge, 1982); Michael Apple, *Official Knowledge: Democratic Education in a Conservative Age* (New York: Routledge, 1993); Peter McLaren, *Critical Pedagogy and Predatory Culture* (New York: Routledge, 1995); Henry Giroux and Peter McLaren, "Teacher Education and the Politics of Engagement: The Case for Democratic Schooling," *Harvard Educational Review* 56, no. 3 (1986): 213–238. Adrienne Rich, *On Lies, Secrets, and Silence: Selected Prose 1966–1978* (New York: Norton), pp. 231–236; bell hooks, *Teaching to Transgress: Education as the Practice of Freedom* (New York: Routledge, 1994).

20. Doug Thomas and Kim Borwege, "A Choice to Charter," *Phi Delta Kappan* 96 (September 1996): 31.

21. Bryan Hassel, "Charter Schools: Politics and Practice in Four States, in Paul Peterson and Bryan Hassel, eds., *Learning from School Choice* (Washington, D.C.: Brookings Institution Press, 1998), pp. 249–274.

22. Larry Cuban, *How Teachers Taught: Constancy and Change in American Classrooms, 1880–1990* (New York: Teachers College Press, 1993); David Tyack and Larry Cuban, *Tinkering toward Utopia: A Century of Public School Reform* (Cambridge, Mass.: Harvard University Press, 1995).

23. Tyack and Cuban, *Tinkering toward Utopia*, pp. 19–20.

24. John Chubb and Terry Moe, *Politics, Markets, and America's Schools.* (Washington, D.C.: Brookings Institution, 1990).

25. Michael Engel, "Privatization and Democratic Values in Public Schools," paper presented at the annual meeting of the Northeastern Political Science Association, November 14, 1996.

8. Breaking Away or Pulling Together?

1. Thanks to Martin Carnoy for stimulating this line of thinking.

2. For a brief review of these political dynamics, see Bruce Fuller, "Will Governor Davis' School Reforms Make the Grade?" *San Francisco Chronicle* March 10, 1999, p. B3.

3. Emile Durkheim, *The Elementary Forms of Religious Life,* trans. Karen E. Fields (New York: Free Press, 1995).

4. For a review of the new "civil society" strategy of the political right, which borrows from the left's old reform playbook, see E. J. Dionne, "Civil Society, Why Now?" *Brookings Review* 15 (1997): 5–8. For discussions of how civil society might be advanced in relation to the central state, see Martin Carnoy, *Political Theory and the State* (Princeton: Princeton University Press, 1984). Bruce Fuller, *Government Confronts Culture* (New York: Garland, Taylor and Francis, 1999).

5. Richard Elmore helped to clarify this framing with "School Decentralization: Who Gains? Who Loses?" in J. Hannaway and M. Carnoy, eds., *Decentralization and School Improvement: Can We Fulfill the Promise?* (San Francisco: Jossey-Bass, 1993), pp. 33–54. Joseph Ellis, *American Sphinx: The Character of Thomas Jefferson* (New York: Vintage Books, 1998); Jack Rakove, *Original Meanings: Politics and Ideas in the Making of the Constitution* (New York: Vintage Books, 1997).

6. A third intended effect is that urban school bureaucracies will become more responsive as they face the competitive pressure of charter schools. Two studies have now found that this is true only in small districts where a significant proportion of the district's children have opted to enroll in a charter school. See Eric Rofes, "How Are Districts Responding to Charter Laws and Charter Schools?" (Berkeley: University of California, Policy Analysis for California Education, 1998). Also see UCLA Charter School Study, *Beyond the Rhetoric of Charter School Reform: A Study of Ten California School Districts* (Los Angeles: UCLA Graduate School of Education and Information Studies, 1998).

7. Milbrey W. McLaughlin, "Learning from Experience: Lessons from Policy Implementation," *Educational Evaluation and Policy Analysis* 9 (1987): 171–178.

8. Abby R. Weiss, *Going It Alone* (Boston: Institute for Responsive Education, Northeastern University, 1997), pp. 12–13; reviewed in Seymour B. Sarason,

Charter Schools: Another Failed Educational Reform? (New York: Teachers College Press, 1998).

9. James Traub, "In Theory: A School of Your Own," *New York Times* (Education Life), April 4, 1999, section 4A, pp. 30–31, 42.

10. See Randall Collins's discussion of the institutional foundations of Adam Smith's market theory in Collins, *Four Sociological Traditions* (New York: Oxford University Press, 1994).

11. Elliot Turiel, moving from the fields of moral development and cultural psychology, argues that proponents of cultural studies largely "fail to recognize that everyone does not participate in the 'culture' in the same ways. Cultural practices affect people of different positions in different ways." See Elliot Turiel, "Conflict, Social Development, and Cultural Change," in Turiel, ed., *Development and Cultural Change: Reciprocal Processes* (San Francisco: Jossey-Bass, 1999), pp. 82, 89.

12. Robert Johnston, "Engler Sees Funding Supplement as Stage for Policies," *Education Week,* (1999) April 21, p. 18.

13. Bruce Fuller et al., *School Choice: Abundant Hopes, Scarce Evidence of Results* (Berkeley: Policy Analysis for California Education, University of California, 1999).

14. After reading an early draft of Patty Yancey's chapter, another scholar, working with a second research team, argued that Yancey had taken the proachievement rhetoric at El-Shabazz at face value, failing to see wide interclassroom variability in teachers' concern with student learning. These differing interpretations underline the scarcity of generalizable data with which claims about achievement can be substantiated. As elsewhere, the quality of teaching will most certainly vary among teachers within charter schools.

15. Christopher Jencks and Meredith Phillips, eds., *The Black-White Test-Store Gap* (Washington, D.C.: Brookings Institution Press, 1998). The recent analysis of family background effects on children's achievement levels was led by Rich Brown and Eva Baker at the UCLA Graduate School of Education and was reviewed by Elaine Woo and Richard Lee Colvin, "Lower Standards, Money, Changing Student Body Are the Challenges," *Los Angeles Times,* May 17, 1998 pp. S1–S3.

16. Roslyn Mickelson, "The Attitude-Achievement Paradox among Black Adolescents," *Sociology of Education* 63 (1990): 44–61.

17. George Will, *Statecraft as Soulcraft: What Government Does* (New York: Simon and Schuster, 1983).

18. For explication of the thesis that the charter school movement is the result of wider social and economic forces beyond the bureaucratic school and state, see Amy Stuart Wells et al., "Charter Schools as Postmodern Paradox: Rethinking Social Stratification in an Age of Deregulated School Choice," *Harvard Educational Review* 69 (1999): 172–204.

19. Alan Wolfe, "The Pursuit of Autonomy," *New York Times Magazine,* May 7, 2000, pp. 53–56.

Contributors

Bruce Fuller is associate professor of education and public policy at the University of California, Berkeley. His work focuses on the dilemmas that arise when institutions—public schools, child care, or family welfare programs—are decentralized to local organizations. He is coauthor, with Susan D. Holloway, of *Through My Own Eyes* (Harvard, 1997) and author of the recent book *Government Confronts Culture* (Taylor and Francis, 1999).

Jennifer Jellison Holme is a research associate with the UCLA Charter School Study and a doctoral candidate in education policy studies at the University of California, Los Angeles. Her research interests are school choice, the politics and implementation of school desegregation, and the connection between housing policy and access to schools.

Luis A. Huerta taught in an elementary school in California's Central Valley before beginning his doctoral studies at Berkeley. His graduate work focuses on school finance reform and choice. He is coauthor of *School Choice: Abundant Hopes, Scarce Evidence* (PACE, University of California, 1999).

Eric Rofes received his doctorate in social and cultural studies at Berkeley. He currently is assistant professor of education at California State University, Humboldt. His work focuses on school reform and charters, as well as on gay and lesbian issues inside schools. His writings have appeared in the *Harvard Educational Review, Rethinking Schools,* and other journals.

Ash Vasudeva is a doctoral student at UCLA. He was a member of Amy Wells's research team and coauthor of the UCLA Charter School Study report *Beyond the Rhetoric of Charter School Reform* (UCLA Graduate School of Education and Information Studies, 1998).

Amy Stuart Wells is associate professor of education policy at UCLA. Her research and writing focus on issues of race and education, including desegregation, tracking, and school choice. She was the principal investigator of a three-year study of charter schools and their host districts in California, funded by the Ford Foundation and the

Annie E. Casey Foundation. Her published work includes *Time to Choose: America at the Crossroads of School Choice Policy* (Hill and Wang, 1993) and, with Robert L. Crain, *Stepping over the Color Line: African-American Students in White Suburban Schools* (Yale University Press, 1997).

Edward Wexler teaches high school in Richmond, California, and is a doctoral student in education policy at Berkeley. He was the lead author on a recent study of California's class-size reduction program, published by the Berkeley research center Policy Analysis for California Education (PACE), and is coauthor of *School Choice: Abundant Hopes, Scarce Evidence* (University of California, 1999).

Patty Yancey received her Ph.D. in social and cultural studies from Berkeley. She is currently adjunct professor of teacher education at the University of San Francisco. She conducted qualitative research for the four-year national evaluation of charter schools and recently published a book on the community mobilization and politics surrounding the creation of two charter schools, *Parents, Choice, and Decentralization* (Peter Lang, 1999).

Kate Zernike, formerly a reporter for the *Boston Globe,* now writes on education at the *New York Times.* A graduate of Columbia University's journalism school, she also served as a features writer for the *Boston Globe Magazine.*

Index